John Timbs

Club Life of London

Vol. 2

John Timbs

Club Life of London
Vol. 2

ISBN/EAN: 9783337294205

Printed in Europe, USA, Canada, Australia, Japan

Cover: Foto ©Thomas Meinert / pixelio.de

More available books at **www.hansebooks.com**

CLUB LIFE OF LONDON

WITH

ANECDOTES OF THE CLUBS, COFFEE-HOUSES

AND TAVERNS OF THE METROPOLIS

DURING THE 17TH, 18TH, AND 19TH CENTURIES.

By JOHN TIMBS, F.S.A.

IN TWO VOLUMES.—VOL. II.

LONDON:

RICHARD BENTLEY, NEW BURLINGTON STREET,

Publisher in Ordinary to Her Majesty.

1866.

CONTENTS.

— ◆ —

𝔆𝔬𝔣𝔣𝔢𝔢-𝔥𝔬𝔲𝔰𝔢𝔰,

Taverns.

x CONTENTS.

CONTENTS.

APPENDIX.

Page

BEEFSTEAK SOCIETY 286

WHITE'S CLUB 287

THE ROYAL ACADEMY CLUB 289

DESTRUCTION OF TAVERNS BY FIRE . . 290

THE TZAR OF MUSCOVY'S HEAD, TOWER-STREET . . 291

ROSE TAVERN, TOWER-STREET 292

THE NAG'S HEAD TAVERN, CHEAPSIDE 293

THE HUMMUMS, COVENT GARDEN 295

ORIGIN OF TAVERN SIGNS 296

INDEX TO THE FIRST VOLUME 305

INDEX TO THE SECOND VOLUME . . . 313

" The Lion's Head," at Button's Coffee-House.

Coffee-houses.

EARLY COFFEE-HOUSES.

Coffee is thus mentioned by Bacon, in his *Sylva Sylvarum:*—"They have in *Turkey* a *drink* called *Coffee*, made of a *Berry* of the same name, as Black as *Soot*, and of a *Strong Sent*, but not *Aromatical;* which they take, beaten into Powder, in *Water*, as Hot as they can *Drink* it; and they take it, and sit at it in their *Coffee Houses*, which are like our *Taverns.* The *Drink* comforteth the *Brain*, and *Heart*, and helpeth *Digestion."*

And in Burton's *Anatomy of Melancholy*, part i., sec. 2, occurs, "Turks in their coffee-houses, which much resemble our taverns." The date is 1621, several years before coffee-houses were introduced into England.

In 1650, Wood tells us, was opened at Oxford, the first coffee-house, by Jacobs, a Jew, " at the Angel, in the parish of St. Peter in the East; and there it was, by some who delighted in novelty, drank."

There was once an odd notion prevalent that coffee was unwholesome, and would bring its drinkers to an untimely end. Yet, Voltaire, Fontenelle, and Fourcroy, who were great coffee-drinkers, lived to a good old age. Laugh at Madame de Sévigné, who foretold that coffee and Racine would be forgotten together !

A manuscript note, written by Oldys, the celebrated antiquary, states that " The use of coffee in England was first known in 1657. [It will be seen, as above, that Oldys is incorrect.] Mr. Edwards, a Turkey merchant, brought from Smyrna to London one Pasqua Rosee, a Ragusan youth, who prepared this drink for him every morning. But the novelty thereof drawing too much company to him, he allowed his said servant, with another of his son-in-law, to sell it publicly, and they set up the first coffee-house in London, in St. Michael's-alley, in Cornhill. The sign was Pasqua Rosee's own head." Oldys is slightly in error here; Rosee commenced his coffee-house in 1652, and one Jacobs, a Jew, as we have just seen, had established a similar undertaking at Oxford, two years earlier. One of Rosee's original shop or hand-bills, the only mode of advertising in those days, is as follows :—

" THE VERTUE OF THE COFFEE DRINK,

" *First made and publickly sold in England by Pasqua Rosee.*

" The grain or berry called coffee, groweth upon little trees only in the deserts of Arabia. It is brought from thence, and drunk generally throughout all the Grand Seignour's dominions. It is a simple, innocent thing, composed into a drink, by being dried in an oven, and ground to powder, and boiled up with spring water, and about half a pint of it to be drunk fasting an hour before, and not eating an hour after, and to be taken as hot as possibly can be endured; the which will never fetch the skin off the mouth, or raise any blisters by reason of that heat.

"The Turks' drink at meals and other times is usually water, and their diet consists much of fruit; the crudities whereof are very much corrected by this drink.

"The quality of this drink is cold and dry; and though it be a drier, yet it neither heats nor inflames more than hot posset. It so incloseth the orifice of the stomach, and fortifies the heat within, that it is very good to help digestion; and therefore of great use to be taken about three or four o'clock afternoon, as well as in the morning. It much quickens the spirits, and makes the heart lightsome; it is good against sore eyes, and the better if you hold your head over it and take in the steam that way. It suppresseth fumes exceedingly, and therefore is good against the head-ache, and will very much stop any defluxion of rheums, that distil from the head upon the stomach, and so prevent and help consumptions and the cough of the lungs.

"It is excellent to prevent and cure the dropsy, gout,* and scurvy. It is known by experience to be better than any other drying drink for people in years, or children that have any running humours upon them, as the king's evil, &c. It is a most excellent remedy against the spleen, hypochondriac winds, and the like. It will prevent drowsiness, and make one fit for business, if one have occasion to watch, and therefore you are not to drink of it after supper, unless you intend to be watchful, for it will hinder sleep for three or four hours.

* In the French colonies, where Coffee is more used than in the English, Gout is scarcely known.

B 2

" It is observed that in Turkey, where this is generally
drunk, that they are not troubled with the stone, gout,
dropsy, or scurvy, and that their skins are exceeding
clear and white. It is neither laxative nor restringent.

> " *Made and sold in St. Michael's-alley, in Cornhill, by*
> *Pasqua Rosee, at the sign of his own head.*"

The new beverage had its opponents, as well as its
advocates. The following extracts from *An invective
against Coffee,* published about the same period, informs
us that Rosee's partner, the servant of Mr. Edwards's
son-in-law, was a coachman ; while it controverts the
statement that hot coffee will not scald the mouth, and
ridicules the broken English of the Ragusan :—

"A BROADSIDE AGAINST COFFEE.

" A coachman was the first (here) coffee made,
    And ever since the rest drive on the trade :
' *Me no good Engalash !* ' and sure enough,
    He played the quack to salve his Stygian stuff ;
' *Ver boon for de stomach, de cough, de phthisick,*'
    And I believe him, for it looks like physic.
Coffee a crust is charred into a coal,
    The smell and taste of the mock china bowl ;
Where huff and puff, they labour out their lungs,
    Lest, Dives-like, they should bewail their tongues.
And yet they tell ye that it will not burn,
    Though on the jury blisters you return ;
Whose furious heat does make the water rise,
    And still through the alembics of your eyes.
Dread and desire, you fall to 't snap by snap,
    As hungry dogs do scalding porridge lap.
But to cure drunkards it has got great fame ;
    Posset or porridge, will 't not do the same ?
Confusion hurries all into one scene,
    Like Noah's ark, the clean and the unclean.

"And now, alas ! the drench has credit got,
And he's no gentleman that drinks it not;
That such a dwarf should rise to such a stature !
But custom is but a remove from nature.
A little dish and a large coffee-house,
What is it but a mountain and a mouse ?"

Notwithstanding this opposition, coffee soon became a favourite drink, and the shops, where it was sold, places of general resort.

There appears to have been a great anxiety that the Coffee-house, while open to all ranks, should be conducted under such restraints as might prevent the better class of customers from being annoyed. Accordingly, the following regulations, printed on large sheets of paper, were hung up in conspicuous positions on the walls :—

" *Enter, Sirs, freely, but first, if you please,*
Peruse our civil orders, which are these.

First, gentry, tradesmen, all are welcome hither,
And may without affront sit down together :
Pre-eminence of place none here should mind,
But take the next fit seat that he can find :
Nor need any, if finer persons come,
Rise up for to assign to them his room ;
To limit men's expense, we think not fair,
But let him forfeit twelve-pence that shall swear :
He that shall any quarrel here begin,
Shall give each man a dish t' atone the sin.;
And so shall he, whose compliments extend
So far to drink in coffee to his friend ;
Let noise of loud disputes be quite forborne,
Nor maudlin lovers here in corners mourn,
But all be brisk and talk, but not too much ;
On sacred things, let none presume to touch,
Nor profane Scripture, nor saucily wrong
Affairs of state with an irreverent tongue :

Let mirth be innocent, and each man see
That all his jests without reflection be ;
To keep the house more quiet and from blame,
We banish hence cards, dice, and every game ;
Nor can allow of wagers, that exceed
Five shillings, which ofttimes do troubles breed ;
Let all that's lost or forfeited be spent
In such good liquor as the house doth vent.
And customers endeavour, to their powers,
For to observe still, seasonable hours.
Lastly, let each man what he calls for pay,
And so you're welcome to come every day."

In a print of the period, five persons are shown in a coffee-house, one smoking, evidently, from their dresses, of different ranks of life; they are seated at a table, on which are small basins without saucers, and tobacco-pipes, while a waiter is serving the coffee.

GARRAWAY'S COFFEE-HOUSE.

This noted Coffee-house, situated in Change-alley, Cornhill, has a threefold celebrity : tea was first sold in England here ; it was a place of great resort in the time of the South Sea Bubble ; and has since been a place of great mercantile transactions. The original proprietor was Thomas Garway, tobacconist and coffee-man, the first who retailed tea, recommending for the cure of all disorders; the following is the substance of his shop bill :—" Tea in England hath been sold in the leaf for six pounds, and sometimes for ten pounds the pound weight, and in respect of its former scarceness and dearness, it hath been only used as a regalia in high treatments and entertainments, and presents made thereof to princes and grandees till the year 1651. The said Thomas Garway did purchase a quantity thereof, and first publicly sold the said tea in leaf and drink, made according to the directions of the most knowing merchants and travellers into those Eastern countries ; and upon knowledge and experience of the said Garway's continued care and industry in obtaining the best tea, and making drink thereof, very many noblemen, physicians, merchants, and gentlemen of quality, have ever since sent to him for the said leaf, and daily resort to his house in Exchange-alley, aforesaid, to drink the drink thereof ; and to the end that all persons of eminence and quality, gentlemen, and others, who have occasion for tea in leaf, may be supplied, these are to give notice that the said Thomas Garway hath tea to sell from " sixteen to fifty shillings per pound." (See the document entire in Ellis's *Letters*, series iv. 58.)

Ogilby, the compiler of the *Britannia*, had his standing lottery of books at Mr. Garway's Coffee-house from April 7, 1673, till wholly drawn off. And, in the *Journey through England*, 1722, Garraway's, Robins's, and Joe's, are described as the three celebrated Coffee-houses: in the first, the People of Quality, who have business in the City, and the most considerable and wealthy citizens, frequent. In the second the Foreign Banquiers, and often even Foreign Ministers. And in the third, the Buyers and Sellers of Stock.

Wines were sold at Garraway's in 1673, " by the candle," that is, by auction, while an inch of candle burns. In *The Tatler*, No. 147, we read : " Upon my coming home last night, I found a very handsome present of

French wine left for me, as a taste of 216 hogsheads, which are to be put to sale at 20l. a hogshead, at Garraway's Coffee-house, in Exchange-alley," &c. The sale by candle is not, however, by candle-light, but during the day. At the commencement of the sale, when the auctioneer has read a description of the property, and the conditions on which it is to be disposed of, a piece of candle, usually an inch long, is lighted, and he who is the last bidder at the time the light goes out is declared the purchaser.

Swift, in his " Ballad on the South Sea Scheme," 1721, did not forget Garraway's :—

> " There is a gulf, where thousands fell,
>   Here all the bold adventurers came,
> A narrow sound, though deep as hell,
>   'Change alley is the dreadful name.
>
> " Subscribers here by thousands float,
>   And jostle one another down,
> Each paddling in his leaky boat,
>   And here they fish for gold and drown.
>
> " Now buried in the depths below,
>   Now mounted up to heaven again,
> They reel and stagger to and fro,
>   At their wits' end, like drunken men.
>
> " Meantime secure on Garway cliffs,
>   A savage race, by shipwrecks fed,
> Lie waiting for the founder'd skiffs,
>   And strip the bodies of the dead."

Dr. Radcliffe, who was a rash speculator in the South Sea Scheme, was usually planted at a table at Garraway's about Exchange time, to watch the turn of the market ; and here he was seated when the footman of his powerful rival, Dr. Edward Hannes, came into Garraway's and inquired, by way of a puff, if Dr. H. was there. Dr. Radcliffe, who was surrounded with several apothecaries and chirurgeons that flocked about him, cried out, "Dr. Hannes was not there," and desired to know "who wanted him?" the fellow's reply was, "such a lord and such a lord;" but he was taken up with the dry rebuke, "No, no, friend, you are mistaken; the Doctor wants those lords." One of Radcliffe's ventures was five thousand guineas upon one South Sea project. When he was told at Garraway's that 'twas all lost, "Why," said he, "'tis but going up five thousand pair of stairs more." "This answer," says Tom Brown, "deserved a statue."

As a Coffee-house, and one of the oldest class, which has withstood, by the well-acquired fame of its proprietors, the ravages of time, and the changes that economy and new generations produce, none can be compared to Garraway's. This name must be familiar with most people in and out of the City; and, notwithstanding our disposition to make allowance for the want of knowledge some of our neighbours of the West-end profess in relation to men and things east of Temple Bar, it must be supposed that the noble personage who said, when asked by a merchant to pay him a visit in one of these places, "that he willingly would, if his friend could tell him where to change horses," had forgotten this establishment, which fostered so great a quantity of dishonoured paper, when in other City coffee-houses it had gone begging at 1s. and 2s. in the pound.*

Garraway's has long been famous as a sandwich and drinking room, for sherry, pale ale, and punch. Tea and coffee are still served. It is said that the sandwich-

* *The City*, 2nd edition.

maker is occupied two hours in cutting and arranging
the sandwiches before the day's consumption commences.
The sale-room is an old fashioned first-floor apartment,
with a small rostrum for the seller, and a few commonly
grained settles for the buyers.   Here sales of drugs,
mahogany, and timber are periodically held.   Twenty
or thirty property and other sales sometimes take place
in a day.   The walls and windows of the lower room are
covered with sale placards, which are unsentimental evidences of the mutability of human affairs.

" In 1840 and 1841, when the tea speculation was at
its height, and prices were fluctuating 6d. and 8d. per
pound, on the arrival of every mail, Garraway's was
frequented every night by a host of the smaller fry of
dealers, when there was more excitement than ever
occurred on 'Change when the most important intelligence arrived.   Champagne and anchovy toasts were
the order of the night; and every one came, ate and
drank, and went, as he pleased without the least question concerning the score, yet the bills were discharged;
and this plan continued for several months."—*The City.*

Here, likewise, we find this redeeming picture :—
" The members of the little *coterie,* who take the dark
corner under the clock, have for years visited this house;
they number two or three old, steady merchants, a
solicitor, and a gentleman who almost devotes the whole
of his time and talents to philanthropic objects,—for
instance, the getting up of a Ball for Shipwrecked
Mariners and their families; or the organization of a
Dinner for the benefit of the Distressed Needlewomen
of the Metropolis; they are a very quiet party, and
enjoy the privilege of their *séance,* uninterrupted by
visitors."

We may here mention a tavern of the South Sea time, where the " Globe *permits*" fraud was very successful. These were nothing more than square pieces of card on which was a wax seal of the sign of the Globe Tavern, situated in the neighbourhood of Change-alley, with the inscription, " Sail-cloth Permits." The possessors enjoyed no other advantage from them than permission to subscribe at some future time to a new sail-cloth manufactory projected by one who was known to be a man of fortune, but who was afterwards involved in the peculation and punishment of the South Sea Directors. These Permits sold for as much as sixty guineas in the Alley.

JONATHAN'S COFFEE-HOUSE.

This is another Change-alley Coffee-house, which is described in the *Tatler*, No. 38, as " the general mart of stock-jobbers;" and the *Spectator*, No. 1, tells us that he " sometimes passes for a Jew in the assembly of stock-jobbers at Jonathan's." This was the rendezvous, where gambling of all sorts was carried on ; notwithstanding a formal prohibition against the assemblage of the jobbers, issued by the City of London, which prohibition continued unrepealed until 1825.

In the *Anatomy of Exchange Alley*, 1719, we read :—
" The centre of the jobbing is in the kingdom of Exchange-alley and its adjacencies. The limits are easily surrounded in about a minute and a half: viz. stepping out of Jonathan's into the Alley, you turn

your face full south; moving on a few paces, and then turning due east, you advance to Garraway's; from thence going out at the other door, you go on still east into Birchin-lane; and then halting a little at the Sword-blade Bank, to do much mischief in fewest words, you immediately face to the north, enter Cornhill, visit two or three petty provinces there in your way west; and thus having boxed your compass, and sailed round the whole stock-jobbing globe, you turn into Jonathan's again; and so, as most of the great follies of life oblige us to do, you end just where you began."

Mrs. Centlivre, in her comedy of *A Bold Stroke for a Wife*, has a scene from Jonathan's at the above period: while the stock-jobbers are talking, the coffee-boys are crying " Fresh coffee, gentlemen, fresh coffee! Bohea tea, gentlemen!"

Here is another picture of Jonathan's, during the South Sea mania; though not by an eye-witness, it groups, from various authorities, the life of the place and the time:—" At a table a few yards off sat a couple of men engaged in the discussion of a newly-started scheme. Plunging his hand impatiently under the deep silver-buttoned flap of his frock-coat of cinnamon cloth and drawing out a paper, the more business-looking of the pair commenced eagerly to read out figures intended to convince the listener, who took a jewelled snuff-box from the deep pocket of the green brocade waistcoat which overflapped his thigh, and, tapping the lid, enjoyed a pinch of perfumed Turkish as he leaned back lazily in his chair. Somewhat further off, standing in the middle of the room, was a keen-eyed lawyer, counting on his fingers the probable results of a certain specu-

lation in human hair, to which a fresh-coloured farmer
from St. Albans, on whose boots the mud of the
cattle market was not dry, listened with a face of stolid
avarice, clutching the stag-horn handle of his thonged
whip as vigorously as if it were the wealth he coveted.
There strode a Nonconformist divine, with S. S. S. in
every line of his face, greedy for the gold that perisheth;
here a bishop, whose truer place was Garraway's,
edged his cassock through the crowd; sturdy ship-
captains, whose manners smack·of blustering breezes,
and who hailed their acquaintance as if through a
speaking-trumpet in a storm—booksellers' hacks from
Grub-street, who were wont to borrow ink-bottles and
just one sheet of paper at the bar of the Black Swan in
St. Martin's-lane, and whose tarnished lace, when not
altogether torn away, showed a suspicious coppery
redness underneath—Jews of every grade, from the
thriving promoter of a company for importing ashes
from Spain or extracting stearine from sunflower seeds
to the seller of sailor slops from Wapping-in-the-Wose,
come to look for a skipper who had bilked him—a
sprinkling of well-to-do merchants—and a host of those
flashy hangers-on to the skirts of commerce, who
brighten up in days of maniacal speculation, and are
always ready to dispose of shares in some unopened
mine or some untried invention—passed and repassed
with continuous change and murmur before the squire's
eyes during the quarter of an hour that he sat there."—
Pictures of the Periods, by W. F. Collier, LL.D.

RAINBOW COFFEE-HOUSE.

The Rainbow, in Fleet-street, appears to have been
the second Coffee-house opened in the metropolis.

"The first Coffee-house in London," says Aubrey
(MS. in the Bodleian Library), "was in St. Michael's-
alley, in Cornhill, opposite to the church, which was set
up by one —— Bowman (coachman to Mr. Hodges, a
Turkey merchant, who putt him upon it), in or about
the yeare 1652. 'Twas about four yeares before any
other was sett up, and that was by Mr. Farr." This
was the Rainbow.

Another account states that one Edwards, a Turkey
merchant, on his return from the East, brought with him
a Ragusian Greek servant, named Pasqua Rosee, who
prepared coffee every morning for his master, and with
the coachman above named set up the first Coffee-house
in St. Michael's-alley; but they soon quarrelled and
separated, the coachman establishing himself in St.
Michael's churchyard.—(See pp. 2 and 4, *ante.*)

Aubrey wrote the above in 1680, and Mr. Farr had
then become a person of consequence. In his *Lives,*
Aubrey notes:—" When coffee first came in, Sir Henry
Blount was a great upholder of it, and hath ever since
been a great frequenter of coffee-houses, especially Mr.
Farre's, at the Rainbowe, by Inner Temple Gate."

Farr was originally a barber. His success as a coffee-
man appears to have annoyed his neighbours; and at
the inquest at St. Dunstan's, Dec. 21st, 1657, among
the presentments of nuisances were the following:—

"We present James Farr, barber, for making and selling of a drink called coffee, whereby in making the same he annoyeth his neighbours by evill smells; and for keeping of fire for the most part night and day, whereby his chimney and chamber hath been set on fire, to the great danger and affrightment of his neighbours." However, Farr was not ousted; he probably promised reform, or amended the alleged annoyance: he remained at the Rainbow, and rose to be a person of eminence and repute in the parish. He issued a token, date 1666—an arched rainbow based on clouds, doubtless, from the Great Fire—to indicate that with him all was yet safe, and the Rainbow still radiant. There is one of his tokens in the Beaufoy collection, at Guildhall, and so far as is known to Mr. Burn, the rainbow does not occur on any other tradesman's token. The house was let off into tenements: books were printed here at this very time "for Samuel Speed, at the sign of the Rainbow, near the Inner Temple Gate, in Fleet-street." The Phœnix Fire Office was established here about 1682. Hatton, in 1708, evidently attributed Farr's nuisance to the *coffee itself*, saying: "Who would have thought London would ever have had three thousand such nuisances, and that coffee would have been (as now) so much drank by the best of quality, and physicians?" The nuisance was in Farr's chimney and carelessness, not in the coffee. Yet, in our statute-book anno 1660 (12 Car. II. c. 24), a duty of 4*d.* was laid upon every gallon of coffee made and sold. A statute of 1663 directs that all Coffee-houses should be licensed at the Quarter Sessions. And in 1675, Charles II. issued a proclamation to shut up the Coffee-houses, charged with being seminaries of sedition; but in a few days he suspended this proclamation by a second.

The *Spectator*, No. 16, notices some gay frequenters
of the Rainbow :—" I have received a letter desiring me
to be very satirical upon the little muff that is now in
fashion ; another informs me of a pair of silver garters
buckled below the knee, that have been lately seen at
the Rainbow Coffee-house in Fleet-street."

Mr. Moncrieff, the dramatist, used to tell that about
1780, this house was kept by his grandfather, Alexander
Moncrieff, when it retained its original title of " The
Rainbow Coffee-house." The old Coffee-room had a
lofty bay-window, at the south end, looking into the
Temple : and the room was separated from the kitchen
only by a glazed partition : in the bay was the table for
the elders. The house has long been a tavern ; all the
old rooms have been swept away, and a large and lofty
dining-room erected in their place.

In a paper read to the British Archæological Association, by Mr. E. B. Price, we find coffee and canary
thus brought into interesting comparison, illustrated by
the exhibition of one of Farr's Rainbow tokens; and
another inscribed " At the Canary House in the Strand,
1*d.*, 1665," bearing also the word " Canary " in the mo-
nogram. Having noticed the prosecution of Farr, and his
triumph over his fellow-parishioners, Mr. Price says :—
"The opposition to coffee continued; people viewed it with
distrust, and even with alarm : and we can sympathize
with them in their alarm, when we consider that they
entertained a notion that coffee would eventually put an
end to the species ; that the *genus homo* would some
day or other be utterly extinguished. With our knowledge of the beneficial effect of this article on the com-
munity, and its almost universal adoption in the present
day, we may smile, and wonder while we smile, at the

bare possibility of such a notion ever having prevailed. That it did so, we have ample evidence in the "Women's Petition against Coffee," in the year 1674, cited by D'Israeli, *Curiosities of Literature*, vol. iv., and in which they complain that coffee " made men as unfruitful as the deserts whence that unhappy berry is said to be brought: that the offspring of our mighty ancestors would dwindle into a succession of apes and pigmies," etc. The same authority gives us an extract from a very amusing poem of 1663, in which the writer wonders that any man should prefer Coffee to Canary, terming them English apes, and proudly referring them to the days of Beaumont and Fletcher and Ben Jonson. *They*, says he,

> " Drank pure nectar as the gods drink too
> Sublimed with rich *Canary ;* say, shall then
> These less than coffee's self, these coffee-men,
> These sons of nothing, that can hardly make
> Their broth for laughing how the jest does take,
> Yet grin, and give ye for the vine's pure blood
> A loathsome potion—not yet understood,
> Syrup of soot, or essence of old shoes,
> Dasht with diurnals or the book of news ?"

One of the weaknesses of "rare Ben" was his *penchant* for canary. And it would seem that the Mermaid, in Bread-street, was the house in which he enjoyed it most:

> " But that which most doth take my muse and me,
> Is a pure cup of rich *Canary wine*,
> Which is the Mermaid's now, but shall be mine."

Granger states that Charles I. raised Ben's pension from 100 marks to 100 pounds, and added a tierce of

canary, which salary and its appendage, he says, have
ever since been continued to poets laureate.

Reverting tot he Rainbow (says Mr. Price), "it has
been frequently remarked by 'tavern-goers,' that many
of our snuggest and most comfortable taverns are hidden
from vulgar gaze, and unapproachable except through
courts, blind alleys, or but half-lighted passages." Of
this description was the house in question. But few of
its many nightly, or rather midnightly patrons and frequenters, knew aught of it beyond its famed " stewed
cheeses," and its " stout," with the various " et ceteras "
of good cheer. They little dreamed, and perhaps as little
cared to know, that, more than two centuries back, the
Rainbow flourished as a bookseller's shop; as appears
by the title-page of Trussell's *History of England*,
which states it to be " printed by M.D., for Ephraim
Dawson, and are to bee sold in Fleet Street, at the signe
of the Rainbowe, neere the Inner-Temple Gate, 1636."

NANDO'S COFFEE-HOUSE

Was the house at the east corner of Inner Temple-lane,
No. 17, Fleet-street, and next-door to the shop of Bernard Lintot, the bookseller; though it has been by
some confused with Groom's house, No. 16. Nando's
was the favourite haunt of Lord Thurlow, before he
dashed into law practice. At this Coffee-house a large
attendance of professional loungers was attracted by the
fame of the punch and the charms of the landlady,
which, with the small wits, were duly admired by and

at the bar. One evening, the famous cause of Douglas *v.* the Duke of Hamilton was the topic of discussion, when Thurlow being present, it was suggested, half in earnest, to appoint him junior counsel, which was done. This employment brought him acquainted with the Duchess of Queensberry, who saw at once the value of a man like Thurlow, and recommended Lord Bute to secure him by a silk gown.

The house, formerly Nando's, has been for many years a hair-dresser's. It is inscribed " Formerly the palace of Henry VIII. and Cardinal Wolsey." The structure is of the time of James I., and has an enriched ceiling inscribed P (triple plumed).

This was the office in which the Council for the Management of the Duchy of Cornwall Estates held their sittings; for in the Calendar of State Papers, edited by Mrs. Green, is the following entry, of the time of Charles, created Prince of Wales four years after the death of Henry :—" 1619, Feb. 25 ; Prince's *Council Chamber, Fleet-street.*—Council of the Prince of Wales to the Keepers of Brancepeth, Raby, and Barnard Castles: The trees blown down are only to be used for mending the pales, and no wood to be cut for firewood, nor browse for the deer."

DICK'S COFFEE-HOUSE.

This old Coffee-house, No. 8, Fleet-street (south side, near Temple Bar), was originally " Richard's," named from Richard Torner, or Turner, to whom the house was let in 1680. The Coffee-room retains its olden paneling, and the staircase its original balusters.

The interior of Dick's Coffee-house is engraved as a frontispiece to a drama, called *The Coffee-house*, performed at Drury-lane Theatre in 1737. The piece met with great opposition on its representation, owing to its being stated that the characters were intended for a particular family (that of Mrs. Yarrow and her daughter), who kept Dick's, the coffee-house which the artist had inadvertently selected as the frontispiece.

It appears that the landlady and her daughter were the reigning toast of the Templars, who then frequented Dick's; and took the matter up so strongly that they united to condemn the farce on the night of its production; they succeeded, and even extended their resentment to every thing suspected to be this author's (the Rev. James Miller) for a considerable time after.

Richard's, as it was then called, was frequented by Cowper, when he lived in the Temple. In his own account of his insanity, Cowper tells us: "At breakfast I read the newspaper, and in it a letter, which, the further I perused it, the more closely engaged my attention. I cannot now recollect the purport of it; but before I had finished it, it appeared demonstratively true to me that it was a libel or satire upon me. The author appeared to be acquainted with my purpose of self-destruction, and to have written that letter on purpose to secure and hasten the execution of it. My mind, probably, at this time began to be disordered; however it was, I was certainly given to a strong delusion. I said within myself, 'Your cruelty shall be gratified; you shall have your revenge,' and flinging down the paper in a fit of strong passion, I rushed hastily out of

the room ; directing my way towards the fields, where
I intended to find some house to die in ; or, if not, determined to poison myself in a ditch, where I could meet
with one sufficiently retired."

It is worth while to revert to the earlier tenancy of the
Coffee-house, which was, wholly or in part, the original
printing office of Richard Tottel, law-printer to Edward
VI., Queens Mary and Elizabeth ; the premises were attached to No. 7, Fleet-street, which bore the sign of
" The Hand and Starre," where Tottel lived, and published the law and other works he printed.   No. 7 was
subsequently occupied by Jaggard and Joel Stephens,
eminent law-printers, temp. Geo. I.—III. ; and at the
present day the house is most appropriately occupied by
Messrs. Butterworth, who follow the occupation Tottel
did in the days of Edward VI., being law-publishers to
Queen Victoria ; and they possess the original leases,
from the earliest grant, in the reign of Henry VIII.,
the period of their own purchase.

THE " LLOYD'S " OF THE TIME OF CHARLES II.

During the reign of Charles II., Coffee-houses grew
into such favour, that they quickly spread over the metropolis, and were the usual meeting-places of the roving
cavaliers, who seldom visited home but to sleep.   The
following song, from Jordan's *Triumphs of London*,
1675, affords a very curious picture of the manners of
the times, and the sort of conversation then usually

met with in a well-frequented house of the sort,—the
" Lloyd's " of the seventeenth century :—

> " You that delight in wit and mirth,
>   And love to hear such news
> That come from all parts of the earth,
>   Turks, Dutch, and Danes, and Jews :
> I'll send ye to the rendezvous,
>   Where it is smoaking new ;
> Go hear it at a coffee-house,
>   It cannot but be true.

> " There battails and sea-fights are fought,
>   And bloudy plots displaid ;
> They know more things than e'er was thought,
>   Or ever was bewray'd :
> No money in the minting-house
>   Is half so bright and new ;
> And coming from the *Coffee-House,*
>   It cannot but be true.

> " Before the navies fell to work,
>   They knew who should be winner ;
> They there can tell ye what the Turk
>   Last Sunday had to dinner.
> Who last did cut Du Ruiter's* corns,
>   Amongst his jovial crew ;
> Or who first gave the devil horns,
>   Which cannot but be true.

> ' A fisherman did boldly tell,
>   And strongly did avouch,
> He caught a shole of mackerell,
>   They parley'd all in Dutch ;

* The Dutch admiral who, in June, 1667, dashed into the
Downs with a fleet of eighty sail, and many fire-ships, blocked
up the mouths of the Medway and Thames, destroyed the
fortifications at Sheerness, cut away the paltry defences of
booms and chains drawn across the rivers, and got to Chatham,
on the one side, and nearly to Gravesend on the other; the
king having spent in debauchery the money voted by Parliament
for the proper support of the English navy.

And cry'd out *Yaw, yaw, yaw, mine hare,*
   And as the draught they drew,
They stunk for fear that Monk* was there :
   This sounds as if 'twere true.

" There's nothing done in all the world,
   From monarch to the mouse ;
But every day or night 'tis hurl'd
   Into the coffee-house :
What Lilly† or what Booker‡ cou'd
   By art not bring about,
At Coffee-house you'll find a brood,
   Can quickly find it out.

" They know who shall in times to come,
   Be either made or undone,
From great St. Peter's-street in Rome,
   To Turnbal-street§ in London.

*   *   *

* General Monk and Prince Rupert were at this time com-
manders of the English fleet.

† Lilly was the celebrated astrologer of the Protectorate, who
earned great fame at that time by predicting, in June, 1645, " if
now we fight, a victory stealeth upon us :" a lucky guess, sig-
nally verified in the King's defeat at Naseby. Lilly thenceforth
always saw the stars favourable to the Puritans.

‡ This man was originally a fishing-tackle-maker in Tower-
street, during the reign of Charles I. ; but turning enthusiast, he
went about prognosticating " the downfall of the King and
Popery ;" and as he and his predictions were all on the popular
side, he became a great man with the superstitious " godly
brethren " of that day.

§ Turnbal, or Turnbull-street as it is still called, had been for
a century previous of infamous repute. In Beaumont and Fletcher's play, the *Knight of the Burning Pestle,* one of the ladies
who is undergoing penance at the barber's, has her character
sufficiently pointed out to the audience, in her declaration, that
she had been " stolen from her friends in Turnbal-street."

"They know all that is good or hurt,
　　To damn ye or to save ye ;
There is the college and the court,
　　The country, camp, and navy.
So great an university,
　　I think there ne'er was any ;
In which you may a scholar be,
　　For spending of a penny.

"Here men do talk of everything,
　　With large and liberal lungs,
Like women at a gossiping,
　　With double tire of tongues,
They'll give a broadside presently,
　　'Soon as you are in view :.
With stories that you'll wonder at,
　　Which they will swear are true.

"You shall know there what fashions are,
　　How perriwigs are curl'd ;
And for a penny you shall hear
　　All novels in the world ;
Both old and young, and great and small,
　　And rich and poor you'll see ;
Therefore let's to the Coffee all,
　　Come all away with me."

LLOYD'S COFFEE-HOUSE.

Lloyd's is one of the earliest establishments of the
kind ; it is referred to in a poem printed in the year
1700, called the *Wealthy Shopkeeper, or Charitable
Christian :*

　　"Now to Lloyd's coffee-house he never fails,
　　To read the letters, and attend the sales."

In 1710, Steele (*Tatler*, No. 246,) dates from Lloyd's

his Petition on Coffee-house Orators and Newsvendors. And Addison, in *Spectator*, April 23, 1711, relates this droll incident :—" About a week since there happened to me a very odd accident, by reason of which one of these my papers of minutes which I had accidentally dropped at Lloyd's Coffee-house, where the auctions are usually kept. Before I missed it, there were a cluster of people who had found it, and were diverting themselves with it at one end of the coffee-house. It had raised so much laughter among them before I observed what they were about, that I had not the courage to own it. The boy of the coffee-house, when they had done with it, carried it about in his hand, asking everybody if they had dropped a written paper; but nobody challenging it, he was ordered by those merry gentlemen who had before perused it, to get up into the auction-pulpit, and read it to the whole room, that if anybody would own it, they might. The boy accordingly mounted the pulpit, and with a very audible voice read what proved to be minutes, which made the whole coffee-house very merry ; some of them concluded it was written by a madman, and others by somebody that had been taking notes out of the *Spectator*. After it was read, and the boy was coming out of the pulpit, the Spectator reached his arm out, and desired the boy to give it him ; which was done according. This drew the whole eyes of the company upon the Spectator; but after casting a cursory glance over it, he shook his head twice or thrice at the reading of it, twisted it into a kind of match, and lighted his pipe with it. ' My profound silence,' says the Spectator, ' together with the steadiness of my countenance, and the gravity of my behaviour during the whole transaction, raised a very loud laugh on all sides of me ; but as I had escaped all suspicion of being the author, I was very well satisfied, and applying myself to my pipe and the *Postman*, took no further notice of anything that passed about me.' "

Nothing is positively known of the original Lloyd; but in 1750, there was issued an Irregular Ode, entitled *A Summer's Farewell to the Gulph of Venice, in the Southwell Frigate*, Captain Manly, jun., commanding, stated to be "printed for Lloyd, well-known for obliging the public with the Freshest and Most Authentic Ship News, and sold by A. More, near St. Paul's, and at the Pamphlet Shops in London and Westminster, MDCCL."

In the *Gentleman's Magazine*, for 1740, we read :— "11 March, 1740, Mr. Baker, Master of Lloyd's Coffee-house, in Lombard-street, waited on Sir Robert Walpole with the news of Admiral Vernon's taking Portobello. This was the first account received thereof, and proving true, Sir Robert was pleased to order him a handsome present."

Lloyd's is, perhaps, the oldest collective establishment in the City. It was first under the management of a single individual, who started it as a room where the underwriters and insurers of ships' cargoes could meet for refreshment and conversation. The Coffee-house was originally in Lombard-street, at the corner of Abchurch-lane; subsequently in Pope's-head-alley, where it was called "New Lloyd's Coffee-house;" but on February 14th, 1774, it was removed to the north-west corner of the Royal Exchange, where it remained until the destruction of that building by fire.

In rebuilding the Exchange, a fine suite of apartments was provided for Lloyd's "Subscription Rooms," which are the rendezvous of the most eminent merchants, ship-owners, underwriters, insurance, stock, and exchange

brokers. Here is obtained the earliest news of the arrival and sailing of vessels, losses at sea, captures, re-
captures, engagements, and other shipping intelligence;
and proprietors of ships and freights are insured by the
underwriters. The rooms are in the Venetian style, with
Roman enrichments. They are—1. The Subscribers'
or Underwriters', the Merchants', and the Captains'
Room. At the entrance of the room are exhibited the
Shipping Lists, received from Lloyd's agents at home
and abroad, and affording particulars of departures or
arrivals of vessels, wrecks, salvage, or sale of property
saved, etc. To the right and left are " Lloyd's Books,"
two enormous ledgers : right hand, ships " spoken with,"
or arrived at their destined ports; left hand : records of
wrecks, fires, or severe collisions, written in a fine Roman
hand, in "double lines." To assist the underwriters in
their calculations, at the end of the room is an Anemo-
meter, which registers the state of the wind day and
night; attached is a rain-gauge.

The life of the underwriter is one of great anxiety and
speculation. "Among the old stagers of the room, there
is often strong antipathy to the insurance of certain
ships. In the case of one vessel it was strangely followed
out. She was a steady trader, named after one of the
most venerable members of the room; and it was a curious coincidence that he invariably refused to ' write
her ' for ' a single line.' Often he was joked upon the
subject, and pressed to ' do a little ' for his namesake;
but he as often declined, shaking his head in a doubtful
manner. One morning the subscribers were reading the
' double lines,' or the losses, and among them was this
identical ship, which had gone to pieces, and become a
total wreck."—*The City*, *2nd edit.*, 1848.

The Merchants' Room is superintended by a master, who can speak several languages: here are duplicate copies of the books in the underwriters' room, and files of English and foreign newspapers.

The Captains' Room is a kind of coffee-room, where merchants and ship-owners meet captains, and sales of ships, etc. take place.

The members of Lloyd's have ever been distinguished by their loyalty and benevolent spirit. In 1802, they voted 2000*l.* to the Life-boat subscription. On July 20, 1803, at the invasion panic, they commenced the Patriotic Fund with 20,000*l.* 3-per-cent. Consols; besides 70,312*l.* 7*s.* individual subscriptions, and 15,000*l.* additional donations. After the battle of the Nile, in 1798, they collected for the widows and wounded seamen 32,423*l.*; and after Lord Howe's victory, June 1, 1794, for similar purposes, 21,281*l.* They have also contributed 5000*l.* to the London Hospital; 1000*l.* for the suffering inhabitants of Russia in 1813; 1000*l.* for the relief of the militia in our North American colonies, 1813; and 10,000*l.* for the Waterloo subscription, in 1815. The Committee vote medals and rewards to those who distinguish themselves in saving life from shipwreck.

Some years since, a member of Lloyd's drew from the books the following lines of names contained therein :—

"A Black and a White, with a Brown and a Green,
And also a Gray at Lloyd's room may be seen ;
With Parson and Clark, then a Bishop and Pryor,
And Water, how Strange adding fuel to fire ;
While, at the same time, 'twill sure pass belief,
There's a Winter, a Garland, Furze, Bud, and a Leaf;
With Freshfield, and Greenhill, Lovegrove, and a Dale ;
Though there's never a Breeze, there's always a Gale.

No music is there, though a Whistler and Harper;
There's a Blunt and a Sharp, many flats, but no sharper.
There's a Danniell, a Samuel, a Sampson, an Abell;
The first and the last write at the same table.
Then there's Virtue and Faith there, with Wylie and Rasch,
Disagreeing elsewhere, yet at Lloyd's never clash,
There's a Long and a Short, Small, Little, and Fatt,
With one Robert Dewar, who ne'er wears his hat:
No drinking goes on, though there's Porter and Sack,
Lots of Scotchmen there are, beginning with Mac;
Macdonald, to wit, Macintosh and McGhie,
McFarquhar, McKenzie, McAndrew, Mackie.
An evangelized Jew, and an infidel Quaker;
There's a Bunn and a Pye, with a Cook and a Baker,
Though no Tradesmen or Shopmen are found, yet herewith
Is a Taylor, a Saddler, a Paynter, a Smyth;
Also Butler and Chapman, with Butter and Glover,
Come up to Lloyd's room their bad risks to cover.
Fox, Shepherd, Hart, Buck, likewise come every day;
And though many an ass, there is only one Bray.
There is a Mill and Miller, A-dam and a Poole,
A Constable, Sheriff, a Law, and a Rule.
There's a Newman, a Niemann, a Redman, a Pitman,
Now to rhyme with the last, there is no other fit man.
These, with Young, Cheap, and Lent, Luckie, Hastie, and
     Slow,
With dear Mr. Allnutt, Allfrey, and Auldjo,
Are all the queer names that at Lloyd's I can show."

Many of these individuals are now deceased; but a
frequenter of Lloyd's in former years will recognize the
persons mentioned.

THE JERUSALEM COFFEE-HOUSE,

Cornhill, is one of the oldest of the City news-rooms, and is frequented by merchants and captains connected with the commerce of China, India, and Australia.

"The subscription-room is well-furnished with files of the principal Canton, Hongkong, Macao, Penang, Singapore, Calcutta, Bombay, Madras, Sydney, Hobart Town, Launceston, Adelaide, and Port Phillip papers, and Prices Current: besides shipping lists and papers from the various intermediate stations or ports touched at, as St. Helena, the Cape of Good Hope, etc. The books of East India shipping include arrivals, departures, casualties, etc. The full business is between two and three o'clock, p.m. In 1845, John Tawell, the Slough murderer, was captured at [traced to] the Jerusalem, which he was in the habit of visiting, to ascertain information of the state of his property in Sydney."— *The City*, 2nd edit., 1848.

BAKER'S COFFEE-HOUSE,

Change-alley, is remembered as a tavern some forty years since. The landlord, after whom it is named, may possibly have been a descendant from "Baker," the master of Lloyd's Rooms. It has been, for many years, a chop-house, with direct service from the grid-

iron, and upon pewter; though on the first-floor, joint
dinners are served : its post-prandial punch was formerly much drunk.   In the lower room is a portrait of
James, thirty-five years waiter here.

COFFEE-HOUSES OF THE EIGHTEENTH CENTURY.

Of Ward's *Secret History* of the Clubs of his time
we have already given several specimens. Little is known
of him personally.   He was, probably, born in 1660,
and early in life he visited the West Indies.   Sometime
before 1669, he kept a tavern and punch-house, next
door to Gray's Inn, of which we shall speak hereafter.
His works are now rarely to be met with.   His doggrel
secured him a place in the *Dunciad,* where not only his
elevation to the pillory is mentioned, but the fact is also
alluded to that his productions were extensively shipped
to the Plantations or Colonies of those days,—

" Nor sail with Ward to ape-and-monkey climes,
    Where vile mundungus trucks for viler rhymes,"

the only places, probably, where they were extensively
read. In return for the doubtful celebrity thus conferred
upon his rhymes, he attacked the satirist in a wretched
production, intituled *Apollo's Maggot in his Cups ;* his
expiring effort, probably, for he died, as recorded in the
pages of our first volume, on the 22nd of June, 1731.
His remains were buried in the churchyard of Old St.
Pancras, his body being followed to the grave solely by
his wife and daughter, as directed by him in his poetical

will, written some six years before. We learn from Noble that there are no less than four engraved portraits of Ned Ward. The structure of the *London Spy*, the only work of his that at present comes under our notice, is simple enough. The author is self-personified as a countryman, who, tired with his " tedious confinement to a country hutt," comes up to London ; where he fortunately meets with a quondam school-fellow,—a " man about town," in modern phrase,—who undertakes to introduce him to the various scenes, sights, and mysteries of the, even then, " great metropolis :" much like the visit, in fact, from Jerry Hawthorn to Corinthian Tom, only anticipated by some hundred and twenty years. " We should not be at all surprised (says the *Gentleman's Magazine,*) to find that the stirring scenes of Pierce Egan's *Life in London* were first suggested by more homely pages of the *London Spy.*"

At the outset of the work we have a description—not a very flattering one, certainly—of a common coffee-house of the day, one of the many hundreds with which London then teemed. Although coffee had been only known in England some fifty years, coffee-houses were already among the most favourite institutions of the land ; though they had not as yet attained the political importance which they acquired in the days of the *Tatler* and *Spectator*, some ten or twelve years later :—

" ' Come,' says my friend, 'let us step into this coffee-house here ; as you are a stranger in the town, it will afford you some diversion.' Accordingly in we went, where a parcel of muddling muckworms were as busy as so many rats in an old cheese-loft ; some going, some coming, some scribbling, some talking, some drinking, some smoking, others jangling; and the whole room stinking of tobacco, like a Dutch scoot [schuyt], or a boatswain's cabin. The walls were hung round with gilt frames, as a farrier's shop with horse-shoes; which contained abundance of rarities, viz., Nectar and Ambrosia, May-dew, Golden Elixirs, Popular Pills, Liquid Snuff, Beautifying Waters, Dentifrices, Drops, and Lozenges; all as infallible as the Pope, ' Where every one (as the famous Saffold^e has it) above the rest, Deservedly has gain'd the name of best:' every medicine being so catholic, it pretends to nothing less than universality. So that, had not my friend told me 'twas a coffee-house, I should have taken it for Quacks' Hall, or the parlour of some eminent moun-tebank. We each of us stuck in our mouths a pipe of sotweed, and now began to look about us."

A description of Man's Coffee-house, situate in Scot-land-yard, near the water-side, is an excellent picture of a fashionable coffee-house of the day. It took its name from the proprietor, Alexander Man, and was sometimes known as Old Man's, or the Royal Coffee-house, to dis-tinguish it from Young Man's and Little Man's minor establishments in the neighbourhood :—

" We now ascended a pair of stairs, which brought us into an old-fashioned room, where a gaudy crowd of odoriferous *Tom-Essences* were walking backwards and forwards with their hats in their hands, not daring to convert them to their intended use, lest it should put the foretops of their wigs into some disorder. We squeezed through till we got to the end of the room, where, at a small table, we sat down, and observed that it was as great a rarity to hear anybody call for a dish of *Politician's porridge*, or any other liquor, as it is to

hear a beau call for a pipe of tobacco ; their whole exercise being to charge and discharge their nostrils, and
keep the curls of their periwigs in their proper order.
The clashing of their snush-box lids, in opening and
shutting, made more noise than their tongues. Bows
and cringes of the newest mode were here exchanged,
'twixt friend and friend, with wonderful exactness. They
made a humming like so many hornets in a country
chimney, not with their talking, but with their whisper-
ing over their new *Minuets* and *Bories*, with their hands
in their pockets, if only freed from their snush-box.
We now began to be thoughtful of a pipe of tobacco ;
whereupon we ventured to call for some instruments of
evaporation, which were accordingly brought us, but
with such a kind of unwillingness, as if they would much
rather have been rid of our company ; for their tables
were so very neat, and shined with rubbing, like the
upper-leathers of an alderman's shoes, and as brown as
the top of a country housewife's cupboard. The floor
was as clean swept as a Sir Courtly's dining-room, which
made us look round, to see if there were no orders
hung up to impose the forfeiture of so much Mop-
money upon any person that should spit out of the
chimney-corner. Notwithstanding we wanted an example to encourage us in our porterly rudeness, we
ordered them to light the wax-candle, by which we
ignified our pipes and blew about our whiffs ; at which
several Sir Foplins drew their faces into as many peevish
wrinkles, as the beaux at the Bow-street Coffee-house,
near Covent-garden did, when the gentleman in masquerade came in amongst them, with his oyster-barrel
muff and turnip-buttons, to ridicule their fopperies."

COFFEE-HOUSES OF THE EIGHTEENTH CENTURY.

A cabinet picture of the Coffee-house life of a century and a half since is thus given in the well-known *Journey through England* in 1714: "I am lodged," says the tourist, "in the street called Pall Mall, the ordinary residence of all strangers, because of its vicinity to the Queen's Palace, the Park, the Parliament House, the Theatres, and the Chocolate and Coffee-houses, where the best company frequent. If you would know our manner of living, 'tis thus: we rise by nine, and those that frequent great men's levees, find entertainment at them till eleven, or, as in Holland, go to tea-tables; about twelve the *beau monde* assemble in several Coffee or Chocolate houses: the best of which are the Cocoa-tree and White's Chocolate-houses, St. James's, the Smyrna, Mrs. Rochford's, and the British Coffee-houses; and all these so near one another, that in less than an hour you see the company of them all. We are carried to these places in chairs (or sedans), which are here very cheap, a guinea a week, or a shilling per hour, and your chairmen serve you for porters to run on errands, as your gondoliers do at Venice.

"If it be fine weather, we take a turn into the Park till two, when we go to dinner; and if it be dirty, you are entertained at piquet or basset at White's, or you may talk politics at the Smyrna or St. James's. I must not forget to tell you that the parties have their different places, where, however, a stranger is always well re-

ceived ; but a Whig will no more go to the Cocoa-tree or
Ozinda's, than a Tory will be seen at the Coffee-house,
St. James's.

"The Scots go generally to the British, and a mixture of all sorts to the Smyrna.   There are other little
Coffee-houses much frequented in this neighbourhood,
—Young Man's for officers, Old Man's for stock-jobbers,
pay-masters, and courtiers, and Little Man's for sharpers.   I never was so confounded in my life as when I
entered into this last : I saw two or three tables full at
faro, heard the box and dice rattling in the room above
stairs, and was surrounded by a set of sharp faces, that
I was afraid would have devoured me with their eyes.
I was glad to drop two or three half crowns at faro to
get off with a clear skin, and was overjoyed I so got
rid of them.

"At two, we generally go to dinner; ordinaries are
not so common here as abroad, yet the French have set
up two or three good ones for the convenience of
foreigners in Suffolk-street, where one is tolerably well
served ; but the general way here is to make a party at
the Coffee-house to go to dine at the tavern, where we
sit till six, when we go to the play ; except you are invited
to the table of some great man, which strangers are
always courted to, and nobly entertained."

We may here group the leading Coffee-houses,* the
principal of which will be more fully described hereafter :

"Before 1715, the number of Coffee-houses in London
was reckoned at two thousand.   Every profession, trade,
class, party, had its favourite Coffee-house.   The lawyers discussed law or literature, criticized the last new
play, or retailed the freshest Westminster Hall "bite"

* From the *National Review*, No. 8.

at Nando's or the Grecian, both close on the purlieus
of the Temple. Here the young bloods of the Inns-of-
Court paraded their Indian gowns and lace caps of a
morning, and swaggered in their lace coats and Mechlin
ruffles at night, after the theatre. The Cits met to dis-
cuss the rise and fall of stocks, and to settle the rate of
insurance, at Garraway's or Jonathan's; the parsons
exchanged university gossip, or commented on Dr.
Sacheverel's last sermon at Truby's or at Child's in St.
Paul's Churchyard; the soldiers mustered to grumble
over their grievances at Old or Young Man's, near
Charing Cross; the St. James's and the Smyrna were
the head-quarters of the Whig politicians, while the
Tories frequented the Cocoa-tree or Ozinda's, all in St.
James's-street; Scotchmen had their house of call at
Forrest's, Frenchmen at Giles's or Old Slaughter's, in
St. Martin's-lane; the gamesters shook their elbows in
White's and the Chocolate-houses round Covent Garden;
the *virtuosi* honoured the neighbourhood of Gresham
College; and the leading wits gathered at Will's, Button's, or Tom's, in Great Russell-street, where after the
theatre was playing at piquet and the best of conversation till midnight. At all these places, except a few
of the most aristocratic Coffee or Chocolate-houses of
the West-End, smoking was allowed. A penny was
laid down at the bar on entering, and the price of a dish
of tea or coffee seems to have been two-pence: this
charge covered newspapers and lights. The established
frequenters of the house had their regular seats, and
special attention from the fair lady at the bar, and the
tea or coffee boys.

" To these Coffee-houses men of all classes, who had
either leisure or money, resorted to spend both ; and in

them, politics, play, scandal, criticism, and business, went on hand-in-hand. The transition from Coffee-house to Club was easy. Thus Tom's, a Coffee-house till 1764, in that year, by a guinea subscription, among nearly seven hundred of the nobility, foreign ministers, gentry, and geniuses of the age, became the place of meeting for the subscribers exclusively.* In the same way, White's and the Cocoa-tree changed their character from Chocolate-house to Club. When once a house had customers enough of standing and good repute, and acquainted with each other, it was quite worth while—considering the characters who, on the strength of as-surance, tolerable manners, and a laced coat, often got a footing in these houses while they continued open to the public, to purchase power of excluding all but subscribers."

Thus, the chief places of resort were at this period Coffee and Chocolate-houses, in which some men almost lived, as they do at the present day, at their Clubs. Whoever wished to find a gentleman commonly asked, not where he resided, but which coffee-house he fre-quented. No decently attired idler was excluded, pro-vided he laid down his penny at the bar ; but this he could seldom do without struggling through the crowd of beaux who fluttered round the lovely bar-maid. Here the proud nobleman or country squire was not to be distinguished from the genteel thief and daring high-wayman. " Pray, sir," says Aimwell to Gibbet, in Farquhar's *Beaux Stratagem*, " ha'n't I seen your face at Will's Coffee-house ?" The robber's reply is : " Yes, Sir, and at White's too."

* We question whether the Coffee-house general business was entirely given up immediately after the transition.

Three of Addison's papers in the *Spectator*, (Nos. 402, 481, and 568,) are humorously descriptive of the Coffee-houses of this period. No. 403 opens with the remark that "the courts of two countries do not so much differ from one another, as the Court and the City, in their peculiar ways of life and conversation. In short, the inhabitants of St. James's, notwithstanding they live under the same laws, and speak the same language, are a distinct people from those of Cheapside, who are likewise removed from those of the Temple on the one side, and those of Smithfield on the other, by several climates and degrees in their way of thinking and conversing together." For this reason, the author takes a ramble through London and Westminster, to gather the opinions of his ingenious countrymen upon a current report of the King of France's death. " I know the faces of all the principal politicians within the bills of mortality; and as every Coffee-house has some particular statesman belonging to it, who is the mouth of the street where he lives, I always take care to place myself near him, in order to know his judgment on the present posture of affairs. And, as I foresaw, the above report would produce a new face of things in Europe, and many curious speculations in our British Coffee-houses, I was very desirous to learn the thoughts of our most eminent politicians on that occasion.

"That I might begin as near the fountain-head as possible, I first of all called in at St. James's, where I found the whole outward room in a buzz of politics; the speculations were but very indifferent towards the door, but grew finer as you advanced to the upper end of the room, and were so much improved by a knot of theorists, who sat in the inner room, within the steams of the coffee-pot, that I there heard the whole Spanish monarchy disposed of, and all the line of Bourbons provided for in less than a quarter of an hour.

" I afterwards called in at Giles's, where I saw a board of French gentlemen sitting upon the life and death of their grand monarque. Those among them who had espoused the Whig interest very positively affirmed that he had departed this life about a week since, and therefore, proceeded without any further delay to the release of their friends in the galleys, and to their own re-establishment ; but, finding they could not agree among themselves, I proceeded on my intended progress.

" Upon my arrival at Jenny Man's I saw an alert young fellow that cocked his hat upon a friend of his, who entered just at the same time with myself, and accosted him after the following manner : ' Well, Jack, the old prig is dead at last. Sharp's the word. Now or never, boy. Up to the walls of Paris, directly;' with several other deep reflections of the same nature.

" I met with very little variation in the politics between Charing Cross and Covent Garden. And, upon my going into Will's, I found their discourse was gone off, from the death of the French King, to that of Monsieur Boileau, Racine, Corneille, and several other poets, whom they regretted on this occasion as persons who would have obliged the world with very noble elegies on the death of so great a prince, and so eminent a patron of learning.

" At a Coffee-house near the Temple, I found a couple of young gentlemen engaged very smartly in a dispute on the succession to the Spanish monarchy. One of them seemed to have been retained as advocate for the Duke of Aujou, the other for his Imperial Majesty.

They were both for regarding the title to that kingdom by the statute laws of England : but finding them going out of my depth, I pressed forward to Paul's Churchyard, where I listened with great attention to a learned man, who gave the company an account of the deplorable state of France during the minority of the deceased King.

"I then turned on my right hand into Fish-street, where the chief politician of that quarter, upon hearing the news, (after having taken a pipe of tobacco, and ruminated for some time,) 'If,' says he, 'the King of France is certainly dead, we shall have plenty of mackerel this season : our fishery will not be disturbed by privateers, as it has been for these ten years past.' He afterwards considered how the death of this great man would affect our pilchards, and by several other remarks infused a general joy into his whole audience.

"I afterwards entered a by-coffee-house that stood at the upper end of a narrow lane, where I met with a conjuror, engaged very warmly with a laceman who was the great support of a neighbouring conventicle. The matter in debate was whether the late French King was most like Augustus Cæsar, or Nero. The controversy was carried on with great heat on both sides, and as each of them looked upon me very frequently during the course of their debate, I was under some apprehension that they would appeal to me, and therefore laid down my penny at the bar, and made the best of my way to Cheapside.

"I here gazed upon the signs for some time before I found one to my purpose. The first object I met in the coffee-room was a person who expressed a great grief for the death of the French King ; but upon his explaining himself, I found his sorrow did not arise from the loss of the monarch, but for his having sold out of the Bank about three days before he heard the news of it. Upon which a haberdasher, who was the oracle of the Coffee-house, and had his circle of admirers about him, called several to witness that he had declared his opinion, above a week before, that the French King was certainly dead ; to which he added, that, considering the late advices we had received from France, it was impossible that it could be otherwise. As he was laying these toge-ther, and debating to his hearers with great authority, there came a gentleman from Garraway's, who told us that there were several letters from France just come in, with advice that the King was in good health, and was gone out a hunting the very morning the post came away; upon which the haberdasher stole off his hat that hung upon a wooden peg by him, and retired to his shop with great confusion. This intelligence put a stop to my travels, which I had prosecuted with so much satisfaction; not being a little pleased to hear so many different opinions upon so great an event, and to observe how naturally, upon such a piece of news, every one is apt to consider it to his particular interest and advantage."

COFFEE-HOUSE SHARPERS IN 1776.

The following remarks by Sir John Fielding* upon the dangerous classes to be found in our metropolitan Coffee-houses three-quarters of a century since, are de-

* 'The Magistrate : Description of London and Westminster,' 1776.

scribed as "necessary Cautions to all Strangers resorting thereto."

"A stranger or foreigner should particularly frequent the Coffee-houses in London. These are very numerous in every part of the town; will give him the best insight into the different characters of the people, and the justest notion of the inhabitants in general, of all the houses of public resort these are the least dangerous. Yet, some of these are not entirely free from sharpers. The deceivers of this denomination are generally descended from families of some repute, have had the groundwork of a genteel education, and are capable of making a tolerable appearance. Having been equally profuse of their own substance and character, and learned, by having been undone, the ways of undoing, they lie in wait for those who have more wealth and less knowledge of the town. By joining you in discourse, by admiring what you say, by an officiousness to wait upon you, and to assist you in anything you want to have or know, they insinuate themselves into the company and acquaintance of strangers, whom they watch every opportunity of fleecing. And if one finds in you the least inclination to cards, dice, the billiard-table, bowling-green, or any other sort of gaming, you are morally sure of being taken in. For this set of gentry are adepts in all the arts of knavery and tricking. If, therefore, you should observe a person, without any previous acquaintance, paying you extraordinary marks of civility; if he puts in for a share of your conversation with a pretended air of deference; if he tenders his assistance, courts your acquaintance, and would be suddenly thought your friend, avoid him as a pest; for these are the usual baits by which the unwary are caught."

DON SALTERO'S COFFEE-HOUSE.

Among the curiosities of Old Chelsea, almost as well
known as its china, was the Coffee-house and Museum,
No. 18, Cheyne Walk, opened by a barber, named
Salter, in 1695. Sir Hans Sloane contributed some
of the refuse gimcracks of his own collection; and
Vice-Admiral Munden, who had been long on the coast
of Spain, where he had acquired a fondness for Spanish
titles, named the keeper of the house *Don Saltero,* and
his coffee-house and museum, *Don Saltero's.*

The place, however, would, in all probability, have
enjoyed little beyond its local fame, had not Sir Richard
Steele immortalized the Don and Don Saltero's in *The
Tatler,* No. 34, June 28, 1700; wherein he tells us of
the necessity of travelling to know the world by his
journey for fresh air, no further than the village of
Chelsea, of which he fancied that he could give an
immediate description, from the five fields, where the
robbers lie in wait, to the Coffee-house, where the
literati sit in council. But he found, even in a place
so near town as this, there were enormities and persons of eminence, whom he before knew nothing of.

The Coffee-house was almost absorbed by the Museum. "When I came into the Coffee-house," says
Steele, "I had not time to salute the company, before
my eyes were diverted by ten thousand gimcracks
round the room, and on the ceiling. When my first
astonishment was over, comes to me a sage of thin
and meagre countenance, which aspect made me doubt

whether reading or fretting had made it so philoso-
phic; but I very soon perceived him to be of that
sort which the ancients call 'gingivistee,' in our language 'tooth-drawers.' I immediately had a respect
for the man; for these practical philosophers go upon
a very practical hypothesis, not to cure, but to take
away the part affected. My love of mankind made
me very benevolent to Mr. Salter, for such is the name
of this eminent barber and antiquary."

The Don was famous for his punch and his skill on
the fiddle; he also drew teeth, and wrote verses; he
described his museum in several stanzas, one of which
is—

"Monsters of all sorts are seen:
    Strange things in nature as they grew so;
Some relicks of the Sheba Queen,
    And fragments of the fam'd Bob Crusoe."

Steele then plunges into a deep thought why bar-
bers should go further in hitting the ridiculous than any
other set of men; and maintains that Don Saltero is
descended in a right line, not from John Tradescant,
as he himself asserts, but from the memorable companion of the Knight of Mancha. Steele then certifies
that all the worthy citizens who travel to see the Don's
rarities, his double-barrelled pistols, targets, coats of
mail, his sclopeta, and sword of Toledo, were left to
his ancestor by the said Don Quixote, and by his ancestor to all his progeny down to Saltero. Though
Steele thus goes far in favour of Don Saltero's great
merit, he objects to his imposing several names (without
his licence) on the collection he has made, to the abuse
of the good people of England; one of which is particularly calculated to deceive religious persons, to the

great scandal of the well-disposed, and may introduce
heterodox opinions. [Among the curiosities presented
by Admiral Munden was a coffin, containing the body
or relics of a Spanish saint, who had wrought miracles.]
" He shows you a straw hat, which," says Steele, " I
know to be made by Madge Peskad, within three miles
of Bedford; and tells you ' It is Pontius Pilate's wife's
chambermaid's sister's hat.' To my knowledge of this
very hat, it may be added that the covering of straw
was never used among the Jews, since it was demanded
of them to make bricks without it. Therefore, this is
nothing but, under the specious pretence of learning
and antiquities, to impose upon the world. There are
other things which I cannot tolerate among his rarities, as, the china figure of the lady in the glass-case;
the Italian engine, for the imprisonment of those who
go abroad with it; both of which I hereby order to be
taken down, or else he may expect to have his letters
patent for making punch superseded, be debarred wearing his muff next winter, or ever coming to London
without his wife." Babillard says that Salter had an
old grey muff, and that, by wearing it up to his nose,
he was distinguishable at the distance of a quarter of a
mile. His wife was none of the best, being much addicted to scolding; and Salter, who liked his glass, if
he could make a trip to London by himself, was in no
haste to return.

Don Saltero's proved very attractive as an exhibition,
and drew crowds to the coffee-house. A catalogue was published, of which were printed more than forty editions.
Smollett, the novelist, was among the donors. The catalogue, in 1760, comprehended the following rarities:—
Tigers' tusks; the Pope's candle; the skeleton of a

Guinea-pig; a fly-cap monkey; a piece of the true Cross; the Four Evangelists' heads cut on a cherry-stone; the King of Morocco's tobacco-pipe; Mary Queen of Scots' pincushion; Queen Elizabeth's prayer-book; a pair of Nun's stockings; Job's ears, which grew on a tree; a frog in a tobacco-stopper; and five hundred more odd relics! The Don had a rival, as appears by "A Catalogue of the Rarities to be seen at Adams's, at the Royal Swan, in Kingsland-road, leading from Shoreditch Church, 1756." Mr. Adams exhibited, for the entertainment of the curious, "Miss Jenny Cameron's shoes; Adam's eldest daughter's hat; the heart of the famous Bess Adams, that was hanged at Tyburn with Lawyer Carr, January 18, 1736–7; Sir Walter Raleigh's tobacco-pipe; Vicar of Bray's clogs; engine to shell green peas with; teeth that grew in a fish's belly; Black Jack's ribs; the very comb that Abraham combed his son Isaac and Jacob's head with; Wat Tyler's spurs; rope that cured Captain Lowry of the head-ach, ear-ach, tooth-ach, and belly-ach; Adam's key of the fore and back door of the Garden of Eden, &c., &c." These are only a few out of five hundred others equally marvellous.

The Don, in 1723, issued a curious rhyming advertisement of his Curiosities, dated "Chelsea Knackatory," and in one line he calls it "My Museum Coffee-house."

In Dr. Franklin's _Life_ we read:—"Some gentlemen from the country went by water to see the College, and Don Saltero's Curiosities, at Chelsea." They were shown in the coffee-room till August, 1799, when the collection was mostly sold or dispersed; a few gimcracks were left until about 1825, when we were informed on the premises, they were thrown away! The house is now a tavern, with the sign of "The Don Saltero's Coffee-house."

The success of Don Saltero, in attracting visitors to his coffee-house, induced the proprietor of the Chelsea Bun-house to make a similar collection of rarities, to attract customers for the buns; and to some extent it was successful.

SALOOP-HOUSES.

What was, in our time, occasionally sold at stalls in the streets of London, with this name, was a decoction of sassafras; but it was originally made from Salep, the roots of *Orchis mascula*, a common plant of our meadows, the tubers of which, being cleaned and peeled, are lightly browned in an oven. Salep was much recommended in the last century by Dr. Percival, who stated that salep had the property of concealing the taste of salt water, which property it was thought might be turned to account in long sea-voyages. The root has been considered as containing the largest portion of nutritious matter in the smallest space; and when boiled, it was much used in this country before the introduction of tea and coffee, and their greatly reduced prices. Salep is now almost entirely disused in Great Britain; but we remember many saloop-stalls in our streets. We believe the last house in which it was sold, to have been Read's Coffee-house, in Fleet-street. The landlord of the noted Mug-house, in Salisbury-square, was one Read. (See CLUBS, p. 52.)

THE SMYRNA COFFEE-HOUSE,

In Pall Mall, was, in the reign of Queen Anne, famous for "that cluster of wise-heads" found sitting every evening, from the left side of the fire to the door. The following announcement in the *Tatler*, No. 78, is amusing: "This is to give notice to all ingenious gentlemen in and about the cities of London and Westminster, who have a mind to be instructed in the noble sciences of music, poetry, and politics, that they repair to the Smyrna Coffee-house, in Pall Mall, betwixt the hours of eight and ten at night, where they may be instructed gratis, with elaborate essays by word of mouth," on all or any of the above-mentioned arts. The disciples are to prepare their bodies with three dishes of bohea, and to purge their brains with two pinches of snuff. If any young student gives indication of parts, by listening attentively, or asking a pertinent question, one of the professors shall distinguish him, by taking snuff out of his box in the presence of the whole audience.

"N.B. The seat of learning is now removed from the corner of the chimney on the left hand towards the window, to the round table in the middle of the floor over against the fire; a revolution much lamented by the porters and chairmen, who were much edified through a pane of glass that remained broken all the last summer."

Prior and Swift were much together at the Smyrna: we read of their sitting there two hours, "receiving acquaintance;" and one entry of Swift's tells us that he walked a little in the Park till Prior made him go with him to the Smyrna Coffee-house. It seemed to be the place to *talk politics ;* but there is a more agreeable record of it in association with our " Poet of the Year," thus given by Cunningham : " In the printed copy of Thomson's proposals for publishing, by subscription, the Four Seasons, with a Hymn on their succession, the following note is appended :—' Subscriptions now taken in by the author, at the Smyrna Coffee-house, Pall Mall.' "* We find the Smyrna in a list of Coffee-Houses in 1810.

ST. JAMES'S COFFEE-HOUSE.

This was the famous Whig Coffee-house from the time of Queen Anne till late in the reign of George III. It was the last house but one on the south-west corner of St. James's-street, and is thus mentioned in No. 1 of the *Tatler :* "Foreign and Domestic News you will have from St. James's Coffee-house." It occurs also in the passage quoted at page 39, from the *Spectator.* The St. James's was much frequented by Swift; letters for him were left here. In his Journal to Stella he says : " I met Mr. Harley, and he asked me how long I had learnt the trick of writing to myself? He had seen your letter through the glass case at the Coffee-house, and would swear it was my hand." The letters from Stella were enclosed under cover to Addison.

* The Dane Coffee-house, between the Upper and Lower Malls, Hammersmith, was frequented by Thomson, who wrote here a part of his *Winter.* On the Terrace resided, for many years, Arthur Murphy, and Loutherbourg, the painter. The latter died there, in 1812.

Elliot, who kept the coffee-house, was, on occasions, placed on a friendly footing with his guests.[1] Swift, in his Journal to Stella, Nov. 19, 1710, records an odd instance of this familiarity : "This evening I christened our coffee-man Elliot's child; when the rogue had a most noble supper, and Steele and I sat amongst some scurvy company over a bowl of punch."

In the first advertisement of Lady Mary Wortley Montagu's *Town Eclogues*, they are stated to have been read over at the St. James's Coffee-house, when they were considered by the general voice to be productions of a Lady of Quality. From the proximity of the house to St. James's Palace, it was much frequented by the Guards; and we read of its being no uncommon circumstance to see Dr. Joseph Warton at breakfast in the St. James's Coffee-house, surrounded by officers of the Guards, who listened with the utmost attention and pleasure to his remarks.

To show the order and regularity observed at the St. James's, we may quote the following advertisement, appended to the *Tatler*, No. 25 :—"To prevent all mistakes that may happen among gentlemen of the other end of the town, who come but once a week to St. James's Coffee-house, either by miscalling the servants, or requiring such things from them as are not properly within their respective provinces; this is to give notice that Kidney, keeper of the book-debts of the outlying customers, and observer of those who go off without paying, having resigned that employment, is succeeded by John Sowton; to whose place of enterer of messages and first coffee-grinder, William Bird is promoted; and Samuel Burdock comes as shoe-cleaner in the room of the said Bird."

But the St. James's is more memorable as the house where originated Goldsmith's celebrated poem, *Retaliation*. The poet belonged to a temporary association of men of talent, some of them members of the Club, who dined together occasionally here. At these dinners he was generally the last to arrive. On one occasion, when he was later than usual, a whim seized the company to write epitaphs on him as "the late Dr. Goldsmith," and several were thrown off in a playful vein. The only one extant was written by Garrick, and has been preserved, very probably, by its pungency :—

> "Here lies poet Goldsmith, for shortness called Noll ;
> He wrote like an angel, but talked like poor Poll."

Goldsmith did not relish the sarcasm, especially coming from such a quarter; and, by way of *retaliation*, he produced the famous poem, of which Cumberland has left a very interesting account, but which Mr. Forster, in his *Life of Goldsmith*, states to be "pure romance." The poem itself, however, with what was prefixed to it when published, sufficiently explains its own origin. What had formerly been abrupt and strange in Goldsmith's manners, had now so visibly increased, as to become matter of increased sport to such as were ignorant of its cause ; and a proposition made at one of the dinners, when he was absent, to write a series of epitaphs upon him (his "country dialect" and his awkward person) was agreed to and put in practice by several of the guests. The active aggressors appear to have been Garrick, Doctor Bernard, Richard Burke, and Caleb Whitefoord. Cumberland says he, too, wrote an epitaph ; but it was complimentary and grave, and hence the grateful return he received. Mr. Forster considers Garrick's epitaph to indicate the tone of all. This, with the rest, was read to Goldsmith when he next appeared at the St. James's Coffee-house, where Cumberland, however, says he never again met his friends. But "the Doctor was called on for Retaliation," says the friend who published the poem with that name, "and at their next meeting, produced the following, which I think adds one leaf to his immortal wreath." "*Retaliation*," says Sir Walter Scott, "had the effect of placing the author on a more equal footing with his Society than he had ever before assumed."

Cumberland's account differs from the version formerly received, which intimates that the epitaphs were written before Goldsmith arrived: whereas the pun, "the late Dr. Goldsmith," appears to have suggested the writing of the epitaphs. In the *Retaliation*, Goldsmith has not spared the characters and failings of his associates, but has drawn them with satire, at once pungent and good-humoured. Garrick is smartly chastised; Burke, the Dinner-bell of the House of Commons, is not let off; and of all the more distinguished names of the Club, Thomson, Cumberland, and Reynolds alone escape the lash of the satirist. The former is not mentioned, and the two latter are even dismissed with unqualified and affectionate applause.

Still, we quote Cumberland's account of the *Retaliation*, which is very amusing from the closely circumstantial manner in which the incidents are narrated, although they have so little relationship to truth :—" It was upon a proposal started by Edmund Burke, that a party of friends who had dined together at Sir Joshua Reynolds's and my house, should meet at the St. James's Coffee-house, which accordingly took place, and was repeated occasionally with much festivity and good fellowship. Dr. Bernard, Dean of Derry; a very amiable and old friend of mine, Dr. Douglas, since Bishop of Salisbury; Johnson, David Garrick, Sir Joshua Reynolds, Oliver Goldsmith, Edmund and Richard Burke, Hickey, with two or three others, constituted our party. At one of these meetings an idea was suggested of extemporary epitaphs upon the parties present: pen and ink were called for, and Garrick, off-hand, wrote an epitaph with a good deal of humour, upon poor Goldsmith, who was the first in jest, as he proved to be in reality, that we committed to the grave. The Dean also gave him an epitaph, and Sir Joshua illuminated the Dean's verses with a sketch of his bust in pen-and-ink, inimitably caricatured. Neither Johnson nor Burke wrote anything, and when I perceived that Oliver was rather sore, and seemed to watch me with that kind of attention which indicated his expectation of something in the same kind of burlesque with theirs; I thought it time to press the joke no further, and wrote a few couplets at a side-table, which, when I had finished, and was called upon by the company to exhibit, Goldsmith, with much agitation, besought me to spare him; and I was about to tear them, when Johnson wrested them out of my hand, and in a loud voice read them at the table. I have now lost recollection of them, and, in fact, they were little worth remembering; but as they were serious and complimentary, the effect upon Goldsmith was the more pleasing, for being so entirely unexpected. The concluding line, which was the only one I can call to mind, was :—

"'All mourn the poet, I lament the man.'

This I recollect, because he repeated it several times, and seemed much gratified by it. At our next meeting he

produced his epitaphs, as they stand in the little posthu-
mous poem above mentioned, and this was the last time
he ever enjoyed the company of his friends."*

Mr. Cunningham tells us that the St. James's was
closed about 1806; and a large pile of building looking
down Pall Mall, erected on its site.

The globular oil-lamp was first exhibited by its inven-
tor, Michael Cole, at the door of the St. James's Coffee-
house, in 1709; in the patent he obtained, it is mentioned
as " a new kind of light."

THE BRITISH COFFEE-HOUSE,

In Cockspur-street, " long a house of call for Scotchmen," has been fortunate in its landladies. In 1759, it
was kept by the sister of Bishop Douglas, so well known
for his works against Lauder and Bower, which may
explain its Scottish fame. At another period it was
kept by Mrs. Anderson, described in Mackenzie's *Life
of Home* as " a woman of uncommon talents, and the
most agreeable conversation."†

The British figures in a political faction of 1750, at
which date Walpole writes to Sir Horace Mann : " The
Argyll carried all the Scotch against the turnpike; they
were willing to be carried, for the Duke of Bedford, in
case it should have come into the Lords, had writ to
the sixteen Peers, to solicit their votes; but with so
little difference, that he enclosed all the letters under one
cover directed to the British Coffee-house."

* *Cumberland's Memoirs*, vol. i.
† *Cunningham's Walpole*, vol. ii. p. 196, note.

WILL'S COFFEE-HOUSE.*

Will's, the predecessor of Button's, and even more celebrated than that Coffee-house, was kept by William Urwin, and was the house on the north side of Russell-street at the end of Bow-street—the corner house—now occupied as a ham and beef shop, and numbered twenty-three. " It was Dryden who made Will's Coffee-house the great resort of the wits of his time." (*Pope* and *Spence*). The room in which the poet was accustomed to sit was on the first floor; and his place was the place of honour by fire-side in the winter; and at the corner of the balcony, looking over the street, in fine weather; he called the two places his winter and his summer seat. This was called the dining-room floor in the last century. The company did not sit in boxes, as subsequently, but at various tables which were dispersed through the room. Smoking was permitted in the public room : it was then so much in vogue that it does not seem to have been considered a nuisance. Here, as in other similar places of meeting, the visitors divided themselves into parties; and we are told by Ward, that the young beaux and wits, who seldom approached the principal

* Will's Coffee-house first had the title of the Red Cow, then of the Rose, and, we believe, is the same house alluded to in the pleasant story in the second number of the *Tatler* :—

"Supper and friends expect we at the Rose."

The Rose, however, was a common sign for houses of public entertainment.

table, thought it a great honour to have a pinch out of Dryden's snuff-box.

Dean Lockier has left this life-like picture of his interview with the presiding genius at Will's :—" I was about seventeen when I first came up to town," says the Dean, "an odd-looking boy, with short rough hair, and that sort of awkwardness which one always brings up at first out of the country with one. However, in spite of my bashfulness and appearance, I used, now and then, to thrust myself into Will's, to have the pleasure of seeing the most celebrated wits of that time, who then resorted thither. The second time that ever I was there, Mr. Dryden was speaking of his own things, as he frequently did, especially of such as had been lately published. ' If anything of mine is good,' says he, ' 'tis *Mac-Flecno*; and I value myself the more upon it, because it is the first piece of ridicule written in heroics.' On hearing this I plucked up my spirit so far as to say, in a voice but just loud enough to be heard, ' that *Mac-Flecno* was a very fine poem, but that I had not imagined it to be the first that was ever writ that way.' On this, Dryden turned short upon me, as surprised at my interposing ; asked me how long ' I had been a dealer in poetry ; ' and added, with a smile, ' Pray, Sir, what is it that you did imagine to have been writ so before ? '—I named Boileau's *Lutrin*, and Tassoni's *Secchia Rapita*, which I had read, and knew Dryden had borrowed some strokes from each. ' 'Tis true,' said Dryden, ' I had forgot them.' A little after, Dryden went out, and in going, spoke to me again, and desired me to come and see him the next day. I was highly delighted with the invitation ; went to see him accordingly ; and was well acquainted with him after, as long as he lived."

Will's Coffee-house was the open market for libels and lampoons, the latter named from the established burden formerly sung to them :—

"Lampone, lampone, camerada lampone."

There was a drunken fellow, named Julian, who was a characterless frequenter of Will's, and Sir Walter Scott has given this account of him and his vocation :—

" Upon the general practice of writing lampoons, and the necessity of finding some mode of dispersing them, which should diffuse the scandal widely while the authors remained concealed, was founded the self-erected office of Julian, Secretary, as he calls himself, to the Muses. This person attended Will's, the Wits' Coffee-house, as it was called; and dispersed among the crowds who frequented that place of gay resort copies of the lampoons which had been privately communicated to him by their authors. ' He is described,' says Mr. Malone, ' as a very drunken fellow, and at one time was confined for a liable.' Several satires were written, in the form of addresses to him as well as the following. There is one among the *State Poems* beginning—

> " ' Julian, in verse, to ease thy wants I write,
> Not moved by envy, malice, or by spite,
> Or pleased with the empty names of wit and sense,
> But merely to supply thy want of pence :
> This did inspire my muse, when out at heel,
> She saw her needy secretary reel ;
> Grieved that a man, so useful to the age,
> Should foot it in so mean an equipage ;
> A crying scandal that the fees of sense
> Should not be able to support the expense
> Of a poor scribe, who never thought of wants,
> When able to procure a cup of Nantz.'

Another, called a 'Consoling Epistle to Julian,' is said to have been written by the Duke of Buckingham.

" From a passage in one of the *Letters from the Dead to the Living*, we learn, that after Julian's death, and the madness of his successor, called Summerton, lampoon felt a sensible decay ; and there was no more that brisk spirit of verse, that used to watch the follies and vices of the men and women of figure, that they could not start new ones faster than lampoons exposed them."

How these lampoons were concocted we gather from Bays, in the *Hind and the Panther transversed :*—" 'Tis a trifle hardly worth owning; I was 'tother day at Will's, throwing out something of that nature ; and, i' gad, the hint was taken, and out came that picture ; indeed, the poor fellow was so civil as to present me with a dozen of 'em for my friends ; I think I have here one in my pocket. . . . Ay, ay, I can do it if I list, tho' you must not think I have been so dull as to mind these things myself; but 'tis the advantage of our Coffee-house, that from their talk, one may write a very good polemical discourse, without ever troubling one's head with the books of controversy."

Tom Brown describes " a Wit and a Beau set up with little or no expense. A pair of red stockings and a sword-knot set up one, and peeping once a day in at Will's, and two or three second-hand sayings, the other."

Pepys, one night, going to fetch home his wife, stopped in Covent Garden, at the Great Coffee-house there, as he called Will's, where he never was before : " Where," he adds, " Dryden, the poet (I knew at Cambridge), and all the Wits of the town, and Harris the player, and Mr. Hoole of our College. And had I had time then, or could at other times, it will be good coming thither, for there, I perceive, is very witty and pleasant discourse. But I could not tarry; and, as it was late, they were all ready to go away."

Addison passed each day alike, and much in the manner that Dryden did. Dryden employed his mornings in writing, dined *en famille*, and then went to Will's, "only he came home earlier o' nights."

Pope, when very young, was impressed with such veneration for Dryden, that he persuaded some friends to take him to Will's Coffee-house, and was delighted that he could say that he had seen Dryden. Sir Charles Wogan, too, brought up Pope from the Forest of Windsor, to dress *à la mode*, and introduce at Will's Coffee-house. Pope afterwards described Dryden as "a plump man with a down look, and not very conversible;" and Cibber could tell no more " but that he remembered him a decent old man, arbitor of critical disputes at Will's." Prior sings of—

> "the younger Stiles,
> Whom Dryden pedagogues at Will's!"

Most of the hostile criticisms on his Plays, which Dryden has noticed in his various Prefaces, appear to have been made at his favourite haunt, Will's Coffee-house.

Dryden is generally said to have been returning from Will's to his house in Gerard-street, when he was cudgelled in Rose-street by three persons hired for the purpose by Wilmot, Earl of Rochester, in the winter of 1679. The assault, or "the Rose-alley Ambuscade," certainly took place; but it is not so certain that Dryden was on his way from Will's, and he then lived in Long Acre, not Gerard-street.

It is worthy of remark that Swift was accustomed to speak disparagingly of Will's, as in his *Rhapsody on Poetry* :—

> " Be sure at Will's the following day
> Lie snug, and hear what critics say ;
> And if you find the general vogue
> Pronounces you a stupid rogue,
> Damns all your thoughts as low and little ;
> Sit still, and swallow down your spittle."

Swift thought little of the frequenters of Will's : he used to say, " the worst conversation he everheard in his life was at Will's Coffee-house, where the wits (as they were called) used formerly to assemble; that is to say, five or six men, who had writ plays or at least prologues, or had a share in a miscellany, came thither, and entertained one another with their trifling composures, in so important an air as if they had been the noblest efforts of human nature, or that the fate of kingdoms depended on them."

In the first number of the *Tatler*, Poetry is promised under the article of Will's Coffee-house. The place, however, changed after Dryden's time : " you used to see songs, epigrams, and satires in the hands of every man you met; you have now only a pack of cards ; and instead of the cavils about the turn of the expression, the elegance of the style, and the like, the learned now dispute only about the truth of the game." " In old times, we used to sit upon a play here, after it was acted, but now the entertainment's turned another way."

The *Spectator* is sometimes seen " thrusting his head into a round of politicians at Will's, and listening with great attention to the narratives that are made in these little circular audiences." Then, we have as an instance of no one member of human society but that would have some little pretension for some degree in it, " like him who came to Will's Coffee-house upon the merit of having writ a posie of a ring." And, " Robin, the porter who waits at Will's, is the best man in town for carrying a billet : the fellow has a thin body, swift step, demure looks, sufficient sense, and knows the town."

After Dryden's death in 1701, Will's continued for about ten years to be still the Wits' Coffee-house, as we see by Ned Ward's account, and by that in the *Journey through England* in 1722.

Pope entered with keen relish into society, and courted the correspondence of the town wits and coffee-house critics. Among his early friends was Mr. Henry Cromwell, one of the *cousinry* of the Protector's family : he was a bachelor, and spent most of his time in London ; he had some pretensions to scholarship and literature, having translated several of Ovid's Elegies, for Tonson's Miscellany. With Wycherley, Gay, Dennis, the popular actors and actresses of the day, and with all the frequenters of Will's, Cromwell was familiar. He had done more than take a pinch out of Dryden's snuff-box, which was a point of high ambition and honour at Will's ; he had quarrelled with him about a frail poetess, Mrs. Elizabeth Thomas, whom Dryden had christened Corinna, and who was also known as Sappho. Gay characterized this literary and eccentric beau as

" Honest, hatless Cromwell, with red breeches ;"

it being his custom to carry his hat in his hand when walking with ladies. What with ladies and literature, rehearsals and reviews, and critical attention to the quality of his coffee and Brazil snuff, Henry Cromwell's

* *The Spectator*, No. 398.

time was fully occupied in town. Cromwell was a dangerous acquaintance for Pope at the age of sixteen or seventeen, but he was a very agreeable one. Most of Pope's letters to his friend are addressed to him at the Blue Ball, in Great Wild-street, near Drury-lane; and others to " Widow Hambledon's Coffee-house at the end of Princes-street, near Drury-lane, London." Cromwell made one visit to Binfield ; on his return to London, Pope wrote to him, " referring to the ladies in particular," and to his favourite coffee :

" As long as Mocha's happy tree shall grow,
 While berries crackle, or while mills shall go ;
 While smoking streams from silver spouts shall glide
 Or China's earth receive the sable tide,
 While Coffee shall to British nymphs be dear,
 While fragrant steams the bended head shall cheer,
 Or grateful bitters shall delight the taste,
 So long her honours, name, and praise shall last."

Even at this early period Pope seems to have relied for relief from headache to the steam of coffee, which he inhaled for this purpose throughout the whole of his life.*

The Taverns and Coffee-houses supplied the place of the Clubs we have since seen established. Although no exclusive subscription belonged to any of these, we find by the account which Colley Cibber gives of his first visit to Will's, in Covent Garden, that it required an introduction to this Society not to be considered as an impertinent intruder. There the veteran Dryden had long presided over all the acknowledged wits and poets of the day, and those who had the pretension to be reckoned among them. The politicians assembled at the St. James's Coffee-house, from whence all the ar-

* Carruthers : Life of Pope.

ticles of political news in the first *Tatlers* are dated.
The learned frequented the Grecian Coffee-house in
Devereux-court. Locket's, in Gerard-street, Soho, and
Pontac's, were the fashionable taverns where the young
and gay met to dine : and White's and other chocolate
houses seem to have been the resort of the same company in the morning. Three o'clock, or at latest four,
was the dining-hour of the most fashionable persons in
London, for in the country no such late hours had been
adopted. In London, therefore, soon after six, the men
began to assemble at the coffee-house they frequented
if they were not setting in for hard drinking, which
seems to have been much less indulged in private houses
than in taverns. The ladies made visits to one another,
which it must be owned was a much less waste of time
when considered as an amusement for the evening, than
now, as being a morning occupation.

BUTTON'S COFFEE-HOUSE.

Will's was the great resort for the wits of Dryden's
time, after whose death it was transferred to Button's.
Pope describes the houses as " opposite each other, in
Russell-street, Covent Garden," where Addison established Daniel Button, in a new house, about 1712; and
his fame, after the production of *Cato*, drew many of
the Whigs thither. Button had been servant to the
Countess of Warwick. The house is more correctly
described as " over against Tom's, near the middle of
the south side of the street."

Addison was the great patron of Button's; but it is

,aid that when he suffered any vexation from his Countess, he withdrew the company from Button's house. His chief companions, before he married Lady Warwick, were Steele, Budgell, Philips, Carey, Davenant, and Colonel Brett. He used to breakfast with one or other of them in St. James's-place, dine at taverns with them, then to Button's, and then to some tavern again, for supper in the evening; and this was the usual round of his life, as Pope tells us, in Spence's *Anecdotes;* where Pope also says: "Addison usually studied all the morning, then met his party at Button's, dined there, and stayed five or six hours; and sometimes far into the night. I was of the company for about a year, but found it too much for me: it hurt my health, and so I quitted it." Again: "There had been a coldness between me and Mr. Addison for some time, and we had not been in company together for a good while anywhere but at Button's Coffee-house, where I used to see him almost every day."

Here Pope is reported to have said of Patrick, the lexicographer, that "a dictionary-maker might know the meaning of one word, but not of two put together."

Button's was the receiving-house for contributions to *The Guardian,* for which purpose was put up a lion's head letter-box, in imitation of the celebrated lion at Venice, as humorously announced. Thus :—

"N.B.—Mr. Ironside has, within five weeks last past, muzzled three lions, gorged five, and killed one. On Monday next the skin of the dead one will be hung up, *in terrorem,* at Button's Coffee-house, over against Tom's in Covent Garden."*

"Button's Coffee-house,—

"Mr. Ironside, I have observed that this day you

* *The Guardian,* No. 71.

make mention of Will's Coffee-house, as a place where people are too polite to hold a man in discourse by the button. Everybody knows your honour frequents this house, therefore' they will take an advantage against me, and say if my company was as civil as that at Will's. You would say so. Therefore pray your honour do not be afraid of doing me justice, because people would think it may be a conceit below you on this occasion to name the name of your humble servant, Daniel Button.—The young poets are in the back room, and take their places as you directed."*

"I intend to publish once every week the roarings of the Lion, and hope to make him roar so loud as to be heard over all the British nation.

"I have, I know not how, been drawn into tattle of myself, *more majorum*, almost the length of a whole *Guardian*. I shall therefore fill up the remaining part of it with what still relates to my own person, and my correspondents. Now I would have them all know that on the 20th instant it is my intention to erect a Lion's Head, in imitation of those I have described in Venice, through which all the private commonwealth is said to pass. This head is to open a most wide and voracious mouth, which shall take in such letters and papers as are conveyed to me by my correspondents, it being my resolution to have a particular regard to all such matters as come to my hands through the mouth of the Lion. There will be under it a box, of which the key will be in my own custody, to receive such papers as are dropped into it. Whatever the Lion swallows I shall digest for the use of the publick. This head requires some time to finish, the workmen being re-

* *The Guardian*, No. 85.

solved to give it several masterly touches, and to represent it as ravenous as possible. It will be set up in Button's Coffee-house, in Covent Garden, who is directed to shew the way to the Lion's Head, and to instruct any young author how to convey his works into the mouth of it with safety and secrecy."*

" I think myself obliged to acquaint the publick, that the Lion's Head, of which I advertised them about a fortnight ago, is now erected at Button's Coffee-house, in Russell-street, Covent Garden, where it opens its mouth at all hours for the reception of such intelligence as shall be thrown into it. It is reckoned an excellent piece of workmanship, and was designed by a great hand in imitation of the antique Egyptian lion, the face of it being compounded out of that of a lion and a wizard. The features are strong and well furrowed. The whiskers are admired by all that have seen them. It is planted on the western side of the Coffee-house, holding its paws under the chin, upon a box, which contains everything that he swallows. He is, indeed, a proper emblem of knowledge and action, being all head and paws."†

" Being obliged, at present, to attend a particular affair of my own, I do empower my printer to look into the arcana of the lion, and select out of them such as may be of publick utility ; and Mr. Button is hereby authorized and commanded to give my said printer free ingress and egress to the lion, without any hindrance, lest, or molestation whatsoever, until such time as he shall receive orders to the contrary. And, for so doing, this shall be his warrant."‡

" My Lion, whose jaws are at all times open to in-

* *The Guardian*, No. 93. † *The Guardian*, No. 114.
‡ *The Guardian*, No. 142.

telligence, informs me that there are a few enormous
weapons still in being; but that they are to be met
with only in gaming-houses and some of the obscure
retreats of lovers, in and about Drury-lane and Covent
Garden."*

This memorable Lion's Head was tolerably well
carved: through the mouth the letters were dropped
into a till at Button's; and beneath were inscribed
these two lines from Martial:—

> " Cervantur magnis isti Cervicibus ungues :
> Non nisi delictâ pascitur ille ferâ."

The head was designed by Hogarth, and is etched in
Ireland's *Illustrations*. Lord Chesterfield is said to have
once offered for the Head fifty guineas. From Button's
it was removed to the Shakspeare's Head Tavern, under
the Piazza, kept by a person named Tomkyns; and in
1751, was, for a short time, placed in the Bedford
Coffee-house immediately adjoining the Shakspeare, and
there employed as a letter-box by Dr. John Hill, for his
Inspector. In 1769, Tomkyns was succeeded by his
waiter, Campbell, as proprietor of the tavern and lion's
head, and by him the latter was retained until Nov. 8,
1804, when it was purchased by Mr. Charles Richardson, of Richardson's Hotel, for £17. 10s., who also
possessed the original sign of the Shakspeare's Head.
After Mr. Richardson's death in 1827, the Lion's Head
devolved to his son, of whom it was bought by the Duke
of Bedford, and deposited at Woburn Abbey, where it
still remains.

Pope was subjected to much annoyance and insult at
Button's. Sir Samuel Garth wrote to Gay, that everybody was pleased with Pope's Translation, " but a few

* *The Guardian*, No. 171.

at Button's;" to which Gay adds, to Pope, "I am confirmed that at Button's your character is made very free
with, as to morals, etc."

Cibber, in a letter to Pope, says:—"When you used
to pass your hours at Button's, you were even there remarkable for your satirical itch of provocation; scarce
was there a gentleman of any pretension to wit, whom
your unguarded temper had not fallen upon in some
biting epigram, among which you once caught a pastoral
Tartar, whose resentment, that your punishment might
be proportionate to the smart of your poetry, had stuck
up a birchen rod in the room, to be ready whenever you
might·come within reach of it; and at this rate you writ
and rallied and writ on, till you rhymed yourself quite
out of the coffee-house." The "pastoral Tartar" was
Ambrose Philips, who, says Johnson, "hung up a rod
at Button's, with which he threatened to chastise Pope."

Pope, in a letter to Craggs, thus explains the affair:—
"Mr. Philips did express himself with much indignation against me one evening at Button's Coffee-house,
(as I was told,) saying that I was entered into a cabal
with Dean Swift and others, to write against the Whig
interest, and in particular to undermine his own reputation and that of his friends, Steele and Addison; but
Mr. Philips never opened his lips to my face, on this or
any like occasion, though I was almost every night in
the same room with him, nor ever offered me any inde-
corum. Mr. Addison came to me a night or two after
Philips had talked in this idle manner, and assured me
of his disbelief of what had been said, of the friendship
we should always maintain, and desired I would say
nothing further of it. My Lord Halifax did me the
honour to stir in this matter, by speaking to several peo-

ple to obviate a false aspersion, which might have done me no small prejudice with one party. However, Philips did all he could secretly to continue the report with the Hanover Club, and kept in his hands the subscriptions paid for me to him, as secretary to that Club. The heads of it have since given him to understand, that they take it ill; but (upon the terms I ought to be with such a man,) I would not ask him for this money, but commissioned one of the players, his equals, to receive it. This is the whole matter; but as to the secret grounds of this malignity, they will make a very pleasant history when we meet."

Another account says that the rod was hung up at the bar of Button's, and that Pope avoided it by remaining at home—"his usual custom." Philips was known for his courage and superior dexterity with the sword : he afterwards became justice of the peace, and used to mention Pope, whenever he could get a man in authority to listen to him, as an enemy to the Government.

At Button's the leading company, particularly Addison and Steele, met in large flowing flaxen wigs. Sir Godfrey Kneller, too, was a frequenter.

The master died in 1731, when in the *Daily Advertiser*, Oct. 5, appeared the following :—" On Sunday morning, died, after three days' illness, Mr. Button, who formerly kept Button's Coffee-house, in Russell-street, Covent Garden ; a very noted house for wits, being the place where the Lyon produced the famous *Tatlers* and *Spectators*, written by the late Mr. Secretary Addison and Sir Richard Steele, Knt., which works will transmit their names with honour to posterity." Mr. Cunningham found in the vestry-books of St. Paul's, Covent Garden : " 1719, April 16. Received of Mr. Daniel Button, for two

places in the pew No. 18, on the south side of the north
Isle,—2*l.* 2*s.*" J. T. Smith states that a few years after
Button, the Coffee-house declined, and Button's name
appeared in the books of St. Paul's, as receiving an
allowance from the parish.

Button's continued in vogue until Addison's death
and Steele's retirement into Wales, after which the
house was deserted; the coffee-drinkers went to the Bedford Coffee-house, the dinner-parties to the Shakspeare.

Among other wits who frequented Button's were
Swift, Arbuthnot, Savage, Budgell, Martin Folkes, and
Drs. Garth and Armstrong. In 1720, Hogarth mentions "four drawings in Indian ink" of the characters at
Button's Coffee-house. In these were sketches of Arbuthnot, Addison, Pope, (as it is conjectured,) and a
certain Count Viviani, identified years afterwards by
Horace Walpole, when the drawings came under his
notice. They subsequently came into Ireland's possession.*

Jemmy Maclaine, or M'Clean, the fashionable highwayman, was a frequent visitor at Button's. Mr. John
Taylor, of the *Sun* newspaper, describes Maclaine as a
tall, showy, good-looking man. A Mr. Donaldson told
Taylor that, observing Maclaine paid particular attention
to the bar-maid of the Coffee-house, the daughter of the
landlord, he gave a hint to the father of Maclaine's
dubious character. The father cautioned the daughter
against the highwayman's addresses, and imprudently
told her by whose advice he put her on her guard; she
as imprudently told Maclaine. The next time Donaldson visited the Coffee-room, and was sitting in one of

* From Mr. Sala's vivid "William Hogarth;" Cornhill Magazine, vol. i. p. 428.

the boxes, Maclaine entered, and in a loud tone said,
"Mr. Donaldson, I wish to *spake* to you in a private
room." Mr. D. being unarmed, and naturally afraid of
being alone with such a man, said, in answer, that as
nothing could pass between them that he did not wish
the whole world to know, he begged leave to decline
the invitation. "Very well," said Maclaine, as he left
the room, "we shall meet again." A day or two after,
as Mr. Donaldson was walking near Richmond, in the
evening, he saw Maclaine on horseback ; but, fortunately,
at that moment, a gentleman's carriage appeared in view,
when Maclaine immediately turned his horse towards the
carriage, and Donaldson hurried into the protection of
Richmond as fast as he could. But for the appearance
of the carriage, which presented better prey, it is probable that Maclaine would have shot Mr. Donaldson immediately.

Maclaine's father was an Irish Dean; his brother was
a Calvinist minister in great esteem at the Hague. Maclaine himself has been a grocer in Welbeck-street, but
losing a wife that he loved extremely, and by whom he
had one little girl, he quitted his business with two
hundred pounds in his pocket, which he soon spent, and
then took to the road with only one companion, Plunket,
a journeyman apothecary.

Maclaine was taken in the autumn of 1750, by selling
a laced waistcoat to a pawnbroker in Monmouth-street,
who happened to carry it to the very man who had just
sold the lace. Maclaine impeached his companion, Plunket, but he was not taken. The former got into verse :
Gray, in his *Long Story*, sings :

> " A sudden fit of ague shook him ;
> He stood as mute as poor M'Lean."

Button's subsequently became a private house, and here Mrs. Inchbald lodged, probably, after the death of her sister, for whose support she practised such noble and generous self-denial. Mrs. Inchbald's income was now 172*l.* a year, and we are told that she now went to reside in a boarding-house, where she enjoyed more of the comforts of life. Phillips, the publisher, offered her a thousand pounds for her Memoirs, which she declined. She died in a boarding-house at Kensington, on the 1st of August, 1821 ; leaving about 6000*l.* judiciously divided amongst her relatives. Her simple and parsimonious habits were very strange. " Last Thursday," she writes, " I finished scouring my bedroom, while a coach with a coronet and two footmen waited at my door to take me an airing."

" One of the most agreeable memories connected with Button's," says Leigh Hunt, " is that of Garth, a man whom, for the sprightliness and generosity of his nature, it is a pleasure to name. He was one of the most amiable and intelligent of a most amiable and intelligent class of men—the physicians."

DEAN SWIFT AT BUTTON'S.

It was just after Queen Anne's accession that Swift made acquaintance with the leaders of the wits at Button's. Ambrose Philips refers to him as the strange clergyman whom the frequenters of the Coffee-house had observed for some days. He knew no one, no one knew him. He would lay his hat down on a table, and walk up and down at a brisk pace for half an hour

without speaking to any one, or seeming to pay attention to anything that was going forward. Then he would
snatch up his hat, pay his money at the bar, and walk
off, without having opened his lips. The frequenters of
the room had christened him "the mad parson." One
evening, as Mr. Addison and the rest were observing
him, they saw him cast his eyes several times upon
a gentleman in boots, who seemed to be just come out
of the country. At last, Swift advanced towards this
bucolic gentleman, as if intending to address him.
They were all eager to hear what the dumb parson had
to say, and immediately quitted their seats to get near
him. Swift went up to the country gentleman, and
in a very abrupt manner, without any previous salute,
asked him, " Pray, Sir, do you know any good weather
in the world ?" After staring a little at the singularity
of Swift's manner and the oddity of the question, the
gentleman answered, " Yes, Sir, I thank God I remember a great deal of good weather in my time."—"That
is more," replied Swift, "than I can say ; I never remember any weather that was not too hot or too cold,
too wet or too dry ; but, however God Almighty con-
trives it, at the end of the year 'tis all very well."

Sir Walter Scott gives, upon the authority of Dr.
Wall, of Worcester, who had it from Dr. Arbuthnot
himself, the following anecdote—less coarse than the
version generally told. Swift was seated by the fire at
Button's : there was sand on the floor of the coffee-
room, and Arbuthnot, with a design to play upon this
original figure, offered him a letter, which he had been
just addressing, saying at the same time, " There—sand
that."—" I have got no sand," answered Swift, " but I
can help you to a little *gravel.*" This he said so signifi-

cantly, that Arbuthnot hastily snatched back his letter, to save it from the fate of the capital of Lilliput.

TOM'S COFFEE-HOUSE,

In Birchin-lane, Cornhill, though in the main a mercantile resort, acquired some celebrity from its having been frequented by Garrick, who, to keep up an interest in the City, appeared here about twice in a winter at 'Change time, when it was the rendezvous of young merchants. Hawkins says : " After all that has been said of Mr. Garrick, envy must own that he owed his celebrity to his merit ; and yet, of that himself seemed so diffident, that he practised sundry little but innocent arts, to insure the favour of the public :" yet, he did more. When a rising actor complained to Mrs. Garrick that the newspapers abused him, the widow replied, " You should write your own criticisms ; David always did."

One evening, Murphy was at Tom's, when Colley Cibber was playing at whist, with an old general for his partner. As the cards were dealt to him, he took up every one in turn, and expressed his disappointment at each indifferent one. In the progress of the game he did not follow suit, and his partner said, " What ! have you not a spade, Mr. Cibber ?" The latter, looking at his cards, answered, " Oh yes, a thousand ;" which drew a very peevish comment from the general. On which, Cibber, who was shockingly addicted to swearing, replied, " Don't be angry, for —— I can play ten times worse if I like."

THE BEDFORD COFFEE-HOUSE, IN COVENT GARDEN.

This celebrated resort once attracted so much attention as to have published, "Memoirs of the Bedford Coffee-house," two editions, 1751 and 1763. It stood "under the Piazza, in Covent Garden," in the north-west corner, near the entrance to the theatre, and has long ceased to exist.

In *The Connoisseur*, No. 1, 1754, we are assured that "this Coffee-house is every night crowded with men of parts. Almost every one you meet is a polite scholar and a wit. Jokes and bon-mots are echoed from box to box : every branch of literature is critically examined, and the merit of every production of the press, or performance of the theatres, weighed and determined."

And in the above-named *Memoirs*, we read that "this spot has been signalized for many years as the emporium of wit, the seat of criticism, and the standard of taste.—Names of those who frequented the house :—Foote, Mr. Fielding, Mr. Woodward, Mr. Leone, Mr. Murphy, Mopsy, Dr. Arne. Dr. Arne was the only man in a suit of velvet in the dog-days."

Stacie kept the Bedford when John and Henry Fielding, Hogarth, Churchill, Woodward, Lloyd, Dr. Goldsmith, and many others met there and held a gossiping shilling rubber club. Henry Fielding was a very merry fellow."

The *Inspector* appears to have given rise to this reign of the Bedford, when there was placed here the Lion from Button's, which proved so serviceable to Steele, and once more fixed the dominion of wit in Covent Garden.

The reign of wit and pleasantry did not, however, cease at the Bedford at the demise of the *Inspector*. A race of punsters next succeeded. A particular box was allotted to this occasion, out of the hearing of the lady at the bar, that the *double entendres*, which were sometimes very indelicate, might not offend her.

The Bedford was beset with scandalous nuisances, of which the following letter, from Arthur Murphy to Garrick, April 10, 1769, presents a pretty picture:

"Tiger Roach (who used to bully at the Bedford Coffee-house because his name was Roach) is set up by Wilkes's friends to burlesque Luttrel and his pretensions. I own I do not know a more ridiculous circumstance than to be a joint candidate with the Tiger. O'Brien used to take him off very pleasantly, and perhaps you may, from his representation, have some idea of this important wight. He used to sit with a half-starved look, a black patch upon his cheek, pale with the idea of murder, or with rank cowardice, a quivering lip, and a downcast eye. In that manner he used to sit at a table all alone, and his soliloquy, interrupted now and then with faint attempts to throw off a little saliva, was to the following effect :—' Hut ! hut ! a mercer's 'prentice with a bag-wig ;—d—n my s—l, if I would not skiver a dozen of them like larks ! Hut ! hut ! I don't understand such airs !—I'd cudgel him back, breast, and belly, for three skips of a louse ! —How do you do, Pat ! Hut ! hut ! God's blood—Larry, I'm

glad to see you;—'Prentices! a fine thing indeed!—
Hut! hut! How do you, Dominick!—D—n my s—l,
what's here to do !' These were the meditations of this
agreeable youth. From one of these reveries he started
up one night, when I was there, called a Mr. Bagnell
out of the room, and most heroically stabbed him in
the dark, the other having no weapon to defend himself
with. In this career the Tiger persisted, till at length
a Mr. Lennard brandished a whip over his head, and
stood in a menacing attitude, commanding him to ask
pardon directly. The Tiger shrank from the danger,
and with a faint voice pronounced—'Hut! what signifies it between you and me? Well! well! I ask your
pardon.' 'Speak louder, sir; I don't hear a word you
say.' And indeed he was so very tall, that it seemed as
if the sound, sent feebly from below, could not ascend
to such a height. This is the hero who is to figure at
Brentford."

Foote's favourite Coffee-house was the Bedford. He
was also a constant frequenter of Tom's, and took a lead
in the Club held there, and already described.*

Dr. Barrowby, the well-known newsmonger of the
Bedford, and the satirical critic of the day, has left this
whole-length sketch of Foote: — "One evening (he
says), he saw a young man extravagantly dressed out in
a frock suit of green and silver lace, bag-wig, sword,
bouquet, and point-ruffles, enter the room (at the Bedford), and immediately join the critical circle at the
upper end. Nobody recognised him; but such was the
ease of his bearing, and the point of humour and remark with which he at once took up the conversation,
that his presence seemed to disconcert no one, and a

* See "Club at Tom's Coffee-house," vol. i. pp. 159–164.

sort of pleased buzz of 'who is he?' was still going round the room unanswered, when a handsome carriage stopped at the door; he rose, and quitted the room, and the servants announced that his name was Foote, that he was a young gentleman of family and fortune, a student of the Inner Temple, and that the carriage had called for him on its way to the assembly of a lady of fashion." Dr. Barrowby once turned the laugh against Foote at the Bedford, when he was ostentatiously showing his gold repeater, with the remark — " Why, my watch does not go!" "It soon *will go*," quietly remarked the Doctor. Young Collins, the poet, who came to town in 1744 to seek his fortune, made his way to the Bedford, where Foote was supreme among the wits and critics. Like Foote, Collins was fond of fine clothes, and walked about with a feather in his hat, very unlike a young man who had not a single guinea he could call his own. A letter of the time tells us that "Collins was an acceptable companion everywhere; and among the gentlemen who loved him for a genius, may be reckoned the Doctors Armstrong, Barrowby, Hill, Messrs. Quin, Garrick, and Foote, who frequently took his opinion upon their pieces before they were seen by the public. He was particularly noticed by the geniuses who frequented the Bedford and Slaughter's Coffee-houses."*

Ten years later (1754) we find Foote again supreme in his critical corner at the Bedford. The regular frequenters of the room strove to get admitted to his party at supper; and others got as nearly as they could to the table, as the only humour flowed from Foote's tongue. The Bedford was now in its highest repute.

* Memoir by Moy Thomas, prefixed to Collins's Poetical Works. Bell and Daldy, 1858.

Foote and Garrick often met at the Bedford, and many and sharp were their encounters. They were the two great rivals of the day. Foote usually attacked, and Garrick, who had many weak points, was mostly the sufferer. Garrick, in early life, had been in the wine trade, and had supplied the Bedford with wine; he was thus described by Foote as living in Durham-yard, with three quarts of vinegar in the cellar, calling himself a wine-merchant. How Foote must have abused the Bedford wine of this period!

One night, Foote came into the Bedford, where Garrick was seated, and there gave him an account of a most wonderful actor he had just seen. Garrick was on the tenters of suspense, and there Foote kept him a full hour. At last Foote, compassionating the suffering listener, brought the attack to a close by asking Garrick what he thought of Mr. Pitt's histrionic talents, when Garrick, glad of the release, declared that if Pitt had chosen the stage, he might have been the first actor upon it.

One night, Garrick and Foote were about to leave the Bedford together, when the latter, in paying the bill, dropped a guinea; and not finding it at once, said, "Where on earth can it be gone to?"—"Gone to the devil, I think," replied Garrick, who had assisted in the search.—"Well said, David!" was Foote's reply; "let you alone for making a guinea go further than anybody else."

Churchill's quarrel with Hogarth began at the shilling rubber club, in the parlour of the Bedford; when Hogarth used some very insulting language towards Churchill, who resented it in the *Epistle*. This quarrel showed more venom than wit:—"Never," says Walpole,

" did two angry men of their abilities throw mud with less dexterity."

Woodward, the comedian, mostly lived at the Bedford, was intimate with Stacie, the landlord, and gave him his (W.'s) portrait, with a mask in his hand, one of the early pictures by Sir Joshua Reynolds. Stacie played an excellent game at whist. One morning, about two o'clock, one of his waiters awoke him to tell him that a nobleman had knocked him up, and had desired him to call his master to play a rubber with him for one hundred guineas. Stacie got up, dressed himself, won the money, and was in bed and asleep, all within an hour.

Of two houses in the Piazza, built for Francis, Earl of Bedford, we obtain some minute information from the lease granted in 1634, to Sir Edmund Verney, Knight Marshal to King Charles I.; these two houses being just then erected as part of the Piazza. There are also included in the lease the "yardes, stables, coach-houses, and gardens now layd, or hereafter to be layd, to the said messuages," which description of the premises seems to identify them as the two houses at the southern end of the Piazza, adjoining to Great Russell-street, and now occupied as the Bedford Coffee-house and Hotel. They are either the same premises, or they immediately adjoin the premises, occupied a century later as the Bedford Coffee-house. (Mr. John Bruce, *Archæologia*, xxxv. 195.) The lease contains a minute specification of the landlord's fittings and customary accommodations of what were then some of the most fashionable residences in the metropolis. In the attached schedule is the use of the wainscot, enumerating separately every piece of wainscot on the premises. The tenant is bound to keep in repair the " Portico Walke "

underneath the premises ; he is at all times to have " in-
gresse, egresse and regresse " through the Portico Walk ;
and he may " expel, put, or drive away out of the said
walke any youth or other person whatsoever which shall
eyther play or be in the said Portico Walke in offence or
disturbance to the said Sir Edmund Verney."

The inventory of the fixtures is curious. It enumerates every
apartment, from the beer-cellar, and the strong beer-cellar, the
scullery, the pantry, and the buttery, to the dining and with-
drawing-rooms. Most of the rooms had casement windows, but
the dining-room next Russell-street, and other principal apartments, had "shutting windowes." The principal rooms were
also " double creasted round for hangings," and were wainscoted
round the chimney-pieces, and doors and windows. In one case,
a study, "south towards Russell-street, the whole room was
wainscoted, and the hall in part." Most of the windows had
" soil-boards" attached ; the room-doors had generally " stock
locks," in some places " spring plate locks " and spring bolts.
There is not mentioned anything approaching to a fire-grate in
any of the rooms, except perhaps in the kitchen, where occurs
" a travers barre for the chimney."

MACKLIN'S COFFEE-HOUSE ORATORY.

After Macklin had retired from the stage, in 1754,
he opened that portion of the Piazza-houses, in Covent
Garden, which is now the Tavistock Hotel. Here he
fitted up a large coffee-room, a theatre for oratory,
and other apartments. To a three-shilling ordinary he
added a shilling lecture, or " School of Oratory and
Criticism ;" he presided at the dinner-table, and carved
for the company ; after which he played a sort of
" Oracle of Eloquence." Fielding has happily sketched

him in his *Voyage to Lisbon:* " Unfortunately for the
fishmongers of London, the Dory only resides in the
Devonshire seas; for could any of this company only
convey one to the Temple of luxury under the Piazza,
where Macklin, the high priest, daily serves up his rich
offerings, great would be the reward of that fishmonger."

In the Lecture, Macklin undertook to make each of
his audience an orator, by teaching him how to speak.
He invited hints and discussions; the novelty of the
scheme attracted the curiosity of numbers ; and this
curiosity he still further excited by a very uncommon
controversy, which now subsisted either in imagination
or reality, between him and Foote, who abused one
another very openly—" Squire Sammy " having for his
purpose engaged the Little Theatre in the Haymarket.

Besides this personal attack, various subjects were de-
bated here in the manner of the Robin Hood Society,
which filled the orator's pocket, and proved his rhetoric
of some value.

Here is one of his combats with Foote. The subject
was Duelling in Ireland, which Macklin had illustrated
as far as the reign of Elizabeth.   Foote cried " Order ;"
he had a question to put.   " Well, Sir," said Macklin,
" what have you to say upon this subject ?"   " I think,
Sir," said Foote, " this matter might be settled in a few
words.   What o'clock is it, Sir?"   Macklin could not
possibly see what the clock had to do with a dissertation
upon Duelling, but gruffly reported the hour to be half-
past nine.   " Very well," said Foote, " about this time
of the night every gentleman in Ireland that can possibly afford it is in his third bottle of claret, and therefore in a fair way of getting drunk ; and from drunken-
ness proceeds quarrelling, and from quarrelling, duelling,

and so there's an end of the chapter." The company
were much obliged to Foote for his interference, the hour
being considered; though Macklin did not relish the
abridgment.

The success of Foote's fun upon Macklin's Lectures,
led him to establish a summer entertainment of his own
at the Haymarket. He took up Macklin's notion of applying Greek Tragedy to modern subjects, and the squib
was so successful that Foote cleared by it 500*l.*, in five
nights, while the great Piazza Coffee-room in Covent
Garden was shut up, and Macklin in the *Gazette* as a
bankrupt.

But when the great plan of Mr. Macklin proved abor-
tive, when as he said in a former prologue, upon a
nearly similar occasion—

> " From scheming, fretting, famine, and despair,
> We saw to grace restor'd an exiled player;"

when the town was sated with the seemingly-concocted
quarrel between the two theatrical geniuses, Macklin
locked up his doors, all animosity was laid aside, and
they came and shook hands at the Bedford; the group
resumed their appearance, and, with a new master, a new
set of customers was seen.

TOM KING'S COFFEE-HOUSE.

This was one of the old night-houses of Covent Garden Market: it was a rude shed immediately beneath
the portico of St. Paul's Church, and was one " well

known to all gentlemen to whom beds are unknown." Fielding in one of his Prologues says:

" What rake is ignorant of King's Coffee-house ?"

It is in the background of Hogarth's print of *Morning*, where the prim maiden lady, walking to church, is soured with seeing two fuddled *beaux* from King's Coffee-house caressing two frail women. At the door there is a drunken row, in which swords and cudgels are the weapons.

Harwood's *Alumni Etonenses*, p. 293, in the account of the Boys elected from Eton to King's College, contains this entry: " A.D. 1713, Thomas King, born at West Ashton, in Wiltshire, went away scholar in apprehension that his fellowship would be denied him ; and afterwards kept that Coffee-house in Covent Garden, which was called by his own name."

Moll King was landlady after Tom's death: she was witty, and her house was much frequented, though it was little better than a shed. " Noblemen and the first *beaux*," said Stacie, " after leaving Court, would go to her house in full dress, with swords and bags, and in rich brocaded silk coats, and walked and conversed with persons of every description. She would serve chimney-sweepers, gardeners, and the market-people in common with her lords of the highest rank. Mr. Apreece, a tall thin man in rich dress, was her constant customer. He was called Cadwallader by the frequenters of Moll's." It is not surprising that Moll was often fined for keeping a disorderly house. At length, she retired from business —and the pillory—to Hampstead, where she lived on her ill-earned gains, but paid for a pew in church, and was charitable at appointed seasons, and died in peace in 1747.

It was at that period that Mother Needham, Mother
Douglass (alias, according to Foote's Minor, Mother
Cole), and Moll King, the tavern-keepers and the gam-
blers, took possession of premises abdicated by people of
fashion. Upon the south side of the market-sheds was
the noted "Finish," kept by Mrs. Butler, open all
night, the last of the Garden taverns, and only cleared
away in 1829. This house was originally the Queen's
Head. Shuter was pot-boy here. Here was a picture
of the Hazard Club, at the Bedford: it was painted by
Hogarth, and filled a panel of the Coffee-room.

Captain Laroon, an amateur painter of the time of
Hogarth, who often witnessed the nocturnal revels at
Moll King's, made a large and spirited drawing of the
interior of her Coffee-house, which was at Strawberry
Hill. It was bought for Walpole, by his printer, some
seventy years since. There is also an engraving of the
same room, in which is introduced a whole-length of
Mr. Apreece, in a full court-dress: an impression of
this plate is extremely rare.

Justice Welsh used to say that Captain Laroon, his
friend Captain Montague, and their constant companion,
Little Casey, the Link-boy, were the three most troublesome of all his Bow-street visitors. The portraits of
these three heroes are introduced in Boitard's rare print
of "the Covent Garden Morning Frolic." Laroon is
brandishing an artichoke. C. Montague is seated,
drunk, on the top of Bet Careless's sedan, which is preceded by Little Casey, as a link-boy.

Captain Laroon also painted a large folding-screen;
the figures were full of broad humour, two representing a Quack Doctor and his Merry Andrew, before the
gaping crowd.

Laroon was deputy-chairman, under Sir Robert Walpole, of a Club, consisting of six gentlemen only, who met, at stated times, in the drawing-room of Scott, the marine painter, in Henrietta-street, Covent Garden; and it was unanimously agreed by the members, that they should be attended by Scott's wife only, who was a remarkable witty woman. Laroon made a beautiful conversation drawing of the Club, which is highly prized by J. T. Smith.

PIAZZA COFFEE-HOUSE.

This establishment, at the north-eastern angle of Covent Garden Piazza, appears to have originated with Macklin's; for we read in an advertisement in the *Public Advertiser*, March, 5, 1756: "the Great Piazza Coffee-room, in Covent-Garden."

The Piazza was much frequented by Sheridan; and here is located the well-known anecdote told of his coolness during the burning of Drury-lane Theatre, in 1809. It is said that as he sat at the Piazza, during the fire, taking some refreshment, a friend of his having remarked on the philosophical calmness with which he bore his misfortune, Sheridan replied: "A man may surely be allowed to take a glass of wine *by his own fireside.*"

Sheridan and John Kemble often dined together at the Piazza, to be handy to the theatre. During Kemble's management, Sheridan had occasion to make a complaint, which brought a "nervous" letter from Kemble, to which Sheridan's reply is amusing enough. Thus, he writes: "that the management of a theatre is a situation capable of becoming *troublesome*, is information which I do not want, and a discovery which I thought you had made long ago." Sheridan then treats Kemble's letter as "a nervous flight," not to be noticed seriously, adding his anxiety for the interest of the theatre, and alluding to Kemble's touchiness and reserve; and thus concludes:

" If there is anything amiss in your mind not arising from the *troublesomeness* of your situation, it is childish and unmanly not to disclose it. The frankness with which I have dealt towards you entitles me to expect that you should have done so.

" But I have no reason to believe this to be the case ; and attributing your letter to a disorder which I know ought not to be indulged, I prescribe that thou shalt keep thine appointment at the Piazza Coffee-house, to-morrow at five, and, taking four bottles of claret instead of three, to which in sound health you might stint yourself, forget that you ever wrote the letter, as I shall that I ever received it.

" R. B. Sheridan."

The Piazza façade, and interior, were of Gothic design. The house has been taken down, and in its place was built the Floral Hall, after the Crystal Palace model.

THE CHAPTER COFFEE-HOUSE.

In our first volume, pp. 179–186, we described this as a literary place of resort in Paternoster Row, more especially in connection with the Wittinagemot of the last century.

A very interesting account of the Chapter, at a later period, (1848,) is given by Mrs. Gaskell. The Coffee-house is thus described:—

" Paternoster Row was for many years sacred to publishers. It is a narrow flagged street, lying under the shadow of St. Paul's; at each end there are posts placed, so as to prevent the passage of carriages, and thus preserve a solemn silence for the deliberations of the 'fathers of the Row.' The dull warehouses on each side are mostly occupied at present by wholesale stationers; if they be publishers' shops, they show no attractive front to the dark and narrow street. Halfway up on the left-hand side is the Chapter Coffee-house. I visited it last June. It was then unoccupied; it had the appearance of a dwelling-house two hundred years old or so, such as one sometimes sees in ancient country towns; the ceilings of the small rooms were low, and had heavy beams running across them; the walls were wainscoted breast-high; the staircase was shallow, broad, and dark, taking up much space in the centre of the house. This then was the Chapter Coffee-house, which, a century ago, was the resort of all the booksellers and publishers, and where the literary hacks, the critics, and even the wits used to go in search of ideas or employment. This was the place about which Chatterton wrote, in those delusive letters he sent to his mother at Bristol, while he was starving in London.

" Years later it became the tavern frequented by university men, and country clergymen, who were up in London for a few days, and, having no private friends or access into society, were glad to learn what was going on in the world of letters, from the conversation which they were sure to hear in the coffee-room. It was a place solely frequented by men; I believe there was but one female servant in the house. Few people slept there: some of the stated meetings of the trade were held in it, as they had been for more than a century; and occasionally country booksellers, with now and then a clergyman, resorted to it. In the long, low, dingy room upstairs, the meetings of the trade were held. The high narrow windows looked into the gloomy Row; nothing of motion or of change could be seen in the grim dark houses opposite, so near and close, although the whole breadth of the Row was between. The mighty roar of London was round, like the sound of an unseen ocean, yet every foot-fall on the pavement below might be heard distinctly, in that unfrequented street."

Goldsmith frequented the Chapter, and always occupied one place, which, for many years after was the seat of literary honour there.

There are Leather Tokens of the Chapter Coffee-house in existence.

CHILD'S COFFEE-HOUSE,

In St. Paul's Churchyard, was one of the *Spectator's* houses. "Sometimes," he says, "I smoke a pipe at Child's, and whilst I seem attentive to nothing but the *Postman*, overhear the conversation of every table in the room." It was much frequented by the clergy; for the *Spectator*, No. 609, notices the mistake of a country gentleman in taking all persons in scarfs for Doctors

of Divinity, since only a scarf of the first magnitude entitles him to "the appellation of Doctor from his landlady and the *Boy at Child's*."

Child's was the resort of Dr. Mead, and other professional men of eminence. The Fellows of the Royal Society came here. Whiston relates that Sir Hans Sloane,
Dr. Halley, and he were once at Child's, when Dr. H.,
asked him, W., why he was not a member of the Royal
Society? Whiston answered, because they durst not
choose a heretic. Upon which Dr. H. said, if Sir Hans
Sloane would propose him, W., he, Dr. H., would second
it, which was done accordingly.

The propinquity of Child's to the Cathedral and Doctors' Commons, made it the resort of the clergy, and
ecclesiastical loungers. In one respect, Child's was
superseded by the Chapter, in Paternoster Row.

LONDON COFFEE-HOUSE.

This Coffee-house was established previous to the year
1731, for we find of it the following advertisement :—
"May, 1731.
"Whereas, it is customary for Coffee-houses and other
Public-houses, to take 8*s.* for a quart of Arrack, and 6*s.*
for a quart of Brandy or Rum, made into Punch :
"This is to give Notice,
"That James Ashley has opened, on Ludgate Hill, the
London Coffee-house, Punch-house, Dorchester Beer
and Welsh Ale Warehouse, where the finest and best
old Arrack, Rum, and French Brandy is made into

Punch, with the other of the finest ingredients—viz., A quart of Arrack made into Punch for six shillings; and so in proportion to the smallest quantity, which is half-a-quartern for fourpence halfpenny. A quart of Rum or Brandy made into Punch for four shillings; and so in proportion to the smallest quantity, which is half-a-quartern for fourpence halfpenny; and gentlemen may have it as soon made as a gill of Wine can be drawn."

The premises occupy a Roman site; for, in 1800, in the rear of the house, in a bastion of the City Wall, was found a sepulchral monument, dedicated to Claudina Martina by her husband, a provincial Roman soldier; here also were found a fragment of a statue of Hercules, and a female head. In front of the Coffee-house, immediately west of St. Martin's church, stood Ludgate.

The London Coffee-house (now a tavern) is noted for its publishers' sales of stock and copyrights. It was within the rules of the Fleet prison : and in the Coffee-house are " locked up " for the night such juries from the Old Bailey Sessions, as cannot agree upon verdicts. The house was long kept by the grandfather and father of Mr. John Leech, the celebrated artist.

A singular incident occurred at the London Coffee-house, many years since : Mr. Brayley, the topographer, was present at a party here, when Mr. Broadhurst, the famous tenor, by singing a high note, caused a wine-glass on the table to break, the bowl being separated from the stem.

At the bar of the London Coffee-house was sold Rowley's British Cephalic Snuff.

TURK'S HEAD COFFEE HOUSE

IN CHANGE.ALLEY.

From *The Kingdom's Intelligencer*, a weekly paper, published by authority, in 1662, we learn that there had just been opened a "new Coffee-house," with the sign of the Turk's Head, where was sold by retail "the right Coffee-powder," from 4*s.* to 6*s.* 8*d.* per pound; that pounded in a mortar, 2*s.*; East India berry, 1*s.* 6*d.*; and the right Turkie berry, well garbled, at 3*s.* "The ungarbled for lesse, with directions how to use the same." Also Chocolate at 2*s.* 6*d.* per pound; the perfumed from 4*s.* to 10*s.*; "also, Sherbets made in Turkie, of lemons, roses, and violets perfumed; and Tea, or Chaa, according to its goodness. The house seal was Morat the Great. Gentlemen customers and acquaintances are (the next New Year's Day) invited to the sign of the Great Turk at this new Coffee-house, where Coffee will be on free cost." The sign was also Morat the Great. Morat figures as a tyrant in Dryden's *Aurung Zebe.* There is a token of this house, with the Sultan's head, in the Beaufoy collection.

Another token, in the same collection, is of unusual excellence, probably by John Roettier. It has on the obverse, Morat y[e] Great Men did mee call,—Sultan's head; reverse, Where eare I came I conquered all.— In the field, Coffee, Tobacco, Sherbet, Tea, Chocolat, Retail in Exchange Alee. "The word Tea," says Mr. Burn, "occurs on no other tokens than those issued from 'the Great Turk' Coffee-house, in Exchange-

Alley;" in one of its advertisements, 1662, tea is from
6s. to 60s. a pound.

Competition arose. One Constantine Jennings in
Threadneedle-street, over against St. Christopher's
Church, advertised that coffee, chocolate, sherbet, and
tea, the right Turkey berry, may be had as cheap and
as good of him as is any where to be had for money;
and that people may there be taught to prepare the said
liquors gratis.

Pepys, in his *Diary*, tells, Sept. 25, 1669, of his sending for "a cup of Tea, a China Drink, he had not before
tasted." Henry Bennet, Earl of Arlington, about 1666,
introduced tea at Court. And, in his Sir Charles Sedley's *Mulberry Garden*, we are told that "he who wished
to be considered a man of fashion always drank wine-
and-water at dinner, and a dish of tea afterwards."
These details are condensed from Mr. Burn's excellent
Beaufoy Catalogue. 2nd edition, 1855.

In Gerard-street, Soho, also, was another Turk's
Head Coffee-house, where was held a Turk's Head
Society; in 1777, we find Gibbon writing to Garrick:
"At this time of year, (Aug. 14,) the Society of the
Turk's Head can no longer be addressed as a corporate
body, and most of the individual members are probably
dispersed: Adam Smith in Scotland; Burke in the
shades of Beaconsfield; Fox, the Lord or the devil
knows where."

This place was a kind of head-quarters for the Loyal
Association during the Rebellion of 1745.

Here was founded "The Literary Club," already
described in Vol. I., pp. 204–219.

In 1753, several Artists met at the Turk's Head, and
from thence, their Secretary, Mr. F. M. Newton, dated

a printed letter to the Artists to form a select body for the Protection and Encouragement of Art. Another Society of Artists met in Peter's-court, St. Martin's-lane, from the year 1739 to 1769. After continued squabbles, which lasted for many years, the principal Artists met together at the Turk's Head, where many others having joined them, they petitioned the King (George III.) to become patron of a Royal Academy of Art. His Majesty consented; and the new Society took a room in Pall Mall, opposite to Market-lane, where they remained until the King, in the year 1771, granted them apartments in Old Somerset House.—*J. T. Smith.*

The Turk's Head Coffee-house, No. 142, in the Strand, was a favourite supping-house with Dr. Johnson and Boswell, in whose Life of Johnson are several entries, commencing with 1763—"At night, Mr. Johnson and I supped in a private room at the Turk's Head Coffee-house, in the Strand ; ' I encourage this house,' said he, ' for the mistress of it is a good civil woman, and has not much business.' " Another entry is—" We concluded the day at the Turk's Head Coffee-house very socially." And, August 3, 1673—"We had our last social meeting at the Turk's Head Coffee-house, before my setting out for foreign parts."

The name was afterwards changed to " The Turk's Head, Canada and Bath Coffee-house," and was a well frequented tavern and hotel : it was taken down, and a very handsome lofty house erected upon the site, at the cost of, we believe, eight thousand pounds; it was opened as a tavern and hotel, but did not long continue.

At the Turk's Head, or Miles's Coffee-house, New Palace-yard, Westminster, the noted Rota Club met, founded by Harrington, in 1659: where was a large oval table, with a passage in the middle, for Miles to deliver his coffee. (See *Clubs*, Vol. I., pp. 15, 16).

SQUIRE'S COFFEE-HOUSE.

In Fulwood's (*vulgo* Fuller's) Rents, in Holborn, nearly opposite Chancery-lane, in the reign of James I., lived Christopher Fulwood, in a mansion of some pretension, of which an existing house of the period is said to be the remains. " Some will have it," says Hatton, 1708, " that it is called from being a *woody* place before there were buildings here; but its being called Fullwood's Rents (as it is in deeds and leases), shows it to be the rents of one called Fullwood, the owner or builder thereof." Strype describes the Rents, or court, as running up to Gray's-Inn, " into which it has an entrance through the gate; a place of good resort, and taken up by coffee-houses, ale-houses, and houses of entertainment, by reason of its vicinity to Gray's-Inn. On the east side is a handsome open place, with a handsome freestone pavement, and better built, and inhabited by private house-keepers. At the upper end of this court is a passage into the Castle Tavern, a house of considerable trade, as is the Golden Griffin Tavern, on the West side."

Here was John's, one of the earliest Coffee-houses; and adjoining Gray's-Inn gate is a deep-coloured redbrick house, once Squire's Coffee-house, kept by Squire, " a noted man in Fuller's Rents," who died in 1717.

The house is very roomy; it has been handsome, and has a wide staircase. Squire's was one of the receiving-houses of the *Spectator:* in No. 269, January 8, 1711–1712, he accepts Sir Roger de Coverley's invitation to "smoke a pipe with him over a dish of coffee at Squire's. As I love the old man, I take delight in complying with everything that is agreeable to him, and accordingly waited on him to the Coffee-house, where his venerable figure drew upon us the eyes of the whole room. He had no sooner seated himself at the upper end of the high table, but he called for a clean pipe, a paper of tobacco, a dish of coffee, a wax candle, and the *Supplement* [a periodical paper of that time], with such an air of cheerfulness and good humour, that all the boys in the coffee-room, (who seemed to take pleasure in serving him,) were at once employed on his several errands, insomuch that nobody else could come at a dish of tea, until the Knight had got all his conveniences about him." Such was the coffee-room in the *Spectator's* day.

Gray's-Inn Walks, to which the Rents led, across Field-court, were then a fashionable promenade; and here Sir Roger could "clear his pipes in good air;" for scarcely a house intervened thence to Hampstead. Though Ned Ward, in his *London Spy*, says—"I found none but a parcel of superannuated debauchees, huddled up in cloaks, frieze coats, and wadded gowns, to protect their old carcases from the sharpness of Hampstead air; creeping up and down in pairs and leashes no faster than the hand of a dial, or a county convict going to execution: some talking of law, some of religion, and some of politics. After I had walked two or three times round, I sat myself down in the upper walk, where just before me, on a stone pedestal, we fixed an old rusty horizontal dial, with the gnomon broke short off." Round the sun-dial, seats were arranged in a semicircle.

Gray's-Inn Gardens were resorted to by dangerous classes. Expert pickpockets and plausible ring-droppers found easy prey there on crowded days; and in old plays the Gardens are repeatedly mentioned as a place of negotiation for clandestine lovers, which led to the walks being closed, except at stated hours.

Returning to Fulwood's Rents, we may here describe another of its attractions, the Tavern and punch-house, within one door of Gray's-Inn, apparently the King's Head. From some time before 1699, until his death in 1731, Ward kept this house, which he thus commemorates, or, in another word, puffs, in his *London Spy* : being a vintner himself, we may rest assured that he would have penned this in praise of no other than himself:

"To speak but the truth of my honest friend Ned,
The best of all vintners that ever God made ;
He's free of the beef, and as free of his bread,
And washes both down with his glass of rare red,
That tops all the town, and commands a good trade ;
Such wine as will cheer up the drooping King's head,
And brisk up the soul, though our body's half dead ;
He scorns to draw bad, as he hopes to be paid ;
And now his name's up, he may e'en lie abed ;
For he'll get an estate—there's no more to be said."

We ought to have remarked, that the ox was roasted, cut up, and distributed gratis; a piece of generosity which, by a poetic fiction, is supposed to have inspired the above limping balderdash.

SLAUGHTER'S COFFEE-HOUSE.

This Coffee-house, famous as the resort of painters and sculptors, in the last century, was situated at the upper end of the west side of St. Martin's-lane, three doors from Newport-street. Its first landlord was Thomas Slaughter, 1692. Mr. Cunningham tells us that a second Slaughter's (New Slaughter's), was established in the same street about 1760, when the original establishment adopted the name of "Old Slaughter's," by which designation it was known till within a few years of the final demolition of the house to make way for the new avenue between Long-acre and Leicester-square, formed 1843–44. For many years previous to the streets of London being completely paved, "Slaughter's" was called "The Coffee-house on the Pavement." In like manner, "The Pavement," Moor fields, received its distinctive name. Besides being the resort of artists, Old Slaughter's was the house of call for Frenchmen.

St. Martin's-lane was long one of the head-quarters of the artists of the last century. "In the time of Benjamin West," says J. T. Smith, "and before the formation of the Royal Academy, Greek-street, St. Martin's-lane, and Gerard-street, was their colony. Old Slaughter's Coffee-house, in St. Martin's-lane, was their grand resort in the evenings, and Hogarth was a constant visitor." He lived at the Golden Head, on the eastern side of Leicester Fields, in the northern half of the Sabloniere Hotel. The head he cut out himself from pieces of cork, glued and bound together; it was placed over the street-door. At this time, young Benjamin West was living in chambers, in Bedford-street, Covent Garden, and had there set up his easel; he was married, in 1765, at St. Martin's Church. Roubiliac was often to be found at Slaughter's in early life; probably before he gained the patronage of Sir Edward Walpole, through finding and returning to the baronet the pocket-book of bank-notes, which the young maker of monuments had picked up in Vauxhall Gardens. Sir Edward, to remunerate his integrity, and his skill, of which he showed specimens, promised to patronize Roubiliac through life, and he faithfully performed this promise. Young Gainsborough, who spent three years amid the works of the painters in St. Martin's-lane, Hayman, and Cipriani, who were all eminently convivial, were, in all probability, frequenters of Slaughter's. Smith tells us that Quin and Hayman were inseparable friends, and so convivial, that they seldom parted till daylight.

Mr. Cunningham relates that here, "in early life, Wilkie would enjoy a small dinner at a small cost. I have been told by an old frequenter of the house, that Wilkie was always the last dropper-in for a dinner, and that he was never seen to dine in the house by daylight. The truth is, he slaved at his art at home till the last glimpse of daylight had disappeared."

Haydon was accustomed in the early days of his fitful career, to dine here with Wilkie. In his *Autobiography*, in the year 1808, Haydon writes: "This period of our lives was one of great happiness : painting all day, then dining at the Old Slaughter Chop-house, then going to the Academy until eight, to fill up the evening, then

going home to tea—that blessing of a studious man—
talking over our respective exploits, what he [Wilkie]
had been doing, and what I had done, and then, frequently to relieve our minds fatigued by their eight and
twelve hours' work, giving vent to the most extraordinary absurdities.   Often have we made rhymes on odd
names, and shouted with laughter at each new line that
was added.   Sometimes lazily inclined after a good
dinner, we have lounged about, near Drury-lane or
Covent Garden, hesitating whether to go in, and often
have I (knowing first that there was nothing I wished
to see) assumed a virtue I did not possess, and pretending moral superiority, preached to Wilkie on the weak-
ness of not resisting such temptations for the sake of
our art and our duty, and marched him off to his
studies, when he was longing to see Mother Goose."
    J. T. Smith has narrated some fifteen pages of
characteristic anecdotes of the artistic visitors of Old
Slaughter's, which he refers to as "formerly the rendezvous of Pope, Dryden, and other wits, and much
frequented by several eminently clever men of his
day."
    Thither came Ware, the architect, who, when a little
sickly boy, was apprenticed to a chimney-sweeper, and
was seen chalking the street-front of Whitehall, by a
gentleman, who purchased the remainder of the boy's
time; gave him an excellent education; then sent him
to Italy, and, upon his return, employed him, and introduced him to his friends as an architect.   Ware was
heard to tell this story, while he was sitting to Roubiliac for his bust.   Ware built Chesterfield House and
several other noble mansions, and compiled a Palladio,
in folio : he retained the soot in his skin to the day of

his death. He was very intimate with Roubiliac, who was an opposite eastern neighbour of Old Slaughter's. Another architect, Gwynn, who competed with Mylne for designing and building Blackfriars Bridge, was also a frequent visitor at Old Slaughter's, as was Gravelot, who kept a drawing-school in the Strand, nearly opposite to Southampton-street.

Hudson, who painted the Dilettanti portraits; M'Ardell, the mezzotinto-scraper; and Luke Sullivan, the engraver of Hogarth's March to Finchley, also frequented Old Slaughter's; likewise Theodore Gardell, the portrait painter, who was executed for the murder of his landlady; and Old Moser, keeper of the Drawing Academy in Peter's-court. Richard Wilson, the landscape painter, was not a regular customer here : his favourite house was the Constitution, Bedford-street, Covent Garden, where he could indulge in a pot of porter more freely, and enjoy the fun of Mortimer, the painter.

Parry, the Welsh harper, though totally blind, was one of the first draught-players in England, and occasionally played with the frequenters of Old Slaughter's; and here, in consequence of a bet, Roubiliac introduced Nathaniel Smith (father of John Thomas), to play at draughts with Parry; the game lasted about half an hour : Parry was much agitated, and Smith proposed to give in; but as there were bets depending, it was played out, and Smith won. This victory brought Smith numerous challenges; and the dons of the Barn, a public-house, in St. Martin's-lane, nearly opposite the church, invited him to become a member; but Smith declined. The Barn, for many years, was frequented by all the noted players of chess and draughts; and it was there that they often decided games of the first importance, played between persons of the highest rank, living in different parts of the world.

T. Rawle,* the inseparable companion of Captain Grose, the antiquary, came often to Slaughter's.

It was long asserted of Slaughter's Coffee-house that there never had been a person of that name as master of the house, but that it was named from its having been opened for the use of the men who slaughtered the cattle for the butchers of Newport Market, in an open space then adjoining. "This," says J. T. Smith, "may be the fact, if we believe that coffee was taken as refreshment by slaughtermen, instead of purl or porter; or that it was so called by the neighbouring butchers in derision of the numerous and fashionable Coffee-houses of the day; as, for instance, 'The Old Man's Coffee-house,' and 'The Young Man's Coffee-house.' Be that as it may, in my father's time, and also within memory of the most aged people, this Coffee-house was called 'Old Slaughter's,' and not The Slaughter, or The Slaughterer's Coffee-house."

In 1827, there was sold by Stewart, Wheatley, and

* Rawle was one of his Majesty's accoutrement makers; and after his death, his effects were sold by Hutchins, in King-street, Covent Garden. Among the lots were a helmet, a sword, and several letters, of Oliver Cromwell; also the doublet in which Cromwell dissolved the Long Parliament. Another singular lot was a large black wig, with long flowing curls, stated to have been worn by King Charles II.: it was bought by Suett, the actor, who was a great collector of wigs. He continued to act in this wig for many years, in *Tom Thumb*, and other pieces, till it was burnt when the theatre at Birmingham was destroyed by fire. Next morning, Suett, meeting Mrs. Booth, the mother of the lively actress S. Booth, exclaimed, "Mrs. Booth, my wig's gone!"

Adlard, in Piccadilly, a picture attributed to Hogarth, for 150 guineas; it was described A Conversation over a Bowl of Punch, at *Old* Slaughter's Coffee-house, in St. Martin's-lane, and the figures were said to be portraits of the painter, Doctor Monsey, and the landlord, *Old* Slaughter. But this picture, as J. T. Smith shows, was painted by Highmore, for his father's godfather, Nathaniel Oldham, and one of the artist's patrons; " it is neither a scene at Old Slaughter's, nor are the portraits rightly described in the sale catalogue, but a scene at Oldham's house, at Ealing, with an old schoolmaster, a farmer, the artist Highmore, and Oldham himself."

WILL'S AND SERLE'S COFFEE-HOUSES.

At the corner of Serle-street and Portugal-street, most invitingly facing the passage to Lincoln's Inn New-square, was Will's, of old repute, and thus described in the *Epicure's Almanack*, 1815 : " This is, indubitably, a house of the first class, which dresses very desirable turtle and venison, and broaches many a pipe of mature port, double voyaged Madeira, and princely claret ; wherewithal to wash down the dust of making law-books, and take out the inky blots from rotten parchment bonds ; or if we must quote and parodize Will's, ' hath a sweet oblivious antidote which clears the cranium of that perilous stuff that clouds the cerebellum.' " The Coffee-house has some time being given up.

Serle's Coffee-house is one of those mentioned in No. 49, of the *Spectator :* " I do not know that I meet

in any of my walks, objects which move both my spleen
and laughter so effectually as those young fellows at the
Grecian, Squire's, Serle's, and all other Coffee-houses
adjacent to the Law, who rise for no other purpose but
to publish their laziness."

THE GRECIAN COFFEE-HOUSE,

Devereux-court, Strand, (closed in 1843,) was named
from Constantine, of Threadneedle-street, the *Grecian*
who kept it. In the *Tatler* announcement, all accounts
of learning are to be " under the title of the Grecian ;"
and, in the *Tatler*, No. 6 : " While other parts of the
town are amused with the present actions, [Marl-
borough's,] we generally spend the evening at this table
[at the Grecian], in inquiries into antiquity, and think
anything new, which gives us new knowledge. Thus,
we are making a very pleasant entertainment to ourselves in putting the actions of Homer's Iliad into an
exact journal."

The *Spectator's* face was very well-known at the Grecian, a Coffee-house " adjacent to the law." Occasionally, it was the scene of learned discussion. Thus Dr.
King relates that one evening, two gentlemen, who were
constant companions, were disputing here, concerning
the accent of a Greek word. This dispute was carried
to such a length, that the two friends thought proper to
determine it with their swords : for this purpose they
stepped into Devereux-court, where one of them (Dr.
King thinks his name was Fitzgerald) was run through
the body, and died on the spot.

The Grecian was Foote's morning lounge. It was

handy, too, for the young Templar, Goldsmith, and often
did it echo with Oliver's boisterous mirth; for "it had
become the favourite resort of the Irish and Lancashire
Templars, whom he delighted in collecting around him,
in entertaining with a cordial and unostentatious hospi-
tality, and in occasionally amusing with his flute, or
with whist, neither of which he played very well!" Here
Goldsmith occasionally wound up his " Shoemaker's
Holiday " with supper.

It was at the Grecian that Fleetwood Shephard told
this memorable story to Dr. Tancred Robinson, who
gave Richardson permission to repeat it. " The Earl of
Dorset was in Little Britain, beating about for books to
his taste : there was *Paradise Lost.* He was surprised
with some passages he struck upon, dipping here and
there and bought it; the bookseller begged him to speak
in its favour, if he liked it, for they lay on his hands as
waste paper. Jesus!—Shephard was present. My Lord
took it home, read it, and sent it to Dryden, who in a
short time returned it. 'This man,' says Dryden, 'cuts
us all out, and the ancients too !' "

The Grecian was also frequented by Fellows of the
Royal Society. Thoresby, in his *Diary,* tells us,
22 May, 1712, that "having bought each a pair of
black silk stockings in Westminster Hall, they returned
by water, and then walked, to meet his friend, Dr.
Sloane, the Secretary of the Royal Society, at the
Grecian Coffee-house, by the Temple." And, on June
12th, same year, " Thoresby attended the Royal Society,
where were present, the President, Sir Isaac Newton,
both the Secretaries, the two Professors from Oxford,
Dr. Halley and Kell, with others, whose company we
after enjoyed at the Grecian Coffee-house."

In Devereux-court, also, was Tom's Coffee-house, much resorted to by men of letters; among whom were Dr. Birch, who wrote the History of the Royal Society; also Akenside, the poet; and there is in print a letter of Pope's, addressed to Fortescue, his "counsel learned in the law," at this coffee-house.

GEORGE'S COFFEE-HOUSE,

No. 213, Strand, near Temple Bar, was a noted resort in the last and present century. When it was a coffee-house, one day, there came in Sir James Lowther, who after changing a piece of silver with the coffee-woman, and paying twopence for his dish of coffee, was helped into his chariot, for he was very lame and infirm, and went home: some little time afterwards, he returned to the same coffee-house, on purpose to acquaint the woman who kept it, that she had given him a bad half-penny, and demanded another in exchange for it. Sir James had about 40,000*l.* per annum, and was at a loss whom to appoint his heir.

Shenstone, who found

"The warmest welcome at an inn,"

found George's to be economical. " What do you think," he writes, " must be my expense, who love to pry into everything of the kind? Why, truly one shilling. My company goes to George's Coffee-house, where, for that small subscription I read all pamphlets under a three shillings' dimension; and indeed, any larger would not be fit for coffee-house perusal." Shenstone relates that

Lord Orford was at George's, when the mob that were
carrying his Lordship in effigy, came into the box where
he was, to beg money of him, amongst others: this
story Horace Walpole contradicts, adding that he sup-
poses Shenstone thought that after Lord Orford quitted
his place, he went to the coffee-house to learn news.

Arthur Murphy frequented George's, "where the
town wits met every evening." Lloyd, the law-student,
sings :—

> " By law let others toil to gain renown !
> Florio's a gentleman, a man o' the town.
> He nor courts clients, or the law regarding,
> Hurries from Nando's down to Covent Garden,
> Yet, he's a scholar ; mark him in the pit,
> With critic catcall sound the stops of wit!
> Supreme at George's, he harangues the throng,
> Censor of style, from tragedy to song."

THE PERCY COFFEE-HOUSE,

Rathbone-place, Oxford-street, no longer exists ; but it
will be kept in recollection for its having given name
to one of the most popular publications, of its class, in
our time, namely, the *Percy Anecdotes,* " by Sholto and
Reuben Percy, Brothers of the Benedictine Monastery of
Mont Benger," in 44 parts, commencing in 1820. So
said the title pages, but the names and the locality were
supposé. Reuben Percy was Thomas Byerley, who died
in 1824; he was the brother of Sir John Byerley, and
the first editor of the *Mirror,* commenced by John
Limbird, in 1822. Sholto Percy was Joseph Clinton

Robertson, who died in 1852 ; he was the projector of the *Mechanics' Magazine,* which he edited from its commencement to his death. The name of the collection of Anecdotes was not taken, as at the time supposed, from the popularity of the *Percy Reliques,* but from the Percy Coffee-house, where Byerley and Robertson were accustomed to meet to talk over their joint work. The *idea* was, however, claimed by Sir Richard Phillips, who stoutly maintained that it originated in a suggestion made by him to Dr. Tilloch and Mr. Mayne, to cut the anecdotes from the many years' files of the *Star* newspaper, of which Dr. Tilloch was the editor, and Mr. Byerley assistant editor ; and to the latter overhearing the suggestion, Sir Richard contested, might the *Percy Anecdotes* be traced. They were very successful, and a large sum was realized by the work.

PEELE'S COFFEE-HOUSE,

Nos. 177 and 178, Fleet-street, east corner of Fetter-lane, was one of the Coffee-houses of the Johnsonian period ; and here was long preserved a portrait of Dr. Johnson, on the key-stone of a chimney-piece, stated to have been painted by Sir Joshua Reynolds. Peele's was noted for files of newspapers from these dates: *Gazette,* 1759 ; *Times,* 1780 ; *Morning Chronicle,* 1773 ; *Morning Post,* 1773 ; *Morning Herald,* 1784 ; *Morning Advertiser,* 1794 ; and the evening papers from their commencement. The house is now a tavern.

Taverns.

THE TAVERNS OF OLD LONDON.

THE changes in the manners and customs of our metropolis may be agreeably gathered from such glimpses
as we gain of the history of "houses of entertainment"
in the long lapse of centuries. Their records present
innumerable pictures in little of society and modes, the
interest of which is increased by distance. They show
us how the tavern was the great focus of news long
before the newspaper fully supplied the intellectual
want. Much of the business of early times was trans-
acted in taverns, and it is to some extent in the present
day. According to the age, the tavern reflects the
manners, the social tastes, customs, and recreations;
and there, in days when travelling was difficult and
costly, and not unattended with danger, the traveller
told his wondrous tale to many an eager listener; and
the man who rarely strayed beyond his own parish, was
thus made acquainted with the life of the world. Then,
the old tavern combined, with much of the comfort of an
English home, its luxuries, without the forethought of
providing either. Its come-and-go life presented many
a useful lesson to the man who looked beyond the cheer
of the moment. The master, or taverner, was mostly
a person of substance, often of ready wit and cheerful
manners—to render his public home attractive.

The "win-hous," or tavern, is enumerated among the houses of entertainment in the time of the Saxons; and no doubt existed in England much earlier. The peg-tankard, a specimen of which we see in the Ashmolean Collection at Oxford, originated with the Saxons; the pegs inside denoted how deep each guest was to drink: hence arose the saying, "he is a peg too low," when a man was out of spirits. The Danes were even more convivial in their habits than the Saxons, and may be presumed to have multiplied the number of "guest houses," as the early taverns were called. The Norman followers of the Conqueror soon fell into the good cheer of their predecessors in England. Although wine was made at this period in great abundance from vineyards in various parts of England, the trade of the taverns was principally supplied from France. The traffic for Bordeaux and the neighbouring provinces is said to have commenced about 1154, through the marriage of Henry II. with Eleanor of Aquitaine. The Normans were the great carriers, and Guienne the place whence most of our wines were brought; and which are described in this reign to have been sold in the ships and in the wine-cellars near the public place of cookery, on the banks of the Thames. We are now speaking of the customs of seven centuries since; of which the public wine-cellar, known to our time as *the Shades*, adjoining old London Bridge, was unquestionably a relic.

The earliest dealers in wines were of two descriptions: the *vintners*, or importers; and the *taverners*, who kept taverns for them, and sold the wine by retail to such as came to the tavern to drink it, or fetched it to their own homes.

In a document of the reign of Edward II., we find

mentioned a tenement called Pin Tavern, situated in the Vintry, where the Bordeaux merchants *craned* their wines out of lighters, and other vessels on the Thames; and here was the famous old tavern with the sign of the *Three Cranes.* Chaucer makes the apprentice of this period loving better the tavern than the shop :—

> " A prentis whilom dwelt in our citee,—
> At ev'ry bridale would he sing and hoppe;
> He loved bet' the *tavern* than the shoppe,
> For when ther any riding was in Chepe,
> Out of the shoppe thider would he lepe;
> And til that he had all the sight ysein
> And dancid wil, he wold not com agen."

Thus, the idle City apprentice was a great tavern haunter, which was forbidden in his indenture; and to this day, the apprentice's indenture enacts that he shall not " haunt taverns."

In a play of 1608, the apprentices of old Hobson, a rich citizen, in 1560, frequent the *Rose and Crown*, in the Poultry, and the *Dagger*, in Cheapside.

" *Enter Hobson, Two Prentices, and a Boy.*

" 1 PREN. Prithee, fellow Goodman, set forth the ware, and looke to the shop a little. I'll but drink a cup of wine with a customer, at the Rose and Crown in the Poultry, and come again presently.

" 2 PREN. I must needs step to the *Dagger in Cheape*, to send a letter into the country unto my father. Stay, boy, you are the youngest prentice ; look you to the shop."

In the reign of Richard II., it was ordained by statute that " the wines of Gascoine, of Osey, and of Spain," as well as Rhenish wines, should not be sold above six-pence the gallon; and the taverners of this period frequently became very rich, and filled the highest civic offices, as sheriffs and mayors. The fraternity of vintners and taverners, anciently the Merchant Wine Tonners of Gascoyne, became the Craft of Vintners, incorporated by Henry VI. as the Vintners' Company.

The curious old ballad of London Lyckpenny, written in the reign of Henry V., by Lydgate, a monk of Bury, confirms the statement of the prices in the reign of Richard II. He comes to Cornhill, when the wine-drawer of the Pope's Head tavern, standing without the street-door, it being the custom of drawers thus to waylay passengers, takes the man by the hand, and says,— "Will you drink a pint of wine?" whereunto the countryman answers, "A penny spend I may," and so drank his wine. "For bread nothing did he pay"—for that was given in. This is Stow's account : the ballad makes the taverner, not the drawer, invite the countryman ; and the latter, instead of getting bread for nothing, complains of having to go away hungry :—

> " The taverner took me by the sleeve,
>   ' Sir,' saith he, ' will you our wine assay ? '
> I answered, ' That cannot much me grieve,
>   A penny can do no more than it may ;'
> I drank a pint, and for it did pay ;
> Yet, sore a-hungered from thence I yede,
> And, wanting money, I could not speed," etc.

There was no eating at taverns at this time, beyond a crust to relish the wine; and he who wished to dine before he drank, had to go to the cook's.

The furnishing of the Boar's Head, in Eastcheap, with sack, in Henry IV., is an anachronism of Shakspeare's ; for the vintners kept neither sacks, muscadels, malmseys, bastards, alicants, nor any other wines but white and claret, until 1543. All the other sweet wines before that time, were sold at the apothecaries' shops for no other use but for medicine.

Taking it as the picture of a tavern a century later, we see the alterations which had taken place. The single drawer or taverner of Lydgate's day is now changed to a troop of waiters, besides the under skinker, or tapster. Eating was no longer confined to the cook's row, for we find in Falstaff's bill "a capon 2s. 2d.; sack, two gallons, 5s. 8d.; anchovies and sack, after supper, 2s. 6d.; bread, one halfpenny." And there were evidently *different rooms** for the guests, as Francis† bids a brother waiter "Look down in the Pomgranite;" for which purpose they had windows, or loopholes, affording a view from the upper to the lower apartments. The custom of naming the principal rooms in taverns and hotels is usual to the present day.

Taverns and wine-bibbing had greatly increased in the reign of Edward VI., when it was enacted by statute that no more than 8d. a gallon should be taken for any

* This negatives a belief common in our day that a Covent Garden tavern was the first divided into rooms for guests.

† A successor of Francis, a waiter at the Boar's Head, in the last century, had a tablet with an inscription in St. Michael's Crooked-lane churchyard, just at the back of the tavern; setting forth that he died, "drawer at the Boar's Head Tavern, in Great Eastcheap," and was noted for his honesty and sobriety; in that—

"Tho' nurs'd among full hogsheads he defied
The charms of wine, as well as others' pride."

He also practised the singular virtue of drawing good wine and of taking care to "fill his pots," as appears by the closing lines of the inscription :—

"Ye that on Bacchus have a like dependance,
Pray copy Bob in measure and attendance.'

French wines, and the consumption limited in private houses to ten gallons each person yearly; that there should not be "any more or great number of taverns in London of such tavernes or wine sellers by retaile, above the number of fouretye tavernes or wyne sellers," being less than two, upon an average to each parish. Nor did this number much increase afterwards; for in a return made to the Vintners' Company, late in Elizabeth's reign, there were only one hundred and sixty-eight taverns in the whole city and suburbs.

It seems to have been the fashion among old ballad-mongers, street chroniclers, and journalists, to sing the praises of the taverns in rough-shod verse, and that lively rhyme which, in our day, is termed "patter." Here are a few specimens, of various periods.

In a black-letter poem of Queen Elizabeth's reign, entitled *Newes from Bartholomew Fayre*, there is this curious enumeration:

"There hath been great sale and utterance of Wine,
   Besides Beere, and Ale, and Ipocras fine,
   In every country, region, and nation,
   But chiefly in Billingsgate, at the *Salutation*;
   And the *Bore's Head*, near London Stone;
   The *Swan* at Dowgate, a tavern well knowne;
   The *Miter* in Cheape, and then the *Bull Head*;
   And many like places that make noses red;
   The *Bore's Head* in Old Fish-street; *Three Cranes* in the
      Vintry;
   And now, of late, St. Martins in the Sentree;
   The *Windmill* in Lothbury; the *Ship* at th' Exchange;
   King's Head in New Fish-street, where roysterers do range;
   The *Mermaid* in Cornhill; *Red Lion* in the Strand;
   Three Tuns in Newgate Market; Old Fish-street at the *Swan*."

This enumeration omits the Mourning Bush, adjoining

116 CLUB LIFE OF LONDON.

Aldersgate, containing divers large rooms and lodgings, and shown in Aggas's plan of London, in 1560. There are also omitted The Pope's Head, The London Stone, The Dagger, The Rose and Crown, etc. Several of the above *Signs* have been continued to our time in the very places mentioned; but nearly all the original buildings were destroyed in the Great Fire of 1666; and the few which escaped have been re-built, or so altered, that their former appearance has altogether vanished.

The following list of taverns is given by Thomas Heywood, the author of the fine old play of *A Woman killed with Kindness.* Heywood, who wrote in 1608, is telling us what particular houses are frequented by particular classes of people :—

" The Gentry to the King's Head,
The nobles to the Crown,
The Knights unto the Golden Fleece,
And to the Plough the Clown.
The churchman to the Mitre,
The shepherd to the Star,
The gardener hies him to the Rose,
To the Drum the man of war ;
To the Feathers, ladies you ; the Globe
The seaman doth not scorn ;
The usurer to the Devil, and
The townsman to the Horn.
The huntsman to the White Hart,
To the Ship the merchants go,
But you who do the Muses love,
The sign called River Po.
The banquerout to the World's End,
The fool to the Fortune Pie,
Unto the Mouth the oyster-wife,
The fiddler to the Pie.
The punk unto the Cockatrice,
The Drunkard to the Vine,

The beggar to the Bush, then meet,
And with Duke Humphrey dine."

In the *British Apollo* of 1710, is the following doggrel:—

"I'm amused at the signs,
    As I pass through the town,
To see the odd mixture—
    A Magpie and Crown,
The Whale and the Crow,
    The Razor and the Hen,
The Leg and Seven Stars,
The Axe and the Bottle,
    The Tun and the Lute,
The Eagle and Child,
    The Shovel and Boot."

In *Look about You*, 1600, we read that " the drawers
kept sugar folded up in paper, ready for those who called
for *sack;*" and we further find in another old tract,
that the custom existed of bringing two cups of *silver*
in case the wine should be wanted diluted; and this was
done by rose-water and sugar, generally about a pennyworth. A sharper in the *Bellman of London*, described
as having decoyed a countryman to a tavern, " calls for
two pintes of sundry wines, the drawer setting the wine
with *two cups*, as the custome is, the sharper tastes of
one pinte, no matter which, and finds fault with the
wine, saying, ' 'tis too hard, but rose-water and sugar
would send it downe merrily'—and for that purpose
takes up one of the cups, telling the stranger he is well
acquainted with the boy at the barre, and can have two-
pennyworth of rose-water for a penny of him; and so
steps from his seate : the stranger suspects no harme,
because the fawne guest leaves his cloake at the end of
the table behind him,—but the other takes good care

not to return, and it is then found that he hath stolen ground, and out-leaped the stranger more feet than he can recover in haste, for the cup is leaped with him, for which the wood-cock, that is taken in the springe, must pay fifty shillings, or three pounds, and hath nothing but an old threadbare cloake not worth two groats to make amends for his losses."

Bishop Earle, who wrote in the first half of the seventeenth century, has left this " character " of a tavern of his time.   " A tavern is a degree, or (if you will) a pair of stairs above an alehouse, where men are drunk with more credit and apology.   If the vintner's nose be at the door, it is a sign sufficient, but the absence of this is supplied by the ivy-bush.   It is a broacher of more news than hogsheads, and more jests than news, which are sucked up here by some spungy brain, and from thence squeezed into a comedy.   Men come here to make merry, but indeed make a noise, and this music above is answered with a clinking below. The drawers are the civilest people in it, men of good bringing up, and howsoever we esteem them, none can boast more justly of their high calling.   'Tis the best theatre of natures, where they are truly acted, not played, and the business as in the rest of the world up and down, to wit, from the bottom of the cellar to the great chamber.   A melancholy man would find here matter to work upon, to see heads, as brittle as glasses, and often broken ; men come hither to quarrel, and come here to be made friends ; and if Plutarch will lend me his simile, it is even Telephus's sword that makes wounds, and cures them.   It is the common consumption of the afternoon, and the murderer or the maker away of a rainy day.   It is the torrid zone that scorches the face, and tobacco the gunpowder that blows it up. Much harm would be done if the charitable vintner had not water ready for the flames. A house of sin you may call it, but not a house of darkness, for the candles are never out; and it is like those countries far in the north, where it is as clear at midnight as at mid-day. After a long sitting it becomes like a street in a dashing shower, where the spouts are flushing above, and the conduits running below, etc. To give you the total reckoning of it, it is the busy man's recreation, the idle man's business, the melancholy man's sanctuary, the stranger's welcome, the inns-of-court man's entertainment, the scholar's kindness, and the citizen's courtesy. It is the study of sparkling wits, and a cup of comedy their book, whence we leave them."

The conjunction of vintner and victualler had now become common, and would require other accommodation than those mentioned by the Bishop, as is shown in Massinger's *New Way to pay Old Debts*, where Justice Greedy makes Tapwell's keeping no victuals in his house as an excuse for pulling down his sign:

"Thou never hadst in thy house to stay men's stomachs,
 A piece of Suffolk cheese, or gammon of bacon,
 Or any esculent as the learned call it,
 For their emolument, but *sheer drink only*.
 For which gross fault I here do damn thy licence,
 Forbidding thee henceforth to tap or draw ;
 For instantly I will in mine own person,
 Command the constable to pull down thy sign,
 And do't before I eat."

And the decayed vinter, who afterwards applies to Wellborn for payment of his tavern score, answers, on his inquiring who he is :

" A decay'd vintner, Sir;
That might have thriv'd, but that your worship broke me
With trusting you with muscadine and eggs,
And *five-pound suppers*, with your after-drinkings,
When you lodged upon the Bankside."

Dekker tells us, near this time, of regular ordinaries of three kinds : 1st. An ordinary of the longest reckoning, whither most of your courtly gallants do resort : 2nd. A twelvepenny ordinary, frequented by the justice of the peace, a young Knight; and a threepenny ordinary, to which your London usurer, your stale bachelor, and your thrifty attorney, doth resort. Then Dekker tells us of a custom, especially in the City, to send presents of wine from one room to another, as a complimentary mark of friendship. " Inquire," directs he, " what gallants sup in the next room ; and if they be of your acquaintance, do not, after the City fashion, send them in a pottle of wine and your name." Then, we read of Master Brook sending to the Castle Inn at Windsor, a morning draught of sack.

Ned Ward, in the *London Spy*, 1709, describes several famous taverns, and among them the Rose, anciently, the Rose and Crown, as famous for good wine. " There was no parting," he says, " without a glass ; so we went into the Rose Tavern in the Poultry, where the wine, according to its merit, had justly gained a reputation ; and there, in a snug room, warmed with brash and faggot, over a quart of good claret, we laughed over our night's adventure."

" From hence, pursuant to my friend's inclination, we adjourned to the sign of the Angel, in Fenchurch-street, where the vintner, like a double-dealing citizen, condescended as well to draw carmen's comfort as the consolatory juice of the vine.

"Having at the King's Head well freighted the hold of our vessels with excellent food and delicious wine, at a small expense, we scribbled the following lines with chalk upon the wall." (See page 98.)

The tapster was a male vendor, not "a woman who had the care of the tap," as Tyrwhitt states. In the 17th century ballad, *The Times*, occurs:

> "The bar-boyes and the tapsters
> Leave drawing of their beere,
> And running forth in haste they cry,
> 'See, where Mull'd Sack comes here!'"

The ancient drawers and tapsters were now super-seded by the barmaid, and a number of waiters: Ward describes the barmaid as "all ribbon, lace, and feathers, and making such a noise with her bell and her tongue together, that had half-a-dozen paper-mills been at work within three yards of her, they'd have signified no more to her clamorous voice than so many lutes to a drum, which alarmed two or three nimble fellows aloft, who shot themselves downstairs with as much celerity as a mountebank's mercury upon a rope from the top of a church-steeple, every one charged with a mouthful of coming, coming, coming." The barmaid (generally the vintner's daughter) is described as "bred at the dancing-school, becoming a bar well, stepping a minuet finely, playing sweetly on the virginals, 'John come kiss me now, now, now,' and as proud as she was hand-some."

Tom Brown sketches a flirting barmaid of the same time, "as a fine lady that stood pulling a rope, and screaming like a peacock against rainy weather, pinned up by herself in a little pew, all people bowing to her as they passed by, as if she was a goddess set up to be

worshipped, armed with the chalk and sponge, (which
are the principal badges that belong to that honourable
station you beheld her in,) was the *barmaid*."

Of the nimbleness of the waiters, Ward says in another place —" That the chief use he saw in the Monument was, for the improvement of vintners' boys and
drawers, who came every week to exercise their supporters, and learn the tavern trip, by running up to the
balcony and down again."

Owen Swan, at the Black Swan tavern, Bartholomew
Lane, is thus apostrophized by Tom Brown for the goodness of his wine :—

> " Thee, *Owen*, since the God of wine has made
> Thee steward of the gay carousing trade,
> Whose art decaying nature still supplies,
> Warms the faint pulse, and sparkles in our eyes.
> Be bountiful like him, bring t'other *flask*,
> Were the stairs wider we would have the *cask*.
> This pow'r we from the God of wine derive,
> Draw such as this, and I'll pronounce thou'lt live."

THE BEAR AT THE BRIDGE FOOT.

This celebrated tavern, situated in Southwark, on the
west side of the foot of London Bridge, opposite the end
of St. Olave's or Tooley-street, was a house of considerable antiquity. We read in the accounts of the Steward
of Sir John Howard, March 6th, 1463–4 (Edward IV.),
" Item, payd for red wyn at the Bere in Southwerke,
iij*d*." Garrard, in a letter to Lord Strafford, dated 1633

intimates that " all back-doors to taverns on the Thames are commanded to be shut up, only the Bear at Bridge Foot is exempted, by reason of the passage to Greenwich," which Mr. Burn suspects to have been " the avenue or way called Bear Alley."

The Cavaliers' Ballad on the funeral pageant of Admiral Deane, killed June 2nd, 1653, while passing by water to Henry the Seventh's Chapel, Westminster, has the following allusion :—

> " From Greenwich towards the Bear at Bridge foot,
> He was wafted with wind that had water to't,
> But I think they brought the devil to boot,
>   Which nobody can deny."

Pepys was told by a waterman, going through the bridge, 24th Feb. 1666–7, that the mistress of the Beare Tavern, at the Bridge foot, " did lately fling herself into the Thames, and drown herself."

The Bear must have been a characterless house, for among its gallantries was the following, told by Wycherley to Major Pack, " just for the oddness of the thing." It was this : " There was a house at the Bridge Foot where persons of better condition used to resort for pleasure and privacy. The liquor the ladies and their lovers used to drink at these meetings was canary ; and among other compliments the gentlemen paid their mistresses, this it seems was always one, to take hold of the bottom of their smocks, and pouring the wine through that filter, feast their imaginations with the thought of what gave the zesto, and so drink a health to the toast."

The Bear Tavern was taken down in December, 1761, when the labourers found gold and silver coins, of the time of Elizabeth, to a considerable value. The wall that enclosed the tavern was not cleared away until 1764, when the ground was cleared and levelled quite up to Pepper Alley stairs. There is a Token of the Bear Tavern, in the Beaufoy cabinet, which, with other rare Southwark tokens, was found under the floors in taking down St. Olave's Grammar School in 1839.

MERMAID TAVERNS.

The celebrated Mermaid, in Bread-street, with the history of " the Mermaid Club," has been described in Vol. I. pp. 8–10; its interest centres in this famous company of Wits.

There was another Mermaid, in Cheapside, next to Paul's Gate, and still another in Cornhill. Of the latter we find in Burn's Beaufoy Catalogue, that the vintner, buried in St. Peter's, Cornhill, in 1606, " gave forty shillings yearly to the parson for preaching four sermons every year, so long as the lease of the Mermaid, in Cornhill, (the tavern so called,) should endure. He also gave to the poor of the said parish thirteen penny loaves every Sunday, during the aforesaid lease." There are tokens of both these taverns in the Beaufoy Collection.

THE BOAR'S HEAD TAVERN.

This celebrated Shakspearean tavern was situated in Great Eastcheap, and is first mentioned in the time of Richard II.; the scene of the revels of Falstaff and

Henry V., when Prince of Wales, in Shakspeare's
Henry IV., Part 2. Stow relates a riot in "the cooks'
dwellings" here on St. John's eve, 1410, by Princes
John and Thomas. The tavern was destroyed in the
Great Fire of 1666, but was rebuilt in two years, as
attested by a boar's head cut in stone, with the initials
of the landlord, I. T., and the date 1668, above the first-
floor window. This sign-stone is now in the Guildhall
library. The house stood between Small-alley and St.
Michael's-lane, and in the rear looked upon St. Michael's
churchyard, where was buried a *drawer*, or waiter, at
the tavern, d. 1720: in the church was interred John
Rhodoway, "Vintner at the Bore's Head," 1623.

Maitland, in 1739, mentions the Boar's Head, as
"the chief tavern in London" under the sign. Goldsmith (*Essays*), Boswell (*Life of Dr. Johnson*), and
Washington Irving (*Sketch-book*), have idealized the
house as the identical place which Falstaff frequented,
forgetting its destruction in the Great Fire. The site
of the Boar's Head is very nearly that of the statue of
King William IV.

In 1834, Mr. Kempe, F.S.A., exhibited to the Society
of Antiquaries a carved oak figure of Sir John Falstaff,
in the costume of the 16th century; it had supported
an ornamental bracket over one side of the door of the
Boar's Head, a figure of Prince Henry sustaining that
on the other. The Falstaff was the property of one
Shelton, a brazier, whose ancestors had lived in the shop
he then occupied in Great Eastcheap, since the Great
Fire. He well remembered the last Shakspearean
grand dinner-party at the Boar's Head, about 1784:
at an earlier party, Mr. Wilberforce was present. A
boar's head, with tusks, which had been suspended in a

room of the tavern, perhaps the Half-Moon or Pome-
granate, (see Henry IV. act ii. sc. 4,) at the Great Fire,
fell down with the ruins of the house, and was conveyed
to Whitechapel Mount, where, many years after, it
was recovered, and identified with its former locality.
At a public house, No. 12, Miles-lane, was long preserved a tobacco-box, with a painting of the original
Boar's Head Tavern on the lid.*

In High-street, Southwark, in the rear of Nos. 25 and
26, was formerly the *Boar's Head Inn*, part of Sir John
Falstolf's benefaction to Magdalen College, Oxford. Sir
John was one of the bravest generals in the French wars,
under the fourth, fifth, and sixth Henries; but he is not
the Falstaff of Shakspeare. In the *Reliquiæ Hearnianæ*,
edited by Dr. Bliss, is the following entry relative to this
bequest :—

" 1721. June 2.—The reason why they cannot give so good an
account of the benefaction of Sir John Fastolf to Magd. Coll.
is, because he gave it to the founder, and left it to his management, so that 'tis suppos'd 'twas swallow'd up in his own estate
that he settled it upon the college. However, the college knows
this, that the *Boar's Head* in Southwark, which was then an inn,
and still retains the name, tho' divided into several tenements
(which bring the college about 150*l*. per ann.), was part of Sir
John's gift."

The above property was for many years sublet to the
family of the author of the present Work, at the rent of
150*l*. per annum ; the cellar, finely vaulted, and excellent for wine, extended beneath the entire court, consisting of two rows of tenements, and two end houses,
with galleries, the entrance being from the High-street.
The premises were taken down for the New London

* *Curiosities of London*, p. 265.

Bridge approaches. There was also a noted Boar's Head in Old Fish-street.

Can he forget who has read Goldsmith's nineteenth Essay, his reverie at the Boar's Head?—when, having confabulated with the landlord till long after "the watchman had gone twelve," and suffused in the potency of his wine a mutation in his ideas, of the person of the host into that of Dame Quickly, mistress of the tavern in the days of Sir John, is promptly effected, and the liquor they were drinking seemed shortly converted into sack and sugar. Mrs. Quickly's recital of the history of herself and Doll Tearsheet, whose frailties in the flesh caused their being both sent to the house of correction, charged with having allowed the famed Boar's Head to become a low brothel; her speedy departure to the world of Spirits; and Falstaff's impertinences as affecting Madame Proserpine; are followed by an enumeration of persons who had held tenancy of the house since her time. The last hostess of note was, according to Goldsmith's account, Jane Rouse, who, having unfortunately quarrelled with one of her neighbours, a woman of high repute in the parish for sanctity, but as jealous as Chaucer's Wife of Bath, was by her accused of witchcraft, taken from her own bar, condemned, and executed accordingly!—These were times, indeed, when women could not scold in safety. These and other prudential apophthegms on the part of Dame Quickly, seem to have dissolved Goldsmith's stupor of ideality; on his awaking, the landlord is really the landlord, and not the hostess of a former day, when "Falstaff was in fact an agreeable old fellow, forgetting age, and showing the way to be young at sixty-five. Age, care, wisdom, reflection, begone! I give you to the winds. Let's have t'other bottle.   Here's to the memory of Shakspeare, Falstaff, and all the merry men of Eastcheap."*

THREE CRANES IN THE VINTRY.

This was one of Ben Jonson's taverns, and has already been incidentally mentioned.   Strype describes it as situate in "New Queen-street, commonly called the Three Cranes in the Vintry, a good open street, especially that part next Cheapside, which is best built and inhabited.   At the lowest end of the street, next the Thames, is a pair of stairs, the usual place for the Lord Mayor and Aldermen to take water at, to go to Westminster Hall, for the new Lord Mayor to be sworn before the Barons of the Exchequer.   This place, with the Three Cranes, is now of some account for the costermongers, where they have their warehouse for their fruit."   In Scott's *Kenilworth* we hear much of this Tavern.

LONDON STONE TAVERN.

This tavern, situated in Cannon-street, near the Stone, is stated, but not correctly, to have been the oldest in London.   Here was formed a society, afterwards the famous Robin Hood, of which the history was published in 1716, where it is stated to have originated in a meeting of the editor's grandfather with the great Sir Hugh Myddelton, of New River memory.   King Charles II. was introduced to the society, disguised, by Sir Hugh,

* *Burn's Catalogue of the Beaufoy Tokens.*

and the King liked it so well, that he came thrice afterwards. " He had," continues the narrative, " a piece of
black silk over his left cheek, which almost covered it; and
his eyebrows, which were quite black, he had, by some
artifice or other, converted to a light brown, or rather
flaxen colour ; and had otherwise disguised himself so effectually in his apparel and his looks, that nobody knew
him but Sir Hugh, by whom he was introduced." This is
very circumstantial, but is very doubtful; since Sir Hugh
Myddelton died when Charles was in his tenth year.

THE ROBIN HOOD.

Mr. Akerman describes a Token of the Robin Hood
Tavern :—" IOHN THOMLINSON AT THE. An archer fitting
an arrow to his bow ; a small figure behind, holding an
arrow.—℞. IN CHISWELL STREET, 1667. In the centre,
HIS HALFE PENNY, and I. S. T. Mr. Akerman continues :

" It is easy to perceive what is intended by the representation on the obverse of this token. Though ' Little
John,' we are told, stood upwards of six good English
feet without his shoes, he is here depicted to suit the
popular humour—a dwarf in size, compared with his
friend and leader, the bold outlaw. The proximity of
Chiswell-street to Finsbury-fields may have led to the
adoption of the sign, which was doubtless at a time when
archery was considered an elegant as well as an indis-
pensable accomplishment of an English gentleman. It
is far from obsolete now, as several low public-houses
and beer-shops in the vicinity of London testify. One

of them exhibits Robin Hood and his companion dressed
in the most approved style of ' Astley's,' and underneath
the group is the following irresistible invitation to slake
your thirst :—

> " Ye archers bold and yeomen good,
> Stop and drink with Robin Hood :
> If Robin Hood is not at home,
> Stop and drink with little John."

"Our London readers could doubtless supply the va-
riorum copies of this elegant distich, which, as this is an
age for ' Family Shakspeares,' modernized Chaucers,
and new versions of ' Robin Hood's Garland,' we recommend to the notice of the next editor of the ballads in
praise of the Sherwood freebooter."

PONTACK'S, ABCHURCH LANE.

After the destruction of the White Bear Tavern, in
the Great Fire of 1666, the proximity of the site for all
purposes of business, induced M. Pontack, the son of
the President of Bordeaux, owner of a famous claret
district, to establish a tavern, with all the novelties of
French cookery, with his father's head as a sign, whence
it was popularly called " Pontack's Head." The dinners
were from four or five shillings a head " to a guinea, or
what sum you pleased."

Swift frequented the tavern, and writes to Stella :—
" Pontack told us, although his wine was so good, he
sold it cheaper than others ; he took but seven shillings

a flask. Are not these pretty rates?" In the *Hind and Panther Transversed*, we read of drawers:—

> "Sure these honest fellows have no knack
> Of putting off stum'd claret for Pontack."

The Fellows of the Royal Society dined at Pontack's until 1746, when they removed to the Devil Tavern. There is a Token of the White Bear in the Beaufoy collection; and Mr. Burn tells us, from *Metamorphoses of the Town*, a rare tract, 1731, of Pontack's "guinea ordinary," "ragout of fatted snails," and "chickens not two hours from the shell." In January, 1735, Mrs. Susannah Austin, who lately kept Pontack's, and had acquired a considerable fortune, was married to William Pepys, banker, in Lombard-street.

POPE'S HEAD TAVERN.

This noted tavern, which gave name to Pope's Head Alley, leading from Cornhill to Lombard-street, is mentioned as early as the 4th Edward IV. (1464) in the account of a wager between an Alicant goldsmith and an English goldsmith; the Alicant stranger contending in the tavern that "Englishmen were not so cunning in workmanship of goldsmithry as Alicant strangers;" when work was produced by both, and the Englishman gained the wager. The tavern was left in 1615, by Sir William Craven to the Merchant Tailors' Company. Pepys refers to "the fine painted room" here in 1668-9. In the tavern, April 14, 1718, Quin, the actor, killed in

self-defence, his fellow-comedian, Bowen, a clever but
hot-headed Irishman, who was jealous of Quin's reputation : in a moment of great anger, he sent for Quin to
the tavern, and as soon as he had entered the room,
Bowen placed his back against the door, drew his sword,
and bade Quin draw his.   Quin, having mildly remon-
strated to no purpose, drew in his own defence, and endeavoured to disarm his antagonist.   Bowen received a
wound, of which he died in three days, having acknowledged his folly and madness, when the loss of blood had
reduced him to reason.   Quin was tried and acquitted.
(*Cunningham, abridged.*)   The Pope's Head Tavern was
in existence in 1756.

THE OLD SWAN, THAMES-STREET,

Was more than five hundred years ago a house for
public entertainment: for, in 1323, 16 Edw. II., Rose
Wrytell bequeathed " the tenement of olde tyme called
the Swanne on the Hope in Thames-street," in the
parish of St. Mary-at-hill, to maintain a priest at the
altar of St. Edmund, King and Martyr, " for her soul,
and the souls of her husband, her father, and mother :"
and the purposes of her bequest were established; for,
in the parish book, in 1499, is entered a disbursement
of fourpence, " for a cresset to Rose Wrytell's chantry."
Eleanor Cobham, Duchess of Gloucester, in 1440, in
her public penance for witchcraft and treason, landed at
Old Swan, bearing a large taper, her feet bare, etc.
    Stow, in 1598, mentions the Old Swan as a great
brew-house.   Taylor, the Water-poet, advertised the

professor and author of the Barmoodo and Vtopian tongues, dwelling "at the Old Swanne, neare London Bridge, who will teach them at are willing to learne, with agility and facility."

In the scurrilous Cavalier ballad of Admiral Deane's Funeral, by water, from Greenwich to Westminster, in June, 1653, it is said :—

> " The Old Swan, as he passed by,
>   Said she would sing him a dirge, lye down and die :
>   Wilt thou sing to a bit of a body? quoth I,
>   Which nobody can deny."

The Old Swan Tavern and its landing-stairs were destroyed in the Great Fire ; but rebuilt. Its Token, in the Beaufoy Collection, is one of the rarest, of large size.

COCK TAVERN THREADNEEDLE-STREET.

This noted house, which faced the north gate of the old Royal Exchange, was long celebrated for the excellence of its soups, which were served at an economical price, in silver. One of its proprietors was, it is believed, John Ellis, an eccentric character, and a writer of some reputation, who died in 1791. Eight stanzas addressed to him in praise of the tavern, commenced thus :—

> " When to Ellis I write, I in verse must indite,
>   Come Phœbus, and give me a knock,
>   For on Fryday at eight, all behind ' the 'Change gate,'
>   Master Ellis will be at ' The Cock.' "

After comparing it to other houses, the Pope's Head,

the King's Arms, the Black Swan, and the Fountain, and declaring the Cock the best, it ends :

" 'Tis time to be gone, for the 'Change has struck one :
  O 'tis an impertinent clock !
  For with Ellis I'd stay from December to May ;
  I'll stick to my Friend, and ' The Cock !' "

This house was taken down in 1841 ; when, in a claim for compensation made by the proprietor, the trade in three years was proved to have been 344,720 basins of various soups—viz. 166,240 mock turtle, 3,920 giblet, 59,360 ox-tail, 31,072 bouilli, 84,128 gravy and other soups : sometimes 500 basins of soup were sold in a day.

CROWN TAVERN, THREADNEEDLE-STREET.

Upon the site of the present chief entrance to the Bank of England, in Threadneedle-street, stood the Crown Tavern, " behind the 'Change :" it was frequented by the Fellows of the Royal Society, when they met at Gresham College hard by. The Crown was burnt in the Great Fire, but was rebuilt ; and about a century since, at this tavern, " it was not unusual to draw a butt of mountain wine, containing 120 gallons, in gills, in a morning."—*Sir John Hawkins.*

Behind the Change, we read in the *Connoisseur,* 1754, a man worth a plum used to order a twopenny mess of broth with a boiled chop in it ; placing the chop between the two crusts of a half-penny roll, he would wrap it up in his check handkerchief, and carry it away for the morrow's dinner.

THE KING'S HEAD TAVERN, IN THE POULTRY.

This Tavern, which stood at the western extremity of the Stocks' Market, was not first known by the sign of the King's Head, but the Rose: Machin, in his Diary, Jan. 5, 1560, thus mentions it : " A gentleman arrested for debt; Master Cobham, with divers gentlemen and serving-men, took him from the officers, and carried him to the Rose Tavern, where so great a fray, both the sheriffs were feign to come, and from the Rose Tavern took all the gentlemen and their servants, and carried them to the Compter."

The house was distinguished by the device of a large, well-painted Rose, erected over a doorway, which was the only indication in the main street of such an establishment. In the superior houses of the metropolis in the sixteenth century, room was gained in the rear of the street-line, the space in front being economized, so that the line of shops might not be interrupted. Upon this plan, the larger taverns in the City was constructed, wherever the ground was sufficiently spacious behind : hence it was that the Poultry tavern of which we are speaking, was approached through a long, narrow, covered passage, opening into a well-lighted quadrangle, around which were the tavern-rooms. The sign of the Rose appears to have been a costly work, since there was the fragment of a leaf of an old account-book preserved, when the ruins of the honse were cleared after the Great Fire, on which were written these entries:—"Pd. to Hoggestreete, the Duche Paynter, for ye Picture of a Rose, wth a Standing-bowle and Glasses, for a Signe, xxli. besides Diners and Drinkings. Also for a large Table of Walnut-tree, for a Frame; and for Iron-worke and Hanging the Picture, vli." The artist who is referred to in this memorandum, could be no other than Samuel Van Hoogstraten, a painter of the middle of the seventeenth century, whose works in England are very rare.   He was one of the many excellent artists of the period, who, as Walpole contemptuously says, " painted still-life, oranges and lemons, plate, damask curtains, cloth-of-gold, and that medley of familiar objects that strike the ignorant vulgar."

But, beside the claims of the painter, the sign of the Rose cost the worthy tavern-keeper, a still further outlay, in the form of divers treatings and advances made to a certain rather loose man of letters of his acquaintance, possessed of more wit than money, and of more convivial loyalty than either discretion or principle.   Master Roger Blythe frequently patronized the Rose Tavern as his favourite ordinary.   Like Falstaff, he was " an infinite thing " upon his host's score ; and, like his prototype also, there was no probability of his ever discharging the account.   When the Tavern-sign was about to be erected, this Master Blythe contributed the poetry to it, after the fashion of the time, which he swore was the envy of all the Rose Taverns in London, and of all the poets who frequented them.   " There's your Rose at Temple Bar, and your Rose in Covent-garden, and the Rose in Southwark : all of them indifferent good for wits, and for drawing neat wines too; but, smite me, Master King," he would say, " if I know one of them all fit to be set in the same hemisphere

with yours! No! for a bountiful host, a most sweet
mistress, unsophisticated wines, honest measures, a
choicely-painted sign, and a witty verse to set it forth
withal,—commend me to the Rose Tavern in the
Poultry!"

Even the tavern-door exhibited a joyous frontispiece;
since the entrance was flanked by two columns twisted
with vines carved in wood, which supported a small
square gallery over the portico surrounded by handsome
iron-work. On the front of this gallery was erected the
sign, in a frame of similar ornaments. It consisted of
a central compartment containing the Rose, behind
which appeared a tall silver cup, called in the language
of the time " a standing-bowl," with drinking-glasses.
Beneath the painting was this inscription :—

" THIS IS

THE ROSE TAVERNE
IN THE POULTREY :
KEPT BY
WILLIAM KING,
CITIZEN AND VINTNER.

" This Taverne's like its Signe—a lustie Rose,
   A sight of joy that sweetness doth enclose :
The daintie Flow're well-pictur'd here is seene,
   But for its rarest sweetes—Come, Searche Within !"

The authorities of St. Peter-upon-Cornhill soon determined, on the 10th of May, 1660, in Vestry, " that the
King's Arms, in painted-glass, should be refreshed, and
forthwith be set up by the Churchwarden at the parish-
charges; with whatsoever he giveth to the glazier as a
gratuity, for his care in keeping of them all this while."

The host of the Rose resolved at once to add a Crown
to his sign, with the portrait of Charles, wearing it in

the centre of the flower, and openly to name his tavern
" The Royal Rose and King's Head." He effected his
design, partly by the aid of one of the many excellent
pencils which the time supplied, and partly by the inven-
tive muse of Master Blythe, which soon furnished him
with a new poesy. There is not any further information
extant concerning the painting, but the following remains
of an entry on another torn fragment of the old account-
book already mentioned, seem to refer to the poetical
inscription beneath the picture:— .... " on ye Night
when he made ye Verses for my new Signe, a Soper, and
v. Peeces." The verses themselves were as follow :—

> " Gallants, Rejoice !—This Flow're is now full-blowne ;
> 'Tis a Rose-Noble better'd by a Crowne ;
> All you who love the Embleme and the Signe,
> Enter, and prove our Loyaltie and Wine."

Beside this inscription, Master King also recorded the
auspicious event referred to, by causing his painter to
introduce into the picture a broad-sheet, as if lying on
the table with the cup and glasses—on which appeared
the title " A Kalendar for this Happy Yeare of Restaura-
tion 1660, now newly Imprinted."

As the time advanced when Charles was to make his
entry into the metropolis, the streets were resounding
with the voices of ballad-singers pouring forth loyal
songs, and declaring, with the whole strength of their
lungs, that

> " The King shall enjoy his own again."

Then, there were also to be heard, the ceaseless horns
and proclamations of hawkers and flying-stationers, publishing the latest passages or rumours touching the royal
progress ; which, whether genuine or not, were bought

and read, and circulated, by all parties. At length all
the previous pamphlets and broad-sheets were swallowed
up by a well-known tract, still extant, which the news-
men of the time thus proclaimed :—" Here is *A True
Accompt and Narrative—of his Majestie's safe Arrival
in England—as 'twas reported to the House of Commons,
on Friday, the 25th day of this present May—with the
Resolutions of both Houses thereupon:—Also a Letter
very lately writ from Dover—relating divers remarkable
Passages of His Majestie's Reception there.*"
  On every side the signs and iron-work were either
refreshed, or newly gilt and painted: tapestries and rich
hangings, which had engendered moth and decay from
long disuse, were flung abroad again, that they might be
ready to grace the coming pageant. The paving of the
streets was levelled and repaired for the expected caval-
cade ; and scaffolds for spectators were in the course of
erection throughout all the line of march. Floods of all
sorts of wines were consumed, as well in the streets as
in the taverns ; and endless healths were devotedly and
energetically swallowed, at morning, noon, and night.
  At this time Mistress Rebecca King was about to add
another member to Master King's household: she
received from hour to hour accounts of the proceedings
as they occurred, which so stimulated her curiosity, that
she declared, first to her gossips, and then to her husband, that she " must see the King pass the tavern, or
matters might go cross with her."
  A kind of arbour was made for Mistress Rebecca in
the small iron gallery surmounting the entrance to the
tavern. This arbour was of green boughs and flowers,
hung round with tapestry and garnished with silver
plate ; and here, when the guns at the Tower announced

that Charles had entered London, Mistress King took
her seat, with her children and gossips around her. All
the houses in the main streets from London-bridge to
Whitehall, were decorated like the tavern with rich
silks and tapestries, hung from every scaffold, balcony,
and window; which, as Herrick says, turned the town
into a park, "made green and trimmed with boughs."
The road through London, so far as Temple-Bar, was
lined on the north side by the City Companies, dressed
in their liveries, and ranged in their respective stands,
with their banners; and on the south by the soldiers of
the trained-bands.

One of the wine conduits stood on the south side of
the Stocks' Market, over which Sir Robert Viner subsequently erected a triumphal statue of Charles II.
About this spot, therefore, the crowd collected in the
Market-place, aided by the fierce loyalty supplied from
the conduit, appears for a time to have brought the
procession to a full stop, at the moment when Charles,
who rode between his brothers the Dukes of York and
Gloucester, was nearly opposite to the newly-named
King's Head Tavern. In this most favourable interval,
Master Blythe, who stood upon a scaffold in the doorway, took the opportunity of elevating a silver cup of
wine and shouting out a health to his Majesty. His
energetical action, as he pointed upwards to the gallery,
was not lost; and the Duke of Buckingham, who rode
immediately before the King with General Monk,
directed Charles's attention to Mistress Rebecca, saying,
"Your Majesty's return is here welcomed even by a
subject as yet unborn." As the procession passed by
the door of the King's Head Tavern, the King turned
towards it, raised himself in his stirrups, and gracefully

kissed his hand to Mistress Rebecca. Immediately such a shout was raised from all who beheld it or heard of it, as startled the crowd up to Cheapside conduit; and threw the poor woman herself into such an ecstasy, that she was not conscious of anything more, until she was safe in her chamber and all danger happily over.*

The Tavern was rebuilt after the Great Fire, and flourished many years. It was long a depôt in the metropolis for turtle; and in the quadrangle of the Tavern might be seen scores of turtle, large and lively, in huge tanks of water; or laid upward on the stone floor, ready for their destination. The Tavern was also noted for large dinners of the City Companies and other public bodies. The house was refitted in 1852, but has since been closed.

Another noted Poultry Tavern was the Three Cranes, destroyed in the Great Fire, but rebuilt, and noticed in 1698, in one of the many paper controversies of that day. A fulminating pamphlet, entitled "*Ecclesia et Factio*: a Dialogue between Bow Church Steeple and the Exchange Grasshopper," elicited "An Answer to the Dragon and Grasshopper: in a Dialogue between an Old Monkey and a Young Weasel, at the Three Cranes Tavern, in the Poultry."

THE MITRE, IN WOOD STREET,

Was a noted old Tavern. Pepys, in his *Diary*, Sept. 18, 1660, records his going "to the Mitre Tavern, in Wood-street, (a house of the greatest note in London,) where

* Abridged from an Account of the Tavern, by an Antiquary.

I met W. Symons, D. Scoball, and their wives. Here some of us fell to handicap, a sport I never knew before, which was very good." The tavern was destroyed in the Great Fire.

THE SALUTATION AND CAT TAVERN,

No. 17, Newgate-street (north side), was, according to the tradition of the house, the tavern where Sir Christopher Wren used to smoke his pipe, whilst St. Paul's was re-building. There is more positive evidence of its being a place well frequented by men of letters at the above period. Thus, there exists a poetical invitation to a social feast held here on June 19, 1735–6, issued by the two stewards, Edward Cave and William Bowyer:

"Saturday, Jan. 17, 1735–6.
" Sir,
" You're desir'd on Monday next to meet
At Salutation Tavern, Newgate-street.
Supper will be on table just at eight,
[*Stewards*] One of St. John's [Bowyer], 'tother of St. John's
Gate [Cave]. "

This brought a poetical answer from Samuel Richardson, the novelist, printed *in extenso* in Bowyer's *Anecdotes* :

"For me, I'm much concerned I cannot meet
' At Salutation Tavern, Newgate-street.'
Your notice, like your verse, so sweet and short!
If longer, I'd sincerely thank you for it.
Howe'er, receive my wishes, sons of verse !
May every man who meets, your praise rehearse !

May mirth, as plenty, crown your cheerful board,
And ev'ry one part happy—as a lord !
That when at home, (by such sweet verses fir'd)
Your families may think you all inspir'd.
So wishes he, who pre-engag'd, can't know
The pleasures that would from your meeting flow."

The proper sign is the Salutation and Cat,—a curious combination, but one which is explained by a lithograph, which some years ago hung in the coffee-room. An aged dandy is saluting a friend whom he has met in the street, and offering him a pinch out of the snuff-box which forms the top of his wood-like cane. This box-nob was, it appears, called a " cat "—hence the connection of terms apparently so foreign to each other. Some, not aware of this explanation, have accounted for the sign by supposing that a tavern called " the Cat " was at some time pulled down, and its trade carried to the Salutation, which thenceforward joined the sign to its own; but this is improbable, seeing that we have never heard of *any* tavern called " the Cat " (although we *do* know of " the Barking Dogs ") as a sign. Neither does the *Salutation* take its name from any scriptural or sacred source, as the *Angel and Trumpets*, etc.

More positive evidence there is to show of the " little smoky room at the *Salutation and Cat*," where Coleridge and Charles Lamb sat smoking Oronoko and drinking egg-hot; the first discoursing of his idol, Bowles, and the other rejoicing mildly in Cowper and Burns, or both dreaming of " Pantisocracy, and golden days to come on earth."

"SALUTATION" TAVERNS.

The sign Salutation, from scriptural or sacred source, remains to be explained. Mr. Akerman suspects the original sign to have really represented the Salutation of the Virgin by the Angel—"Ave Maria, gratia plena"— a well-known legend on the jettons of the Middle Ages. The change of representation was properly accommodated to the times. The taverns at that period were the "gossiping shops" of the neighbourhood; and both Puritan and Churchman frequented them for the sake of hearing the news. The Puritans loved the good things of this world, and relished a cup of Canary, or Noll's nose well. holding the maxim—

> "Though the devil trepan
> The Adamical man,
> The saint stands uninfected."

Hence, perhaps, the Salutation of the Virgin was exchanged for the "booin' and scrapin'" scene (two men bowing and greeting), represented on a token which still exists, the tavern was celebrated in the days of Queen Elizabeth. In some old black-letter doggrel, entitled *News from Bartholemew, Fayre* it is mentioned for wine:—

> "There hath been great sale and utterance of wine,
> Besides beere, and ale, and Ipocras fine;
> In every country, region, and nation,
> But chiefly in Billingsgate, *at the Salutation.*"

The Flower-pot was originally part of a symbol of the Annunciation to the Virgin.

QUEEN'S ARMS, ST. PAUL'S CHURCHYARD.

Garrick appears to have kept up his interest in the City by means of clubs, to which he paid periodical visits. We have already mentioned the Club of young merchants, at Tom's Coffee-house, in Cornhill. Another Club was held at the Queen's Arms Tavern, in St. Paul's Churchyard, where used to assemble: Mr. Samuel Sharpe, the surgeon; Mr. Paterson, the City solicitor; Mr. Draper, the bookseller; Mr. Clutterbuck, the mercer; and a few others.

Sir John Hawkins tells us that "they were none of them drinkers, and in order to make a reckoning, called only for French wine." These were Garrick's standing council in theatrical affairs.

At the Queen's Arms, after a thirty years' interval, Johnson renewed his intimacy with some of the members of his old Ivy-lane Club.

Brasbridge, the old silversmith of Fleet-street, was a member of the Sixpenny Card-Club held at the Queen's Arms : among the members was Henry Baldwyn, who, under the auspices of Bonnel Thornton, Colman the elder, and Garrick, set up the *St. James's Chronicle*, which once had the largest circulation of any evening paper this worthy newspaper-proprietor was considerate and generous to men of genius : "Often," says Brasbridge, "at his hospitable board I have seen needy authors, and others connected with his employment, whose abilities, ill-requited as they might have been by the world in general, were by him always appreciated." Among

Brasbridge's acquaintance, also, were John Walker, shopman to a grocer and chandler in Well-street, Rag-fair, who died worth 200,000*l.*, most assuredly not gained by lending money on doubtful security ; and Ben Kenton, brought up at a charity-school, and who realized 300,000*l.*, partly at the Magpie and Crown, in Whitechapel.

DOLLY'S, PATERNOSTER ROW.

This noted tavern, established in the reign of Queen Anne, has for its sign, the cook Dolly, who is stated to have been painted by Gainsborough. It is still a well-appointed chop-house and tavern, and the coffee-room, with its projecting fireplaces, has an olden air. Nearly on the site of Dolly's, Tarlton, Queen Elizabeth's favourite stage-clown, kept an ordinary, with the sign of the Castle. The house, of which a token exists, was destroyed in the Great Fire, but was rebuilt; there the " Castle Society of Music" gave their performances. Part of the old premises were subsequently the Oxford Bible Warehouse, destroyed by fire in 1822, and rebuilt.

The entrance to the Chop-house is in Queen's Head passage; and at Dolly's is a window-pane painted with the head of Queen Anne, which may explain the name of the court.

At Dolly's and Horsman's beef-steaks were eaten with gill-ale.

ALDERSGATE TAVERNS.

Two early houses of entertainment in Aldersgate were the Taborer's Inn and the Crown. Of the former, stated to have been of the time of Edward II., we know nothing but the name. The Crown, more recent, stood at the End of Duck-lane, and is described in Ward's *London Spy*, as containing a noble room, painted by Fuller, with the Muses, the Judgment of Paris, the Contention of Ajax and Ulysses, etc. " We were conducted by the jolly master," says Ward, " a true kinsman of the bacchanalian family, into a large stately room, where at the first entrance, I discerned the master-strokes of the famed Fuller's pencil; the whole room painted by that commanding hand, that his dead figures appeared with such lively majesty that they begat reverence in the spectators towards the awful shadows. We accordingly bade the complaisant waiter oblige us with a quart of his richest claret, such as was fit only to be drank in the presence of such heroes, into whose company he had done us the honour to introduce us. He thereupon gave directions to his drawer, who returned with a quart of such inspiring juice, that we thought ourselves translated into one of the houses of the heavens, and were there drinking immortal nectar with the gods and goddesses:

" Who could such blessings when thus found resign ?
An honest vintner faithful to the vine ;
A spacious room, good paintings, and good wine."

Far more celebrated was the Mourning Bush Tavern, in the cellars of which have been traced the massive

foundations of Aldersgate, and the portion of the City
Wall which adjoins them. This tavern, one of the largest and most ancient in London, has a curious history.
The Bush Tavern, its original name, took for its sign
the *Ivy-bush* hung up at the door. It is believed to have
been the house referred to by Stowe, as follows :—" This
gate (Aldersgate) hath been at sundry times increased
with building; namely, on the south or *inner side*, a
great frame of timber, (or house of wood lathed and
plastered,) hath been added and set up containing divers
large rooms and lodgings," which were an enlarge-
ment of the Bush. Fosbroke mentions the Bush as the
chief sign of taverns in the Middle Ages, (it being ready
to hand,) and so it continued until superseded by " a
thing to resemble one containing three or four tiers of
hoops fastened one above another with vine leaves and
grapes, richly carved and gilt." He adds : " the owner
of the Mourning Bush, Aldersgate, was so affected at the
decollation of Charles I., that he *painted his bush
black*." From this period the house is scarcely mentioned until the year 1719, when we find its name
changed to the Fountain, whether from political feeling
against the then exiled House of Stuart, or the whim of
the proprietor, we cannot learn ; though it is thought to
have reference to a spring on the east side of the gate.
Tom Brown mentions the Fountain satirically, with
four or five topping taverns of the day, whose landlords
are charged with doctoring their wines, but whose trade
was so great that they stood fair for the alderman's gown.
And, in a letter from an old vintner in the City to one
newly set up in Covent Garden, we find the following in
the way of advice : " as all the world are wholly supported
by hard and unintelligible names, you must take care to

christen your wines by some hard name, the further fetched so much the better, and this policy will serve to recommend the most execrable scum in your cellar. I could name several of our brethren to you, who now stand fair to sit in the seat of justice, and sleep in their golden chain at churches, that had been forced to knock off long ago, if it had not been for this artifice. It saved the Sun from being eclipsed; the Crown from being abdicated; the Rose from decaying; and the Fountain from being dry; as well as both the Devils from being confined to utter darkness."

Twenty years later, in a large plan of Aldersgate Ward, 1739–40, we find the Fountain changed to the original Bush. The Fire of London had evidently, at this time, curtailed the ancient extent of the tavern. The exterior is shown in a print of the south side of Aldersgate; it has the character of the larger houses, built after the Great Fire, and immediately adjoins the gate. The last notice of the Bush, as a place of enter- tainment, occurs in Maitland's *History of London*, ed. 1722, where it is described as " the Fountain, commonly called the Mourning Bush, which has a back door into St. Anne's-lane, and is situated near unto Aldersgate." The house was refitted in 1830. In the basement are the original wine-vaults of the old Bush; many of the walls are six feet thick, and bonded throughout with Roman brick. A very agreeable account of the tavern and the antiquities of neighbourhood was published in 1830.

" THE MOURNING CROWN."

In Phœnix Alley, (now Hanover Court,) Long Acre, John Taylor, the Water Poet, kept a tavern, with the sign of " the Mourning Crown," but this being offensive to the Commonwealth (1652), he substituted for a sign his own head with this inscription—

> " There's many a head stands for a sign ;
> Then, gentle reader, why not mine ?"

He died here in the following year; and his widow in 1658.

JERUSALEM TAVERNS, CLERKENWELL.

These houses took their name from the Knights of St. John of Jerusalem, around whose Priory, grew up the village of Clerkenwell. The Priory Gate remains. At the Suppression, the Priory was undermined, and blown up with gunpowder ; the Gate also would pro-bably have been destroyed, but for its serving to define the property. In 1604, it was granted to Sir Roger Wilbraham for his life. At this time Clerkenwell was inhabited by people of condition. Forty years later, fashion had travelled westward ; and the Gate became the printing-office of Edward Cave, who, in 1731, pub-lished here the first number of the *Gentleman's Maga-zine*, which to this day bears the Gate for its vignette. Dr. Johnson was first engaged upon the magazine here by Cave in 1737. At the Gate Johnson first met Richard Savage; and here in Cave's room, when visitors called, he ate his plate of victuals behind the screen, his dress being "so shabby that he durst not make his appearance." Garrick, when first he came to London, frequently called upon Johnson at the Gate. Goldsmith was also a visitor here. When Cave grew rich, he had St. John's Gate painted, instead of his arms, on his carriage, and engraven on his plate. After Cave's death in 1753, the premises became the "Jerusalem" public-house, and the "Jerusalem Tavern."

There was likewise another Jerusalem Tavern, at the corner of Red Lion-street on Clerkenwell-green, which was the original; St. John's Gate public-house, having assumed the name of "Jerusalem Tavern" in consequence of the old house on the Green giving up the tavern business, and becoming the "merchants' house." In its dank and cobwebbed vaults John Britton served an apprenticeship to a wine-merchant; and in reading at intervals by candle-light, first evinced that love of literature which characterized his long life of industry and integrity. He remembered Clerkenwell in 1787, with St. John's Priory-church and cloisters; when Spafields were pasturage for cows; the old garden-mansions of the aristocracy remained in Clerkenwell-close; and Sadler's Wells, Islington Spa, Merlin's Cave, and Bagnigge Wells, were nightly crowded with gay company.

In a friendly note, Sept. 11, 1852, Mr. Britton tells us: "Our house sold wines in *full* quarts, *i.e.* twelve held three gallons, wine measure; and each bottle was marked with four lines cut by a diamond on the neck. Our wines were famed, and the character of the house was high, whence the Gate imitated the bottles and name."

In 1845, by the aid of "the Freemasons of the Church," and Mr. W. P. Griffith, architect, the north and south fronts were restored. The gateway is a good specimen of groining of the 15th century, with moulded ribs, and bosses ornamented with shields of the arms of the Priory, Prior Docwra, etc. The east basement is the tavern-bar, with a beautifully moulded ceiling. The stairs are Elizabethan. The principal room over the arch has been despoiled of its window-mullions and groined roof. The foundation-wall of the Gate face is 10 feet 7 inches thick, and the upper walls are nearly 4 feet, hard red brick, stone-cased: the view from the top of the staircase-turret is extensive. In excavating there have been discovered the original pavement, three feet below the Gate; and the Priory walls, north, south, and west. In 1851, there was published, by B. Foster, proprietor of the Tavern, *Ye History of ye Priory and Gate of St. John.* In the principal room of the Gate, over the great arch, meet the Urban Club, a society, chiefly of authors and artists, with whom originated the proposition to celebrate the tercentenary of the birth of Shakespeare, in 1864.

WHITE HART TAVERN, BISHOPSGATE WITHOUT.

About forty years since there stood at a short distance north of St. Botolph's Church, a large old *hostelrie,*

according to the date it bore (1480,) towards the close
of the reign of Edward IV. Stow, in 1598, describes
it as " a fair inn for receipt of travellers, next unto the
Parish Church of St. Botolph without Bishopsgate."
It preserved much of its original appearance, the main
front consisting of three bays of two storeys, which,
with the interspaces, had throughout casements ; and
above which was an overhanging storey or attic, and the
roof rising in three points. Still, this was not the
original front, which was altered in 1787 : upon the old
inn yard was built White Hart Court. In 1829, the
Tavern was taken down, and rebuilt, in handsome modern style ; when the entrance into Old Bedlam, and
formerly called Bedlam Gate, was widened, and the
street re-named Liverpool-street. A lithograph of the
old Tavern was published in 1829.

   Somewhat lower down, is the residence of Sir Paul
Pindar, now wine-vaults, with the sign of Paul Pindar's
Head, corner of Half-moon-alley, No. 160, Bishopsgate-
street Without. Sir Paul was a wealthy merchant, contemporary with Sir Thomas Gresham. The house was
built towards the end of the 16th century, with a wood-
framed front and caryatid brackets; and the principal
windows bayed, their lower fronts enriched with panels
of carved work. In the first-floor front room is a fine
original ceiling in stucco, in which are the arms of Sir
Paul Pindar. In the rear of these premises, within a
garden, was formerly a lodge, of corresponding date,
decorated with four medallions, containing figures in
Italian taste. In Half-moon-alley, was the Half-moon
Brewhouse, of which there is a token in the Beaufoy
Collection.

THE MITRE, IN FENCHURCH STREET,

Was one of the political taverns of the Civil War, and was kept by Daniel Rawlinson, who appears to have been a staunch royalist : his Token is preserved in the Beaufoy collection. Dr. Richard Rawlinson, whose Jacobite principles are sufficiently on record, in a letter to Hearne, the nonjuring antiquary at Oxford, says of "Daniel Rawlinson, who kept the Mitre Tavern in Fenchurch-street, and of whose being suspected in the Rump time, I have heard much. The Whigs tell this, that upon the King's murder, January 30th, 1649, he hung his sign in mourning : he certainly judged right; the honour of the mitre was much eclipsed by the loss of so good a parent to the Church of England ; these rogues [the Whigs] say, this endeared him so much to the Churchmen, that he strove amain, and got a good estate."

Pepys, who expressed great personal fear of the Plague, in his Diary, August 6, 1666, notices that notwithstanding Dan Rowlandson's being all last year in the country, the sickness in a great measure past, one of his men was then dead at the Mitre of the pestilence ; his wife and one of his maids both sick, and himself shut up, which, says Pepys, " troubles me mightily. God preserve us !"

Rawlinson's tavern, the Mitre, appears to have been destroyed in the Great Fire, and immediately after, rebuilt; as Horace Walpole, from Vertue's notes, states that "Isaac Fuller was much employed to paint the great taverns in London ; particularly the Mitre, in Fenchurch-street, where he adorned all the sides of a great room, in panels, as was then the fashion ;" " the figures being as large as life ; over the chimney, a Venus, Satyr, and sleeping Cupid ; a boy riding a goat, and another fallen down :" this was, he adds, " the best part of the performance. Saturn devouring a child, the colouring raw, and the figure of Saturn too muscular ; Mercury, Minerva, Diana, and Apollo ; Bacchus, Venus, and Ceres, embracing ; a young Silenus fallen down, and holding a goblet into which a boy was pouring wine. The Seasons between the windows, and on the ceiling, in a large circle, two angels supporting a mitre."

Yet, Fuller was a wretched painter, as borne out by Elsum's *Epigram on a Drunken Sot :*—

> " His head does on his shoulder lean,
> His eyes are sunk, and hardly seen :
> Who sees this sot in his own colour
> Is apt to say, 'twas done by Fuller."
>
> *Burn's Beaufoy Catalogue.*

THE KING'S HEAD, FENCHURCH STREET.

No. 53 is a place of historic interest; for, the Princess Elizabeth, having attended service at the church of Allhallows Staining, in Langbourn Ward, on her release from the Tower, on the 19th of May, 1554, dined off pork and peas afterwards, at the King's Head in Fenchurch Street, where the metal dish and cover she is said to have used are still preserved. The Tavern has been of late years enlarged and embellished, in taste accordant with its historical association; the ancient character of the building being preserved in the smoking-room, 60 feet in length, upon the walls of which are displayed corslets, shields, helmets, and knightly arms.

THE ELEPHANT, FENCHURCH STREET.

In the year 1826 was taken down the old Elephant Tavern, which was built before the Great Fire, and narrowly escaped its ravages. It stood on the north side of Fenchurch-street, and was originally the Elephant and Castle. Previous to the demolition of the premises there were removed from the wall two pictures, which Hogarth is said to have painted while a lodger there. About this time, a parochial entertainment which had hitherto been given at the Elephant, was removed to the King's Head (Henry VIII.) Tavern nearly opposite. At this Hogarth was annoyed, and he went over to the King's Head, when an altercation ensued, and he left, threatening to *stick them all up* on the Elephant taproom; this he is said to have done, and on the opposite wall subsequently painted the Hudson's Bay Company's Porters going to dinner, representing Fenchurch-street a century and a half ago. The first picture was set down as Hogarth's first idea of his Modern Midnight Conversation, in which he is supposed to have represented the parochial party at the King's Head, though it differs from Hogarth's print. There was a third picture, Harlequin and Pierrot, and on the wall of the *Elephant* first-floor was found a picture of Harlow Bush Fair, coated over with paint.

Only two of the pictures were-claimed as Hogarth's. The *Elephant* has been engraved; and at the foot of the print, the information as to Hogarth having executed these paintings is rested upon the evidence of Mrs. Hibbert, who kept the house between thirty and forty years, and received her information from persons at that time well acquainted with Hogarth. Still, his biographers do not record his abode in Fenchurch-street. The Tavern has been rebuilt.

THE AFRICAN, ST. MICHAEL'S ALLEY.

Another of the Cornhill taverns, the African, or Cole's Coffee-house, is memorable as the last place at which Professor Porson appeared. He had, in some measure, recovered from the effects of the fit in which he had fallen on the 19th of September, 1808, when he was brought in a hackney-coach to the London Institution, in the Old Jewry. Next morning he had a long discussion with Dr. Adam Clarke, who took leave of him at its close; and this was the last conversation Porson was ever capable of holding on any subject.

Porson is thought to have fancied himself under restraint, and to convince himself of the contrary, next morning, the 20th, he walked out, and soon after went to the African, in St. Michael's Alley, which was one of his City resorts. On entering the coffee-room, he was so exhausted that he must have fallen, had he not caught hold of the curtain-rod of one of the boxes, when he was recognized by Mr. J. P. Leigh, a gentleman with whom he had frequently dined at the house. A chair was given him ; he sat down, and stared around, with a vacant and ghastly countenance, and he evidently did not recollect Mr. Leigh. He took a little wine, which revived him, but previously to this his head lay upon his breast, and he was continually muttering something, but in so low and indistinct a tone as scarcely to be audible. He then took a little jelly dissolved in warm brandy-and-water, which considerably roused him. Still he could make no answer to questions addressed to him, except these words, which he repeated, probably, twenty times :—" The gentleman said it was a lucrative piece of business, and *I* think so too,"—but in a very low tone. A coach was now brought to take him to the London Institution, and he was helped in, and accompanied by the waiter; he appeared quite senseless all the way, and did not utter a word ; and in reply to the question where they should stop, he put his head out of the window, and waved his hand when they came opposite the door of the Institution. Upon this Dr. Clarke touchingly observes : " How quick the transition from the highest degree of intellect to the lowest apprehensions of sense ! On what a precarious tenure does frail humanity hold even its choicest and most necessary gifts."

Porson expired on the night of Sunday, September 20, with a deep groan, exactly as the clock struck twelve, in the forty-ninth year of his age.

THE GRAVE MAURICE TAVERN.

There are two taverns with this name,—in St. Leo-
nard's-road, and Whitechapel-road. The history of the
sign is curious. Many years ago the latter house had
a written sign, " The Grave Morris," but this has been
amended.

But the original was the famous Prince of Orange,
Grave Maurice, of whom we read in Howel's *Familiar
Letters*. In Junius's *Etymologicon*, Grave is explained
to be Comes, or Count, as Palsgrave is Palatine Count;
of which we have an instance in Palsgrave Count, or
Elector Palatine, who married Princess Elizabeth,
daughter of James I. Their issue were the Palsgrave
Charles Louis, the Grave Count or Prince Palatine
Rupert, and the Grave Count or Prince Maurice, who
alike distinguished themselves in the Civil Wars.

The two princes, Rupert and Maurice, for their
loyalty and courage, were after the Restoration, very
popular; which induced the author of the *Tavern Anecdotes* to conjecture : " As we have an idea that the
Mount at Whitechapel was raised to overawe the City,
Maurice, before he proceeded to the west, might have
the command of the work on the east side of the metropolis, and a temporary residence on the spot where his
sign was so lately exhibited." At the close of the troubles
of the reign, the two princes retired. In 1652, they
were endeavouring to annoy the enemies of Charles II.
in the West Indies; when the Grave Maurice lost his
life in a hurricane.

The sign of the Grave Maurice remained against the house in the Whitechapel-road till the year 1806, when it was taken down to be repainted. It represented a soldier in a hat and feather, and blue uniform. The tradition of the neighbourhood is, that it is the portrait of a prince of Hesse, who was a great warrior, but of so inflexible a countenance, that he was never seen to smile in his life; and that he was, therefore, most properly termed *Grave*.

MATHEMATICAL SOCIETY, SPITAL-FIELDS.

It is curious to find that a century and a half since, science found a home in Spitalfields, chiefly among the middle and working classes; they met at small taverns in that locality. It appears that a Mathematical Society, which also cultivated electricity, was established in 1717, and met at the Monmouth's Head in Monmouth-street, until 1725, when they removed to the White Horse Tavern, in Wheeler-street; from thence, in 1735, to Ben Jonson's Head in Pelham-street; and next to Crispin-street, Spitalfields. The members were chiefly tradesmen and artisans; among those of higher rank were Canton, Dollond, Thomas Simpson, and Crossley. The Society lent their instruments (air-pumps, reflecting telescopes, reflecting microscopes, electrical machines, surveying-instruments, etc.) with books for the use of them, on the borrowers giving a note of hand for the value thereof. The number of members was not to exceed the square of seven, except such as were abroad or in the country; but this was increased to the squares of eight and nine. The members met on Saturday evenings: each present was to employ himself in some mathematical exercise, or forfeit one penny; and if he refused to answer a question asked by another in mathematics, he was to forfeit twopence. The Society long cherished a taste for exact science among the residents in the neighbourhood of Spitalfields, and accumulated a library of nearly 3000 volumes; but in 1845, when on the point of dissolution, the few remaining members made over their books, records, and memorials to the Royal Astronomical Society, of which these members were elected Fellows.* This amalgamation was chiefly negotiated by Captain, afterwards Admiral Smyth.

GLOBE TAVERN, FLEET-STREET.

In the last century, when public amusements were comparatively few, and citizens dwelt in town, the Globe in Fleet-street was noted for its little clubs and card-parties. Here was held, for a time, the Robin Hood Club, a Wednesday Club, and later, Oliver Goldsmith and his friends often finished their Shoemaker's Holiday by supping at the Globe. Among the company was a surgeon, who, living on the Surrey side of the Thames (Blackfriars Bridge was not then built), had to take a boat every night, at 3s. or 4s. expense, and the risk of his life; yet, when the bridge was built, he grumbled at having a penny to pay for crossing it.

* Curiosities of London, p. 678.

Other frequenters of the Globe were Archibald Hamilton, "with a mind fit for a lord chancellor;" Carnan, the bookseller, who defeated the Stationers' Company upon the almanac trial; Dunstall, the comedian; the veteran Macklin; Akerman, the keeper of Newgate, who always thought it most prudent not to venture home till daylight; and William Woodfall, the reporter of the parliamentary debates. Then there was one Glover, a surgeon, who restored to life a man who had been hung in Dublin, and who ever after was a plague to his deliverer. Brasbridge, the silversmith of Fleet-street, was a frequenter of the Globe. In his eightieth year he wrote his *Fruits of Experience*, full of pleasant gossip about the minor gaieties of St. Bride's. He was more fond of following the hounds than his business, and failure was the ill consequence: he tells of a sporting party of four—that he and his partner became bankrupt; the third, Mr. Smith, became Lord Mayor; and the fourth fell into poverty, and was glad to accept the situation of patrol before the house of his Lordship, whose associate he had been only a few years before. Smith had 100,000*l.* of bad debts on his books, yet died worth one-fourth of that sum. We remember the Globe, a handsomely-appointed tavern, some forty years since; but it has long ceased to be a tavern.

THE DEVIL TAVERN.

This celebrated Tavern is described in the present work, Vol. I., pp. 10–15, as the meeting-place of the Apollo Club. Its later history is interesting.

Mull Sack, *alias* John Cottington, the noted highway-man of the time of the Commonwealth, is stated to have been a constant visitor at the Devil Tavern. In the garb and character of a man of fashion, he appears to have levied contributions on the public as a pick-pocket and highwayman, to a greater extent than perhaps any other individual of his fraternity on record. He not only had the honour of picking the pocket of Oliver Crom-well, when Lord Protector, but he afterwards robbed King Charles II., then living in exile at Cologne, of plate valued at £1500. Another of his feats was his robbing the wife of the Lord General Fairfax. "This lady," we are told, "used to go to a lecture on a week-day, to Ludgate Church, where one Mr. Jacomb preached, being much followed by the precisians. Mull Sack, observing this,—and that she constantly wore her watch hanging by a chain from her waist,—against the next time she came there, dressed himself like an officer in the army; and having his comrades attending him like troopers, one of them takes out the pin of a coach-wheel that was going upwards through the gate, by which means, it falling off, the passage was obstructed; so that the lady could not alight at the church-door, but was forced to leave her coach without. Mull Sack, taking advantage of this, readily presented himself to her ladyship; and having the impudence to take her from her gentleman usher, who attended her alighting, led her by the arm into the church; and by the way, with a pair of keen or sharp scissors for the purpose, cut the chain in two, and got the watch clear away : she not missing it till sermon was done, when she was going to see the time of the day." At the Devil Tavern Mull Sack could mix with the best society, whom he probably

M 2

occasionally relieved of their watches and purses. There is extant a very rare print of him, in which he is represented partly in the garb of a chimney-sweep, his original avocation, and partly in the fashionable costume of the period.*

In the Apollo chamber, at the Devil Tavern, were rehearsed, with music, the Court-day Odes of the Poets Laureate: hence Pope, in the *Dunciad* :

> " Back to the Devil the loud echoes roll,
>   And ' Coll !' each butcher roars at Hockley Hole."

The following epigram on the Odes rehearsals is by a wit of those times :

> " When Laureates make Odes, do you ask of what sort?
>   Do you ask if they're good, or are evil ?
> You may judge—From the Devil they come to the Court,
>   And go from the Court to the Devil."

St. Dunstan's, or the Devil Tavern, is mentioned as a house of old repute, in the interlude, *Jacke Jugeler*, 1563, where Jack, having persuaded his cousin Jenkin,

> " As foolish a knave withall,
> As any is now, within London wall,"

that he was not himself, thrusts him from his master's door, and in answer to Jenkin's sorrowful question— where his master and he were to dwell, replies,

> " At the Devyll yf you lust, I can not tell !"

Ben Jonson being one night at the Devil Tavern, a country gentleman in the company was obtrusively loquacious touching his land and tenements ; Ben, out of patience, exclaimed, " What signifies to us your dirt

---

* Jesse's ' London and its Celebrities.'

and your clods? Where you have an acre of land I
have ten acres of wit!" "Have you so," retorted the
countryman, "good Mr. Wise-acre?" "Why, how
now, Ben?" said one of the party, "you seem to be
quite stung!" "I was never so pricked by a hobnail
before," grumbled Ben.

There is a ludicrous reference to this old place in
a song describing the visit of James I. to St. Paul's
Cathedral on Sunday, 26th of March, 1620:

"The Maior layd downe his mace, and cry'd,
 ' God save your Grace,
 And keepe our King from all evill!'
With all my hart I then wist, the good mace
 had been in my fist,
To ha' pawn'd it for supper at the *Devill!*"

We have already given the famous Apollo "Welcome,"
but not immortal Ben's Rules, which have been thus
happily translated by Alexander Brome, one of the wits
who frequented the Devil, and who left *Poems and Songs*,
1661: he was an attorney in the Lord Mayor's Court:

"*Ben Jonson's Sociable Rules for the Apollo.*

"Let none but guests, or clubbers, hither come.
Let dunces, fools, sad sordid men keep home.
Let learned, civil, merry men, b' invited,
And modest too; nor be choice ladies slighted.
Let nothing in the treat offend the guests;
More for delight than cost, prepare the feast.
The cook and purvey'r must our palates know;
And none contend who shall sit high or low.
Our waiters must quick-sighted be, and dumb,
And let the drawers quickly hear and come.
Let not our wine be mix'd, but brisk and neat,
Or else the drinkers may the vintners beat.
And let our only emulation be,

Not drinking much, but talking wittily.
Let it be voted lawful to stir up
Each other with a moderate chirping cup ;
Let not our company be, or talk too much ;
On serious things, or sacred, let's not touch
With sated heads and bellies.　Neither may
Fiddlers unask'd obtrude themselves to play.
With laughing, leaping, dancing, jests, and songs,
And whate'er else to grateful mirth belongs,
Let's celebrate our feasts ; and let us see
That all our jests without reflection be.
Insipid poems let no man rehearse,
Nor any be compelled to write a verse.
All noise of vain disputes must be forborne,
And let no lover in a corner mourn.
To fight and brawl, like hectors, let none dare,
Glasses or windows break, or hangings tear.
Whoe'er shall publish what's here done or said
From our society must be banishèd ;
Let none by drinking do or suffer harm,
And, while we stay, let us be always warm."

We must now say something of the noted hosts.
Simon Wadlow appears for the last time, as a licensed
vintner, in the Wardmote return, of December, 1626;
and the burial register of St. Dunstan's records:
" March 30th, 1627, Symon Wadlowe, vintner, was
buried out of Fleet-street."　On St. Thomas's Day, in
the last-named year, the name of " the widow Wadlowe " appears; and in the following year, 1628, of the
eight licensed victuallers, five were widows.　The widow
Wadlowe's name is returned for the last time by the
Wardmote on December 21st, 1629.

The name of John Wadlow, apparently the son of
old Simon, appears first as a licensed victualler, in the
Wardmote return, December 21, 1646.　He issued his

token, showing on its obverse St. Dunstan holding the devil by his nose, his lower half being that of a satyr, the devil on the signboard was as usual, *sable ;* the origin of the practice being thus satisfactorily explained by Dr. Jortin : " The devils used often to appear to the monks in the figure of Ethiopian boys or men ; thence probably the painters learned to make the devil black." Hogarth, in his print of the Burning of the Rumps, represents the hanging of the effigy against the signboard of the Devil Tavern.

In a ludicrous and boasting ballad of 1650, we read :

> " Not the Vintry Cranes, nor St. Clement's Danes,
> Nor the Devill can put us down-a."

John Wadlow's name occurs for the last time in the Wardmote return of December, 1660. After the Great Fire, he rebuilt the Sun Tavern, behind the Royal Exchange : he was a loyal man, and appears to have been sufficiently wealthy to have advanced money to the Crown ; his autograph was attached to several receipts among the Exchequer documents lately destroyed.

Hollar's Map of London, 1667, shows the site of the Devil Tavern, and its proximity to the barrier designated Temple Bar, when the house had become the resort of lawyers and physicians. In the rare volume of *Cambridge Merry Jests,* printed in the reign of Charles II., the will of a tavern-hunter has the bequeathment of " ten pounds to be drank by lawyers and physicians at the Devil's Tavern, by Temple Bar."

The Tatler, October 11, 1709, contains Bickerstaff's account of the wedding entertainment at the Devil Tavern, in honour of his sister Jenny's marriage. He mentions " the Rules of Ben's Club in gold letters over the chimney;" and this is the latest notice of this celebrated ode. When, or by whom, the board was taken from "over the chimney," Mr. Burn has failed to discover.

Swift tells Stella that Oct. 12, 1710, he dined at the Devil Tavern with Mr. Addison and Dr. Garth, when the doctor treated.

In 1746, the Royal Society held here their Annual Dinner; and in 1752, concerts of vocal and instrumental music were given in the great room.

A view of the exterior of the Devil Tavern, with its gable-pointed front, engraved from a drawing by Wale, was published in Dodsley's *London and its Environs*, 1761. The sign-iron bears its pendent sign — the Saint painted as a half-length, and the devil behind him grinning grimly over his shoulder. On the removal of projecting signs, by authority, in 1764, the Devil Tavern sign was placed flat against the front, and there remained till the demolition of the house.

Brush Collins, in March, 1775, delivered for several evenings, in the great room, a satirical lecture on Modern Oratory. In the following year, a Pandemonium Club was held here; and, according to a notice in Mr. Burn's possession, " the first meeting was to be on Monday, the 4th of November, 1776. These devils were lawyers, who were about commencing term, to the annoyance of many a hitherto happy *bon-vivant.*"

From bad to worse, the Devil Tavern fell into disuse, and Messrs. Child, the bankers, purchased the freehold in 1787, for £2800. It was soon after demolished, and the site is now occupied by the houses called Child's-place.

We have selected and condensed these details from

Mr. Burn's exhaustive article on the Devil Tavern, in the Beaufoy Catalogue.

There is a token of this tavern, which is very rare. The initials stand for Simon Wadloe, embalmed in Squire Western's favourite air "Old Sir Simon the King:"—" AT THE D. AND DVNSTANS. The representation of the saint standing at his anvil, and pulling the nose of the ' D.' with his pincers.—R. WITHIN TEMPLE BARRE. In the field, I. S. W."

THE YOUNG DEVIL TAVERN.

The notoriety of the Devil Tavern, as common in such cases, created an opponent on the opposite side of Fleet-street, named "The Young Devil." The Society of Antiquaries, who had previously met at the Bear Tavern, in the Strand, changed their rendezvous Jan. 9, 1707–8, to the Young Devil Tavern; but the host failed, and as Browne Willis tells us, the Antiquaries, in or about 1709, "met at the Fountain Tavern, as we went down into the Inner Temple, against Chancery Lane."

Later, a music-room, called the Apollo, was attempted, but with no success : an advertisement for a concert, December 19, 1737, intimated " tickets to be had at Will's Coffee-house, formerly the Apollo, in Bell Yard, near Temple Bar." This may explain the Apollo Court, in Fleet-street, unless it is found in the next page.

COCK TAVERN, FLEET-STREET.

The Apollo Club, at the Devil Tavern, is kept in remembrance by Apollo Court, in Fleet-street, nearly opposite; next door eastward of which is an old tavern nearly as well known. It is, perhaps, the most primitive place of its kind in the metropolis : it still possesses a fragment of decoration of the time of James I., and the writer remembers the tavern half a century ago, with considerably more of its original panelling. It is just two centuries since (1665), when the Plague was raging, the landlord shut up his house, and retired into the country; and there is preserved one of the farthings referred to in this advertisement :—" This is to certify that the master of the Cock and Bottle, commonly called the Cock Alehouse, at Temple Bar, hath dismissed his servants, and shut up his house, for this long vacation, intending (God willing) to return at Michaelmas next ; so that all persons whatsoever who may have any accounts with the said master, or *farthings belonging to the said house*, are desired to repair thither before the 8th of this instant, and they shall receive satisfaction." Three years later, we find Pepys frequenting this tavern : "23rd April, 1668. Thence by water to the Temple, and there to the Cock Alehouse, and drank, and eat a lobster, and sang, and mightily merry. So almost night, I carried Mrs. Pierce home, and then Knipp and I to the Temple again, and took boat, it being now night." The tavern has a gilt signbird over the passage door, stated to have been carved by Gibbons. Over the mantelpiece is some carving, at least of the time of James I.; but we remember the entire room similarly carved, and a huge black-and-gilt clock, and settle. The head-waiter of our time lives in the verse of Laureate Tennyson—"O plump head-waiter of the Cock!" apostrophizes the "Will Water-proof" of the bard, in a reverie wherein he conceives William to have undergone a transition similar to that of Jove's cup-bearer :—

> " And hence (says he) this halo lives about
>   The waiter's hands, that reach
> To each his perfect pint of stout,
>   His proper chop to each.
> He looks not with the common breed,
>   That with the napkin dally;
> I think he came, like Ganymede,
>   From some delightful valley."

And of the redoubtable bird, who is supposed to have performed the eagle's part in this abduction, he says :—

> " The Cock was of a larger egg
>   Than modern poultry drop,
> Stept forward on a firmer leg,
>   And cramm'd a plumper crop."

THE HERCULES' PILLARS TAVERNS.

Hercules Pillars Alley, on the south side of Fleet-street, near St. Dunstan's Church, is described by Strype as "altogether inhabited by such as keep Publick Houses for entertainment, for which it is of note."

The token of the Hercules Pillars is thus described

by Mr. Akerman :—" ED. OLDHAM AT Y HERCVLES.   A
crowned male figure standing erect, and grasping a pillar
with each hand.—℞. PILLERS IN FLEET STREET.   In the
field, HIS HALF PENNY, E. P. O.   " From this example,"
illustratively observes Mr. Akerman, " it would seem that
the locality, called Hercules Pillars Alley, like other places
in London, took its name from the tavern.   The mode of
representing the pillars of Hercules is somewhat novel ;
and, but for the inscription, we should have supposed
the figure to represent Samson clutching the pillars of
temple of Dagon.   At the trial of Stephen Colledge,
for high-treason, in 1681, an Irishman named Haynes,
swore that he walked to the Hercules Pillars with the
accused, and that in a room upstairs Colledge spoke
of his treasonable designs and feeling.   On another occasion the parties walked from Richard's coffee-house *
to this tavern, where it was sworn they had a similar
conference.   Colledge, in his defence, denies the truth
of the allegation, and declares that the walk from the
coffee-house to the tavern is not more than a bow-shot,
and that during such walk the witness had all the conversation to himself, though he had sworn that treasonable expressions had been made use of on their way
thither.

      " Pepys frequented this tavern : in one part of his
Diary he says, ' With Mr. Creed to Hercules Pillars,
where we drank.'   In another, ' In Fleet-street I met
with Mr. Salisbury, who is now grown in less than two
years' time so great a limner that he is become excellent
and gets a great deal of money at it.   I took him to
Hercules Pillars to drink.' "

      Again : " After the play was done, we met with Mr.

* Subsequently " Dick's."

Bateller and W. Hewer, and Talbot Pepys, and they followed us in a hackney-coach ; and we all supped at Hercules Pillars ;. and there I did give the best supper I could, and pretty merry ; and so home between eleven and twelve at night." "At noon, my wife came to me at my tailor's, and I sent her home, and myself and Tom dined at Hercules Pillars."

Another noted "Hercules Pillars" was at Hyde Park Corner, near Hamilton-place, on the site of what is now the pavement opposite Lord Willoughby's. "Here," says Cunningham, "Squire Western put his horses up when in pursuit of Tom Jones ; and here Field Marshal the Marquis of Gransby was often found." And Wycherley, in his *Plain Dealer*, 1676, makes the spendthrift, Jerry Blackacre, talk of picking up his mortgaged silver "out of most of the ale-houses between Hercules Pillars and the Boatswain in Wapping."

Hyde Park Corner was noted for its petty taverns, some of which remained as late as 1805. It was to one of these taverns that Steele took Savage to dine, and where Sir Richard dictated and Savage wrote a pamphlet, which he went out and sold for two guineas, with which the reckoning was paid. Steele then "returned home, having retired that day only to avoid his creditors, and composed the pamphlet only to discharge his reckoning." .

HOLE-IN-THE-WALL TAVERNS.

This odd sign exists in Chancery-lane, at a house on the east side, immediately opposite the old gate of

Lincoln's-Inn; "and," says Mr. Burn, "being supported by the dependants on legal functionaries, appears
to have undergone fewer changes than the law, retain-
ing all the vigour of a new establishment." There is
another "Hole in the Wall" in St. Dunstan's-court,
Fleet-street, much frequented by printers.

Mr. Akerman says:—"It was a popular sign, and
several taverns bore the same designation, which probably originated in a certain tavern being situated in
some umbrageous recess in the old City walls. Many
of the most popular and most frequented taverns of the
present day are located in twilight courts and alleys,
into which Phœbus peeps at Midsummer-tide only when
on the meridian. Such localities may have been selected
on more than one account: they not only afforded good
skulking 'holes' for those who loved drinking better
than work; but beer and other liquors keep better in
the shade. These haunts, like Lady Mary's farm,
were—

'In summer shady, and in winter warm.'

Rawlins, the engraver of the fine and much coveted
Oxford Crown, with a view of the city under the horse,
dates a quaint supplicatory letter to John Evelyn, 'from
the Hole in the Wall, in St. Martin's;' no misnomer,
we will be sworn, in that aggregation of debt and dissipa-
tion, when debtors were imprisoned with a very remote
chance of redemption. In the days of Rye-house and
Meal-Tub plots, philanthropy overlooked such little
matters; and Small Debts Bills were not dreamt of in
the philosophy of speculative legislators. Among other
places which bore the designation of the Hole in the
Wall, there was one in Chandos-street, in which the

famous Duval, the highwayman, was apprehended after an attack on—two bottles of wine, probably drugged by a 'friend' or mistress."

THE MITRE, IN FLEET-STREET.

This was the true Johnsonian Mitre, so often referred to in *Boswell's Life*; but it has earlier fame. Here, in 1640, Lilly met Old Will Poole, the astrologer, then living in Ram-alley. The Royal Society Club dined at the Mitre from 1743 to 1750, the Society then meeting in Crane-court, nearly opposite. The Society of Antiquaries met some time at the Mitre. Dr. Macmichael, in *The Gold-headed Cane*, makes Dr. Radcliffe say :— " I never recollect to have spent a more delightful evening than that at the Mitre Tavern, in Fleet-street, where my good friend Billy Nutly, who was indeed the better half of me, had been prevailed upon to accept of a small temporary assistance, and joined our party, the Earl of Denbigh, Lords Colepeper and Stowel, and Mr. Blackmore."

The house has a token : — WILLIAM PAGET AT THE. A mitre.—℞. MITRE IN FLEET STREET. In the field, W.E.P.

Johnson's Mitre is commonly thought to be the tavern with that sign, which still exists in Mitre-court, over against Fetter-lane; where is shown a cast of Nollekens' bust of Johnson, in confirmation of this house being his resort. Such was not the case ; Boswell distinctly states it to have been the Mitre Tavern *in*

Fleet-street; and the records by Lilly and the Royal Society, alike specify " in Fleet-street," which Mr. Burn, in his excellent account of the Beaufoy Tokens, explains was the house, No. 39, Fleet-street, that Macklin opened, in 1788, as the Poet's Gallery; and lastly, Saunders's auction-rooms. It was taken down to enlarge the site for Messrs. Hoares' new banking-house. The now Mitre Tavern, in Mitre-court, was originally called Joe's Coffee-house; and on the shutting up of the old Mitre, in Fleet-street, took its name; this being four years after Johnson's death.

The Mitre was Dr. Johnson's favourite supper-house, the parties including Goldsmith, Percy, Hawkesworth, and Boswell; there was planned the tour to the Hebrides. Johnson had a strange nervous feeling, which made him uneasy if he had not touched every post between the Mitre and his own lodgings. Johnson took Goldsmith to the Mitre, where Boswell and the Doctor had supped together in the previous month, when Boswell spoke of Goldsmith's " very loose, odd, scrambling kind of life," and Johnson defended him as one of our first men as an author, and a very worthy man;—adding, " he has been loose in his principles, but he is coming right." Boswell was impatient of Goldsmith from the first hour of their acquaintance. Chamberlain Clarke, who died in 1831, aged 92, was the last surviving of Dr. Johnson's Mitre friends. Mr. William Scott, Lord Stowell, also frequented the Mitre.

Boswell has this remarkable passage respecting the house:—" We had a good supper, and port-wine, of which he (Johnson) sometimes drank a bottle. The orthodox high-church sound of THE MITRE—the figure and manner of the celebrated SAMUEL JOHNSON—the extraordinary power and precision of his conversation, and the pride arising from finding myself admitted as his companion, produced a variety of sensations, and a pleasing elevation of mind, beyond what I had ever experienced."

SHIP TAVERN, TEMPLE BAR.

This noted Tavern, the site of which is now denoted by Ship-yard, is mentioned among the grants to Sir Christopher Hatton, 1571. There is, in the Beaufoy Collection, a Ship token, dated 1649, which is evidence that the inner tavern of that sign was then extant. It was also called the Drake, from the ship painted as the sign being that in which Sir Francis Drake voyaged round the world. Faithorne, the celebrated engraver, kept shop, next door to the Drake. "The Ship Tavern, in the Butcher-row, near Temple Bar," occurs in an advertisement so late as June, 1756.

The taverns about Temple Bar were formerly numerous; and the folly of disfiguring sign-boards was then, as at a later date, a street frolic. "Sir John Denham, the poet, when a student at Lincoln's-Inn, in 1635, though generally temperate as a drinker, having stayed late at a tavern with some fellow-students, induced them to join him in 'a frolic,' to obtain a pot of ink and a plasterer's brush, and blot out all the signs between Temple Bar and Charing Cross. Aubrey relates that R. Estcourt, Esq., carried the ink-pot : and that next day it caused great confusion ; but it happened Sir John and his comrades were discovered, and it cost them some moneys."

THE PALSGRAVE HEAD, TEMPLE BAR.

This once celebrated Tavern, opposite the Ship, occupied the site of Palsgrave-place, on the south side of the Strand, near Temple Bar. The Palsgrave Frederick, afterwards King of Bohemia, was affianced to the Princess Elizabeth (only daughter of James I.), in the old banqueting house at Whitehall, December 27, 1612, when the sign was, doubtless, set up in compliment to him. There is a token of the house in the Beaufoy Collection. (See *Burn's Catalogue,* p. 225.)

Here Prior and Montague, in *The Hind and Panther Transversed,* make the Country Mouse and the City Mouse bilk the Hackney Coachman :

" But now at Piccadilly they arrive,
And taking coach, t'wards Temple Bar they drive,
But at St. Clement's eat out the back ;
And slipping through the Palsgrave, bilkt poor hack."

HEYCOCK'S, TEMPLE BAR,

Near the Palsgrave's Head tavern, was Heycock's Ordinary, much frequented by Parliament men and gallants. Andrew Marvell usually dined here : one day, having eaten heartily of boiled beef, with some roasted pigeons and asparagus, he drank his pint of port; and on the coming in of the reckoning, taking a piece of money out of his pocket, held it up, and addressing his associates, certain members of Parliament, known to be in the pay of the Crown, said, " Gentlemen, who would lett himself out for hire, while he can have such a dinner for half-a-crown ?"

THE CROWN AND ANCHOR, STRAND.

This famous tavern extended from Arundel-street eastward to Milford-lane, in the rear of the south side of the Strand, and occupied the site of an older house with the same sign. Strype, in 1729, described it as "the Crown Tavern; a large and curious house, with good rooms and other conveniences fit for entertainments." Here was instituted the Academy of Music in 1710; and here the Royal Society Club, who had previously met at the Mitre in Fleet-street, removed in 1780, and dined here for the first time on December 21, and here they continued until the tavern was converted into a club-house in 1847.

The second tavern was built in 1790. Its first landlord was Thomas Simpkin, a very corpulent man, who, in superintending the serving of a large dinner, leaned over a balustrade, which broke, when he fell from a considerable height to the ground, and was killed. The sign appears to have been originally " The Crown," to which may have been added the Anchor, from its being the emblem of St. Clement's, opposite; or from the Lord High Admiral having once resided on the site. The tavern contained a ball-room, 84 feet by 35 feet

N 2

6 inches; in 1798, on the birthday of C. J. Fox, was given in this house, a banquet to 2000 persons, when the Duke ot Norfolk presided. The large room was noted for political meetings in the stormy Tory and Radical times; and the Crown and Anchor was long the rallying-point of the Westminster electors. The room would hold 2500 persons: one of the latest popular orators who spoke here was Daniel O'Connell, M.P. There was originally an entrance to the house from the Strand, by a long passage, such as was the uusal approach to our old metropolitan taverns. The premises were entirely destroyed by fire, in 1854, but have been rebuilt.*

Here Johnson and Boswell occasionally supped; and here Johnson quarrelled with Percy about old Dr. Monsey. Thither was brought the altar-piece (St. Cecilia), painted by Kent for St. Clement's Church, whence it was removed, in 1725, by order of Bishop Gibson, on the supposition that the picture contained portraits of the Pretender's wife and children.

THE CANARY-HOUSE, IN THE STRAND.

There is a rare Token of this house, with the date, 1665. The locality of the "Canary House in the Strande," says Mr. E. B. Price, "is now, perhaps, impossible to trace; and it is, perhaps, as vain to attempt a description of the wine from which it took its name, and which was so celebrated in that and the preceding century. Some have erroneously identified it with sack.

* See Whittington Club, Vol. I. p. 313.

We find it mentioned among the various drinks which Gascoyne so virtuously inveighs against in his *Delicate Diet for daintie mouthde Droonkardes*, published in 1576 : " *We* must have March beere, dooble-dooble Beere, Dagger ale, Bragget, Renish wine, White wine, French wine, Gascoyne wine, Sack, Hollocke, Canaria wine, *Vino greco, Vinum amabile*, and al the wines that may be gotten. Yea, wine ʌf its selfe is not sufficient; but Suger, Limons, and sundry sortes of Spices must be drowned therein." The bibbers of this famed wine were wont to be termed " Canary birds." Of its qualities we can perhaps form the best estimate from the colloquy between " mine hostess of the Boar's Head and Doll Tearsheet ;" in which the former charges the latter with having " drunk too much *Canaries ;* and that's a *marvellous searching wine, and it perfumes the blood ere one can say, What's this ?*"*

THE FOUNTAIN TAVERN,

Strand, now the site of Nos. 101 and 102, Ries's Divan, gave the name to the Fountain Club, composed of political opponents of Sir Robert Walpole. Strype describes it as " a very fine Tavern, with excellent vaults, good rooms for entertainment, and a curious kitchen for dressing of meat, which, with the good wine

* We learn from Collier's *Roxburghe Ballads* (*Lit. Gaz.* No. 1566) that in the reign of James I. " sparkling sack " was sold at 1*s.* 6*d.* per quart, and " Canary—pure French wine," at 7 pence.

there sold, make it well resorted to." Dennis, the Critic, describes his supping here with Loggan, the painter, and others, and that after supper they "drank Mr. Wycherley's health by name of Captain Wycherley."

Here, Feb. 12, 1742, was held a great meeting, at which near 300 members of both Houses of Parliament were present, to consider the ministerial crisis, when the Duke of Argyll observed to Mr. Pulteney, that a grain of honesty was worth a cart-load of gold. The meeting was held too late to be of any avail, to which Sir Charles Hanbury Williams alludes in one of his odes to Pulteney, invoking his Muse thus:—

> "Then enlarge on his cunning and wit;
>   Say, how he harang'd at the Fountain;
>   Say, how the old patriots were bit,
>   And a mouse was produc'd by a mountain."

Upon the Tavern site was a Drawing Academy, of which Cosway and Wheatley were pupils; here also was the lecture-room of John Thelwall, the political elocutionist. At No. 101, Ackermann, the printseller, illuminated his gallery with cannel coal, when gas-lighting was a novelty.

In Fountain-court, named from the Tavern, is the Coal-hole Tavern, upon the site of a coal-yard; it was much resorted to by Edmund Kean, and was one of the earliest night taverns for singing.

TAVERN LIFE OF SIR RICHARD STEELE.

Among the four hundred letters of Steele's preserved in the British Museum, are some written from his tavern haunts, a few weeks after marriage, to his "Dearest being on earth :"

> "*Eight o'clock*, Fountain Tavern, Oct. 22, 1707.
> "My dear,
> "I beg of you not to be uneasy; for I have done a great deal of business to-day very successfully, and wait an hour or two about my *Gazette*."

In the next, he does "not come home to dinner, being obliged to attend to some business abroad." Then he writes from the Devil Tavern, Temple Bar, January 3, 1707–8, as follows:—

> "I have partly succeeded in my business, and enclose two guineas as earnest of more. Dear Prue, I cannot come home to dinner; I languish for your welfare, and will never be a moment careless more.
> "Your faithful husband," etc.

Within a few days, he writes from a Pall Mall tavern:—

> "Dear Wife,
> "Mr. Edgecombe, Ned Ask, and Mr. Lumley, have desired me to sit an hour with them at the George, in Pall Mall, for which I desire your patience till twelve o'clock, and that you will go to bed," etc.

When money-matters were getting worse, Steele found it necessary to sleep away from home for a day or two, and he writes:—

> "Tennis-court Coffee-house, May 5, 1708.
> "Dear Wife,
> "I hope I have done this day what will be pleasing to you; in the meantime shall lie this night at a baker's, one Leg, over against the Devil Tavern, at Charing Cross. I shall be able to confront the fools who wish me uneasy, and shall have the satisfaction to see thee cheerful and at ease.
> "If the printer's boy be at home, send him hither; and let Mr. Todd send by the boy my night-gown, slippers, and clean linen. You shall hear from me early in the morning," etc.

He is found excusing his coming home, being " invited to supper at Mr. Boyle's." " Dear Prue," he says on this occasion, " do not send after me, for I shall be ridiculous." There were *Caudles* in those days.*

CLARE MARKET TAVERNS.

Clare Market lying between the two great theatres, its butchers were the arbiters of the galleries, the leaders of theatrical rows, the musicians at actresses' marriages, the chief mourners at players' funerals. In and around the market were the signs of the Sun; the Bull and Butcher, afterwards Spiller's Head ; the Grange ; the Bull's Head, where met " the Shepherd and his Flock Club," and where Dr. Radcliffe was carousing when he received news of the loss of his 5000*l.* venture. Here met weekly a Club of Artists, of which society Hogarth was a member, and he engraved for them a silver tankard with a shepherd and his flock. Next is the Black Jack in Portsmouth-street, the haunt of Joe Miller, the comedian, and where he uttered his time-honoured " Jests : " the house remains, but the sign has disappeared. Miller died in 1738, and was buried in St. Clement's upper ground, in Portugal-street, where his gravestone was inscribed with the following epitaph, written by Stephen Duck : " Here lie the remains of honest Joe Miller, who was a tender husband, a sincere friend, a facetious companion, and an excellent comedian. He departed this life the 15th day of August, 1738, aged 54 years.

* Lives of Wits and Humourists, vol. i. p. 134.

" If humour, wit, and honesty could save
The humorous, witty, honest, from the grave,
This grave had not so soon its tenant found,
With honesty, and wit, and humour crown'd.
Or could esteem and love preserve our health,
And guard us longer from the stroke of Death,
The stroke of Death on him had later fell,
Whom all mankind esteem'd and loved so well."

The stone was restored by the parish grave-digger at the close of the last century; and in 1816, a new stone was set up by Mr. Jarvis Buck, churchwarden, who added S. Duck to the epitaph. The burial-ground has been cleared away, and the site has been added to the grounds of King's College Hospital.

At the Black Jack, also called the Jump, (from Jack Sheppard having once jumped out of a first-floor window, to escape his pursuers, the thief-takers,) a Club known as " the Honourable Society of Jackers," met until 1816. The roll of the fraternity " numbers many of the popular actors since the time of Joe Miller, and some of the wits; from John Kemble, Palmer, and Theodore Hook down to Kean, Liston, and the mercurial John Pritt Harley. Since the dissolution of this last relic of the sociality of the Joe Miller age, 'wit-combats' have been comparatively unknown at the Old Black Jack."*

THE CRAVEN HEAD, DRURY LANE.

This modern Tavern was part of the offices of Craven House, and the adjoining stabling belonged to the man-

* Jo. Miller; a Biography, 1848.

sion ; the extensive cellars still remain, though blocked up.

Craven House was built for William Lord Craven, the hero of Creutznach, upon part of the site of Drury House, and was a large square pile of brick, four storeys high, which occupied the site of the present Craven-buildings, built in 1723. That portion of the mansion abutting on Magpie-alley, now Newcastle-street, was called Bohemia House, and was early in the last century, converted into a tavern, with the sign of the head of its former mistress, the Queen of Bohemia. But a destructive fire happening in the neighbourhood, the tavern was shut up, and the building suffered to decay; till, at length, in 1802, what remained of the dilapidated mansion was pulled down, and the materials sold ; and upon the ground, in 1803, Philip Astley erected his Olympic Pavilion, which was burnt down in 1849.

The Craven Head was some time kept by William Oxberry, the comedian, who first appeared on the stage in 1807 ; he also edited a large collection of dramas. Another landlord of the Craven Head was Robert Hales, "the Norfolk Giant" (height 7 ft. 6 in.), who, after visiting the United States, where Barnum made a speculation of the giant, and 28,000 persons flocked to see him in ten days,—in January, 1851, returned to England, and took the Craven Head Tavern. On April 11th Hales had the honour of being presented to the Queen and Royal Family, when Her Majesty gave him a gold watch and chain, which he wore to the day of his death. His health had been much impaired by the close confinement of the caravans in which he exhibited. He died in 1863, of consumption. Hales was cheerful and well-informed. He had visited several Continental capitals, and had been presented to Louis Philippe, King of the French.

THE COCK TAVERN, IN BOW-STREET.

This Tavern, of indecent notoriety, was situated about the middle of the east side of Bow-street, then consisting of very good houses, well inhabited, and resorted to by gentry for lodgings.   Here Wycherley and his first wife, the Countess of Drogheda, lodged over against the Cock, "whither, if he at any time were with his friends, he was obliged to leave the windows open, that the lady might see there was no woman in the company, or she would be immediately in a downright raving condition." (*Dennis's Letters.*)

The Cock Tavern was the resort of the rakes and Mohocks of that day, when the house was kept by a woman called "Oxford Kate."   Here took place the indecent exposure, which has been told by Johnson, in his life of Sackville, Lord Dorset.   "Sackville, who was then Lord Buckhurst, with Sir Charles Sedley, and Sir Thomas Ogle, got drunk at the Cock, in Bow-street, by Covent-garden, and going into the balcony, exposed themselves to the company in very indecent postures. At last, as they grew warmer, Sedley stood forth naked, and harangued the populace in such profane language, that the public indignation was awakened; the crowd attempted to force the door, and being repulsed, drove in the performers with stones, and broke the windows of the house.   For this misdemeanour they were indicted, and Sedley was fined five hundred pounds; what was the sentence of the others is not known. Sedley employed Killegrew and another to procure a remission of the King, but (mark the friendship of the dissolute!) they begged the fine for themselves, and exacted it to the last groat."

Sir John Coventry had supped at the Cock Tavern, on the night when, in his way home, his nose was cut to the bone, at the corner of Suffolk-street, in the Haymarket, "for reflecting on the King, who, therefore, determined to *set a mark* upon him: " he was watched; when attacked, he stood up to the wall, and snatched the flambeau out of the servant's hands, and with that in one hand, and the sword in the other, he defended himself, but was soon disarmed, and his nose was cut to the bone; it was so well sewed up, that the scar was scarce to be discerned. This attempt at assassination occasioned the Coventry Act, 22 and 23 Car. II. c. 1, by which specific provisions were made against the offence of maiming, cutting off, or disabling, a limb or member.

THE QUEEN'S HEAD, BOW-STREET.

This Tavern, in Duke's Court, was once kept by a facetious person, named Jupp, and is associated with a piece of humour, which may either be matter of fact, or interpreted as a pleasant satire upon etymological fancies. One evening, two well-known characters, Annesley Shay and Bob Todrington (the latter caricatured by Old Dighton), met at the Queen's Head, and at the bar asked for "half a quartern" each, with a little cold water. They continued to drink until they had swallowed four-and-twenty half-quarterns in water, when Shay said to the other, "Now, we'll go." "Oh, no," replied he, "we'll have another, and then go." This did not satisfy the Hibernians, and they continued drinking on till three in the morning, when they both agreed to GO; so that under the idea of going they made a long stay, and this was the origin of drinking, or calling for, goes of liquor; but another, determined to eke out the measure his own way, used to call for a quartern at a time, and these, in the exercise of his humour, he called *stays*. We find the above in the very pleasant *Etymological Compendium*, third edition, revised and improved by Merton A. Thoms, 1853.

THE SHAKSPEARE TAVERN.

Of this noted theatrical tavern, in the Piazza, Covent Garden, several details were received by Mr. John Green, in 1815, from Twigg, who was apprentice at the Shakspeare. They had generally fifty turtles at a time; and upon an average from ten to fifteen were dressed every week; and it was not unusual to send forty quarts of turtle soup a-week into the country, as far as Yorkshire.

The sign of Shakspeare, painted by Wale, cost nearly 200*l*.: it projected at the corner, over the street, with very rich iron-work. Dick Milton was once landlord; he was a great gamester, and once won 40,000*l*. He would frequently start with his coach-and-six, which he would keep about six months, and then sell it. He was so much reduced, and his credit so bad, at times, as to send out for a dozen of wine for his customers; it was sold at 16s. a bottle. This is chronicled as the first tavern in London that had rooms; and from this house the other taverns were supplied with waiters. Here were held three clubs—the Madras, Bengal, and Bombay.

Twigg was cook at the Shakspeare. The largest dinner ever dressed here consisted of 108 made-dishes, besides hams, etc., and vegetables; this was the dinner to Admiral Keppel, when he was made First Lord of the Admiralty. Twigg told of another dinner to Sir Richard Simmons, of Earl's Court, Mr. Small, and three other gentlemen; it consisted of the following dishes:—A turbot, of 40lb., a Thames salmon, a haunch of venison, French beans and cucumbers, a green goose, an apricot tart, and green peas. The dinner was dressed by Twigg, and it came to about seven guineas a head.

The Shakspeare is stated to have been the first tavern in Covent Garden. Twigg relates of Tomkins, the landlord, that his father had been a man of opulence in the City, but failed for vast sums. Tomkins kept his coach and his country-house, but was no gambler, as has been reported. He died worth 40,000l. His daughter married Mr. Longman, the music-seller. Tomkins had never less than a hundred pipes of wine in his cellar; he kept seven waiters, one cellar-man, and a boy. Each waiter was smartly dressed in his ruffles, and thought it a bad week if he did not make 7l. Stacie, who partly served his apprenticeship to Tomkins, told Twigg, that he had betted nearly 3000l. upon one of his race-horses of the name of Goldfinder. Stacie won, and afterwards sold the horse for a large sum.

There was likewise a Shakspeare Tavern in Little Russell-street, opposite Drury-lane Theatre; the sign was altered in 1828, to the Albion.

SHUTER, AND HIS TAVERN-PLACES.

Shuter, the actor, at the age of twelve, was pot-boy at the Queen's Head (afterwards Mrs. Butler's), in Covent Garden, where he was so kind to the rats in the cellar, by giving them sops from porter, (for, in his time, any person might have a toast in his beer,) that they would creep about him and upon him; he would carry them about between his shirt and his waistcoat, and even call them by their names. Shuter was next pot-boy at the Blue Posts, opposite Brydges-street, then kept by Ellidge, and afterwards by Carter, who played well at billiards, on account of the length of his arms. Shuter used to carry beer to the players, behind the scenes at Drury-lane Theatre, and elsewhere, and being noticed by Hippisley, was taken as his servant, and brought on the stage. He had also been at the house next the Blue Posts,—the Sun, in Russell-street, which was frequented by Hippisley. Mr. Theophilus Forrest, when he paid Shuter his money, allowed him in his latter days, two guineas per week, found him calling for gin, and his shirt was worn to half its original size. Latterly, he was hooted by the boys in the street: he became a Methodist, and died at King John's Palace, Tottenham Court Road.

THE ROSE TAVERN, COVENT GARDEN.

This noted Tavern, on the east side of Brydges-street, flourished in the seventeenth and eighteenth centuries, and from its contiguity to Drury-lane Theatre, and close connection with it, was frequented by courtiers and men of letters, of loose character, and other gentry of no character at all. The scenes of *The Morning Ramble, or the Town Humour*, 1672, are laid " at the Rose Tavern, in Covent Garden," which was constantly a scene of drunken broils, midnight orgies, and murderous assaults, by men of fashion, who were designated " Hectors," and whose chief pleasure lay in frequenting taverns for the running through of some fuddled toper, whom wine had made valiant. Shadwell, in his comedy of the *Scowrers*, 1691, written at a time when obedience to the laws was enforced, and these excesses had in consequence declined, observes of these cowardly ruffians : " They were brave fellows, indeed ! In those days a man could not go from the Rose Tavern to the Piazza once, but he must venture his life twice."

Women of a certain freedom of character frequented taverns at the commencement of the last century, and the Rose, doubtless, resembled the box-lobby of a theatre. In the *Rake Reformed*, 1718, this tavern is thus noticed :

" Not far from thence appears a pendent sign,
Whose bush declares the product of the vine,
Whence to the traveller's sight the full-blown Rose
Its dazzling beauties doth in gold disclose ;
And painted faces flock in tally'd clothes."

Dramatists and poets resorted to the house, and about 1726, Gay and other wits, by clubbing verses, concocted the well-known love ditty, entitled *Molly Mogg of the Rose*, in compliment to the then barmaid or waitress. The Welsh ballad, *Gwinfrid Shones*, printed in 1733, has also this tribute to Molly Mogg, as a celebrated toast :

> " Some sing Molly Mogg of the Rose,
> And call her the Oakingham pelle ;
> Whilst others does farces compose,
> On peautiful Molle Lepelle."

Hogarth's third print of the Rake's Progress, published in 1735, exhibits a principal room in the Rose Tavern : Lethercoat, the fellow with a bright pewter dish and a candle, is a portrait; he was for many years a porter attached to the house.

Garrick, when he enlarged Drury-lane Theatre, in 1776, raised the new front designed by Robert Adam, took in the whole of the tavern, as a convenience to the theatre, and retained the sign of the Rose in an oval compartment, as a conspicuous part of the decoration, which is shown in a popular engraving by J. T. Smith.

In D'Urfey's Songs, 1719, we find these allusions to the Rose :

> " *A Song in Praise of Chalk, by W. Pettis.*

> " We the lads at the Rose
> A patron have chose,
> Who's as void as the best is of thinking ;
> And without dedication,
> Will assist in his station,
> And maintains us in eating and drinking."

" *Song.—The Nose.*

" Three merry lads met at the Rose,
To speak in the praises of the nose :
The flat, the sharp, the Roman snout,
The hawk's nose circled round about ;
The crooked nose that stands awry,
The ruby nose of scarlet dye ;
The brazen nose without a face,
That doth the learned college grace.
Invention often barren grows,
Yet still there's matter in the nose."

EVANS'S, COVENT GARDEN.

At the north-west corner of Covent Garden Market
is a lofty edifice, which, with the building that preceded
it, possesses a host of interesting associations. Sir
Kenelm Digby came to live here after the Restoration
of Charles II. : here he was much visited by the philosophers of his day, and built in the garden in the
rear of the house a laboratory. The mansion was
altered, if not rebuilt, for the Earl of Orford, better
known as Admiral Russell, who, in 1692, defeated
Admiral de Tourville, and ruined the French fleet. The
façade of the house originally resembled the forecastle
of a ship. The fine old staircase is formed of part of
the vessel Admiral Russell commanded at La Hogue ;
it has handsomely carved anchors, ropes, and the
coronet and initials of Lord Orford. The Earl died
here in 1727 ; and the house was afterwards occupied
by Thomas, Lord Archer, until 1768 ; and by James

West, the great collector of books, etc., and President of the Royal Society, who died in 1772.

Mr. Twigg recollected Lord Archer's garden (now the site of the singing-room), at the back of the Grand Hotel, about 1765, well stocked; mushrooms and cucumbers were grown there in high perfection.

In 1774, the house was opened by David Low as an hotel; the first family hotel, it is said, in London. Gold, silver, and copper medals were struck, and given by Low, as advertisements of his house; the gold to the princes, silver to the nobility, and copper to the public generally. About 1794, Mrs. Hudson, then proprietor, advertised her hotel, " with stabling for one hundred noblemen and horses." The next proprietors were Richardson and Joy.

At the beginning of the present century, and some years afterwards, the hotel was famous for its large dinner- and coffee-room. This was called the " Star," from the number of men of rank who frequented it. One day a gentleman entered the dining-room, and ordered of the waiter two lamb-chops; at the same time inquiring, " John, have you a cucumber?" The waiter replied in the negative—it was so early in the season; but he would step into the market, and inquire if there were any. The waiter did so, and returned with— " There are a few, but they are half-a-guinea apiece." " Half-a-guinea apiece! are they small or large?" " Why, rather small." " Then buy two," was the reply. This incident has been related of various epicures; it occurred to Charles Duke of Norfolk, who died in 1815.

Evans, of Covent-Garden Theatre, removed here from the Cider Cellar in Maiden-lane, and, using the large dining-room for a singing-room, prospered until 1844, when he resigned the property to Mr. John Green. Meanwhile, the character of the entertainment, by the selection of music of a higher class than hitherto, brought so great an accession of visitors, that Mr. Green built, in 1855, on the site of the old garden (Digby's garden) an extremely handsome hall, to which the former singing-room forms a sort of vestibule. The latter is hung with the collection of portraits of celebrated actors and actresses, mostly of our own time, which Mr. Green has been at great pains to collect.

The *spécialité* of this very agreeable place is the olden music, which is sung here with great intelligence and spirit; the visitors are of the better and more appreciative class, and often include amateurs of rank. The reserved gallery is said to occupy part of the site of the cottage in which the Kembles occasionally resided during the zenith of their fame at Covent-Garden Theatre; and here the gifted Fanny Kemble is said to have been born.

THE FLEECE, COVENT GARDEN.

The Restoration did not mend the morals of the taverns in Covent Garden, but increased their licentiousness, and made them the resort of bullies and other vicious persons. The Fleece, on the west side of Brydges-street, was notorious for its tavern broils; L'Estrange, in his translation of Quevedo's *Visions*, 1667, makes one of the Fleece hectors declare he was never well but either at the Fleece Tavern or Bear at Bridgefoot, stuffing himself "with food and tipple, till the hoops were ready to burst." According to Aubrey, the Fleece was " very unfortunate for homicides ;" there were several killed there in his time; it was a private house till 1692. Aubrey places it in York-street, so that there must have been a back or second way to the tavern—a very convenient resource.

THE BEDFORD HEAD, COVENT GARDEN.

Was a luxurious refectory, in Southampton-street, whose epicurism is commemorated by Pope :—

> " Let me extol a cat on oysters fed,
>   I'll have a party at the Bedford Head."
>   *2nd Sat. of Horace, 2nd Bk.*

> " When sharp with hunger, scorn you to be fed
>   Except on pea-chicks, at the Bedford Head ? "
>   *Pope, Sober Advice.*

Walpole refers to a great supper at the Bedford Head, ordered by Paul Whitehead, for a party of gentlemen dressed like sailors and masked, who, in 1741, on the night of Vernon's birthday, went round Covent Garden with a drum, beating up for a volunteer mob; but it did not take.

THE SALUTATION, TAVISTOCK STREET.

This was a noted tavern in the last century, at the corner of Tavistock-court, Covent Garden. Its original sign was taken down by Mr. Yerrel, the landlord, who informed J. T. Smith, that it consisted of two gentlemen saluting each other, dressed in flowing wigs, and coats with square pockets, large enough to hold folio books, and wearing swords, this being the dress of the time when the sign was put up, supposed to have been about 1707, the date on a stone at the Covent Garden end of the court.

Richard Leveridge, the celebrated singer, kept the Salutation after his retirement from the stage; and here he brought out his *Collection of Songs*, with the music, engraved and printed for the author, 1727.

Among the frequenters of the Salutation was William Cussans, or Cuzzons, a native of Barbadoes, and a most eccentric fellow, who lived upon an income allowed him by his family. He once hired himself as a potman, and then as a coal-heaver. He was never seen to smile. He personated a chimney-sweeper at the Pantheon and Opera-house masquerades, and wrote the popular song of Robinson Crusoe:

" He got all the wood
That ever he could,
And he stuck it together with glue so ;
And made him a hut,
And in it he put
The carcase of Robinson Crusoe."

He was a bacchanalian customer at the Salutation, and his nightly quantum of wine was liberal : he would sometimes take eight pints at a sitting, without being the least intoxicated.

THE CONSTITUTION TAVERN, COVENT GARDEN.

In Bedford-street, near St. Paul's church-gate, was an old tavern, the Constitution (now rebuilt), noted as the resort of working men of letters, and for its late hours; indeed, the sittings here were perennial. Among other eccentric persons we remember to have seen here, was an accomplished scholar named Churchill, who had travelled much in the East, smoked and ate opium to excess, and was full of information. Of another grade were two friends who lived in the same house, and had for many years "turned night into day;" rising at eight o'clock in the evening, and going to bed at eight next morning. They had in common some astrological, alchemical, and *spiritual* notions, and often passed the whole night at the Constitution. This was the favourite haunt of Wilson, the landscape-painter, who then lived in the Garden; he could, at the Constitution, freely indulge in a pot of porter, and enjoy the fun of his brother-painter, Mortimer, who preferred this house, as it was near his own in Church-passage.

THE CIDER CELLAR.

This strange place, upon the south side of Maiden-lane, Covent Garden, was opened about 1730, and is described as a "Midnight Concert Room," in *Adventures Underground*, 1750. Professor Porson was a great

lover of cider, the patronymic drink for which the cellar
was once famed; it became his nightly haunt, for wherever
he spent the evening, he finished the night at the Cider
Cellar. One night, in 1795, as he sat here smoking his
pipe, with his friend George Gordon, he abruptly said,
"Friend George, do you think the widow Lunan an
agreeable sort of personage, as times go?" Gordon
assented. "In that case," replied Porson, "you must
meet me to-morrow morning at St. Martin's-in-the-
Fields, at eight o'clock;" and without saying more,
Porson paid his reckoning, and went home. Next morning, Gordon repaired to the church, and there found
Porson with Mrs. Lunan and a female friend, and the
parson waiting to begin the ceremony. The service being ended, the bride and her friend retired by one door
of the church, and Porson and Gordon by another. The
bride and bridegroom dined together with friends, but
after dinner Porson contrived to slip away, and passed the
rest of the day with a learned friend, and did not leave
till the family were about to retire for the night, when
Porson adjourned to the Cider Cellar, and there stayed
till eight o'clock next morning. One of his companions
here is said to have shouted before Porson, "Dick can
beat us all: he can drink all night and spout all day,"
which greatly pleased the Professor.

We remember the place not many years after Porson's
death, when it was, as its name implied, *a cellar*, and the
fittings were rude and rough: over the mantelpiece was
a large mezzotint portrait of Porson, framed and glazed,
which we take to be the missing portrait named by the
Rev. Mr. Watson, in his Life of the Professor. The
Cider Cellar was subsequently enlarged; but its exhi-
bitions grew to be too sensational for long existence.

OFFLEY'S, HENRIETTA-STREET.

This noted tavern, of our day, enjoyed great and deserved celebrity, though short-lived. It was No. 23, on the south side of Henrietta-street, Covent Garden, and its fame rested upon Burton ale, and the largest supper-room in this theatrical neighbourhood; with no pictures, placards, paper-hangings, or vulgar coffee-room finery, to disturb one's relish of the good things there provided. Offley, the proprietor, was originally at Bellamy's, and " as such, was privileged to watch, and occasionally admitted to assist, the presiding priestess of the gridiron at the exercise of her mysteries." Offley's chop was thick and substantial; the House of Commons' chop was small and thin, and honourable Members sometimes ate a dozen at a sitting. Offley's chop was served with shalots shred, and warmed in gravy, and accompanied by nips of Burton ale, and was a delicious after-theatre supper. The large room at that hour was generally crowded with a higher class of men than are to be seen in taverns of the present day. There was excellent dining up-stairs, with wines really worth drinking—all with a sort of Quakerly plainness, but solid comfort. The fast men came to the great room, where the *spécialité* was singing by amateurs upon one evening of the week; and to prevent the chorus waking the dead in their cerements in the adjoining churchyard, the coffee-room window was double. The " professionals " stayed away. Francis Crew sang Moore's melodies, then in their zenith; sometimes, in a spirit of waggery, an amateur would sing "Chevy Chase" in full; and now and then Offley himself trolled out one of Captain Morris's lyrics. Such was this right joyously convivial place some five-and-forty years since upon the singing night. Upon other evenings, there came to a large round table (a sort of privileged place) a few well-to-do, substantial tradesmen from the neighbourhood, among whom was the renowned surgical-instrument maker from the Strand, who had the sagacity to buy the iron from off the piles of old London Bridge, and convert it (after it had lain for centuries under water) into some of the finest surgical instruments of the day. Offley's, however, declined : the singing was discontinued; Time had thinned the ranks and groups of the bright and buoyant; the large room was mostly frequented by quiet, orderly persons, who kept good hours; the theatre-suppers grew few and far between; the merry old host departed,— when it was proposed to have his portrait painted—but in vain; success had ebbed away, and at length the house was closed.*

Offley's was sketched with a free hand, in *Horæ Offleanæ, Bentley's Miscellany*, March, 1841.

THE RUMMER TAVERN.

The locality of this noted tavern is given by Cunningham, as "two doors from Locket's, between Whitehall and Charing Cross, removed to the water-side of Charing Cross, in 1710, and burnt down Nov. 7th, 1750. It

* Walks and Talks about London, 1865, pp. 180–182.

was kept in the reign of Charles II., by Samuel Prior, uncle of Matthew Prior, the poet, who thus wrote to Fleetwood Shephard :

> " My uncle, rest his soul ! when living,
> Might have contriv'd me ways of thriving :
> Taught me with cider to replenish
> My vats, or ebbing tide of Rhenish.
> So when for hock I drew prickt white-wine,
> Swear't had the flavour, and was right wine."

The Rummer is introduced by Hogarth into his picture of " Night." Here Jack Sheppard committed his first robbery by stealing two silver spoons.

The Rummer, in Queen-street, was kept by Brawn, a celebrated cook, of whom Dr. King, in his *Art of Cookery*, speaks in the same way as Kit-Kat and Locket.

King, also, in his *Analogy between Physicians, Cooks, and Playwrights*, thus describes a visit :—

" Though I seldom go out of my own lodgings, I was prevailed on the other day to dine with some friends at the Rummer in Queen-street. . . . . Sam Trusty would needs have me go with him into the kitchen, and see how matters went there. . . . . He assured me that Mr. Brawn had an art, etc. I was, indeed, very much pleased and surprised with the extraordinary splendour and economy I observed there ; but above all with the great readiness and dexterity of the man himself. His motions were quick, but not precipitate ; he in an instant applied himself from one stove to another, without the least appearance of hurry, and in the midst of smoke and fire preserved an incredible serenity of countenance."

Beau Brummel, according to Mr. Jesse, spoke with a relish worthy a descendant of " the Rummer," of the savoury pies of his aunt Brawn, who then resided at .

Kilburn ; she is said to have been the widow of a grand-
son of the celebrity of Queen-street, who had himself
kept the public-house at the old Mews Gate, at Charing
Cross.—See *Notes and Queries*, 2nd S., no. xxxvi.

We remember an old tavern, "the Rummer," in
1825, which was taken down with the lower portion of
St. Martin's-lane, to form Trafalgar-square.

SPRING GARDEN TAVERNS.

Spring Garden is named from its water-spring or
fountain, set playing by the spectator treading upon its
hidden machinery—an eccentricity of the Elizabethan
garden. Spring Garden, by a patent which is extant,
in 1630 was made a bowling-green by command of
Charles I. "There was kept in it an ordinary of six
shillings a meal (when the king's proclamation allows
but two elsewhere) ; continual bibbing and drinking
wine all day under the trees ; two or three quarrels
every week. It was grown scandalous and insufferable ;
besides, my Lord Digby being reprehended for striking
in the king's garden, he said he took it for a common
bowling-place, where all paid money for their coming
in."—*Mr. Garrard to Lord Strafford.*

In 1634 Spring Garden was put down by the King's
command, and ordered to be hereafter no common
bowling-place. This led to the opening of "a New
Spring Garden" (Shaver's Hall), by a gentleman-barber,
a servant of the lord chamberlain's. The old garden
was, however, re-opened ; for 13th June, 1649, says

Evelyn, " I treated divers ladies of my relations in Spring Gardens;" but 10th May, 1654, he records that Cromwell and his partisans had shut up and seized on Spring Gardens, " wch till now had been ye usual rendezvous for the ladys and gallants at this season."

Spring Garden was, however, once more re-opened; for, in *A Character of England*, 1659, it is described as " The inclosure not disagreeable, for the solemnness of the grove, the warbling of the birds, and as it opens into the spacious walks at St. James's. . . . It is usual to find some of the young company here till midnight; and the thickets of the garden seem to be contrived to all advantages of gallantry, after they have refreshed with the collation, which is here seldom omitted, at a certain cabaret in the middle of this paradise, where the forbidden fruits are certain trifling tarts, neats' tongues, salacious meats, and bad Rhenish."

" The New Spring Garden" at Lambeth (afterwards Vauxhall) was flourishing in 1661-3; when the ground at Charing Cross was built upon, as " Inner Spring Garden" and " Outer Spring Garden." Buckingham-court is named from the Duke of Buckingham, one of the rakish frequenters of the Garden; and upon the site of Drummond's banking-house was " Locket's Ordinary, a house of entertainment much frequented by gentry," and a relic of the Spring Garden gaiety :

" For Locket's stands where gardens once did spring."
Dr. King's *Art of Cookery*, 1709.

Here the witty and beautiful dramatist, Mrs. Centlivre, died, December 1, 1723, at the house of her third husband, Joseph Centlivre, " Yeoman of the Mouth"

(head cook) " to Queen Anne."* In her Prologue to
Love's Contrivances, 1703, we have

> " At Locket's, Brown's, and at Pontack's enquire
> What modish kickshaws the nice beaux desire,
> What famed ragouts, what new invented sallad,
> Has best pretensions to regain the palate."

Locket's was named from its first landlord :† its fame
declined in the reign of Queen Anne, and expired early
in the next reign.

" HEAVEN" AND " HELL" TAVERNS, WESTMINSTER.

At the north end of Lindsay-lane, upon the site of the
Committee-rooms of the House of Commons, was a
tavern called " Heaven ;" and under the old Exchequer
Chamber were two subterraneous passages called "Hell"
and " Purgatory." Butler, in *Hudibras*, mentions the
first as

> " False Heaven at the end of the Hell ;"

Gifford, in his notes on Ben Jonson, says: " Heaven
and Hell were two common alehouses, abutting on
Westminster Hall. Whalley says that they were standing in his remembrance. They are mentioned together

---

* Curiosities of London, pp. 678, 679.
† Edward Locket, in 1693, took the Bowling-green House, on
Putney Heath, where all gentlemen might be entertained. In
a house built on the site of the above, died, Jan. 23, 1806, the
Rt. Hon. William Pitt.

with a third house, called Purgatory, in a grant which I have read, dated in the first year of Henry VII."

Old Fuller quaintly says of Hell: "I could wish it had another name, seeing it is ill jesting with edged tools. I am informed that formerly this place was appointed a prison for the King's debtors, who never were freed thence until they had paid their uttermost due demanded of them. This proverb is since applied to moneys paid into the Exchequer, which thence are irrecoverable, upon what plea or pretence whatever."

Peacham describes Hell as a place near Westminster Hall, "where very good meat is dressed all the term time;" and the Company of Parish Clerks add, it is "very much frequented by lawyers." According to Ben Jonson, Hell appears to have been frequented by lawyers' clerks; for, in his play of the *Alchemist*, Dapper is forbidden

"To break his fast in Heaven or Hell."

Hugh Peters, on his Trial, tells us that he went to Westminster to find out some company to dinner with him, and having walked about an hour in Westminster Hall, and meeting none of his friends to dine with him, he went "to that place called Heaven, and dined there."

When Pride "purged" the Parliament, on Dec. 6, 1648, the forty-one he excepted were shut up for the night in the Hell tavern, kept by a Mr. Duke (*Carlyle*); and which Dugdale calls "their great victualling-house near Westminster Hall, where they kept them all night without any beds."

Pepys, in his *Diary*, thus notes his visit: "28 Jan. 1659-60. And so I returned and went to Heaven, where Ludlin and I dined." Six years later, at the time of the Restoration, four days before the King landed, in one of these taverns, Pepys spent the evening with Locke and Purcell, hearing a variety of brave Italian and Spanish songs, and a new canon of Locke's on the words, " Domine salvum fac Regem."   " Here, out of the windows," he says, " it was a most pleasant sight to see the City, from one end to the other, with a glory about it, so high was the light of the bonfires, and thick round the City, and the bells rang everywhere."

After all, " Hell" may have been so named from its being a prison of the King's debtors, most probably a very bad one : it was also called the Constabulary.   Its Wardenship was valued yearly at the sum of 11s., and Paradise at 4l.

Purgatory appears also to have been an ancient prison, the keys of which, attached to a leathern girdle, says Walcot's *Westminster*, are still preserved.   Herein were kept the ducking-stools for scolds, who were placed in a chair fastened on an iron pivot to the end of a long pole, which was balanced at the middle upon a high trestle, thus allowing the culprit's body to be *ducked* in the Thames.

" BELLAMY'S KITCHEN."

In a pleasantly written book, entitled *A Career in the Commons*, we find this sketch of the singular apartment, in the vicinity of the (Old) House of Commons called " the Kitchen."   " Mr. Bellamy's beer may be unexceptionable, and his chops and steaks may be unrivalled, but the legislators of England delight in eating a dinner in the place where it is cooked, and in the presence of the very fire where the beef hisses and the gravy runs ! Bellamy's kitchen seems, in fact, a portion of the British Constitution. A foreigner, be he a Frenchman, American, or Dutchman, if introduced to the 'kitchen,' would stare with astonishment if you told him that in this plain apartment, with its immense fire, meatscreen, gridirons, and a small tub under the window for washing the glasses, the statesmen of England very often dine, and men, possessed of wealth untold, and with palaces of their own, in which luxury and splendour are visible in every part, are willing to leave their stately dining-halls and powdered attendants, to be waited upon, while eating a chop in Bellamy's kitchen, by two unpretending old women. Bellamy's kitchen, I repeat, is part and parcel of the British Constitution. Baronets who date from the Conquest, and squires of every degree, care nothing for the unassuming character of the 'kitchen,' if the steak be hot and good, if it can be quickly and conveniently dispatched, and the tinkle of the division-bell can be heard while the dinner proceeds. Call England a proud nation, forsooth ! Say that the House of Commons is aristocratic ! Both the nation and its representatives must be, and are, unquestionable patterns of republican humility, if all the pomp and circumstance of dining can be forgotten in Bellamy's kitchen !"*

* At the noted Cat and Bagpipes tavern, at the south-west corner of Downing-street, George Rose used to eat his mutton-chop ; he subsequently became Secretary to the Treasury.

A COFFEE-HOUSE CANARY-BIRD.

Of " a great Coffee-house " in Pall Mall we find the following amusing story, in the *Correspondence of Gray and Mason,* edited by Mitford :

"In the year 1688, my Lord Peterborough had a great mind to be well with Lady Sandwich, Mrs. Bonfoy's old friend. There was a woman who kept a great Coffee-house in Pall Mall, and she had a miraculous canary-bird that piped twenty tunes. Lady Sandwich was fond of such things, had heard of and seen the bird. Lord Peterborough came to the woman, and offered her a large sum of money for it; but she was rich, and proud of it, and would not part with it for love or money. However, he watched the bird narrowly, observed all its marks and features, went and bought just such another, sauntered into the coffee-room, took his opportunity when no one was by, slipped the wrong bird into the cage and the right into his pocket, and went off undiscovered to make my Lady Sandwich happy. This was just about the time of the Revolution ; and, a good while after, going into the same coffee-house again, he saw his bird there, and said, ' Well, I reckon you would give your ears now that you had taken my money.' ' Money !' says the woman, ' no, nor ten times that money now, dear little creature ! for, if your lordship will believe me (as I am a Christian, it is true), it has moped and moped, and never once opened its pretty lips since the day that the poor king went away !'"

STAR AND GARTER, PALL MALL.

FATAL DUEL.

Pall Mall has long been noted for its taverns, as well as for its chocolate- and coffee-houses, and " houses for clubbing." They were resorted to by gay nobility and men of estate; and, in times when gaming and drinking were indulged in to frightful excess, these taverns often proved hot-beds of quarrel and fray. One of the most sanguinary duels on record—that between the Duke of Hamilton and Lord Mohun—was planned at the Queen's Arms, in Pall Mall, and the Rose in Covent Garden; at the former, Lord Mohun supped with his second on the two nights preceding the fatal conflict in Hyde Park.

Still more closely associated with Pall Mall was the fatal duel between Lord Byron and Mr. Chaworth, which was *fought in a room* of the Star and Garter, when the grand-uncle of the poet Lord killed in a duel, or rather scuffle, his relation and neighbour, " who was run through the body, and died next day." The duellists were neighbours in the country, and were members of the Nottinghamshire Club, which met at the Star and Garter once a month.

The meeting at which arose the unfortunate dispute that produced the duel, was on the 26th of January, 1765, when were present Mr. John Hewet, who sat as chairman; the Hon. Thomas Willoughby; Frederick Montagu, John Sherwin, Francis Molyneux, Esqrs., and Lord Byron; William Chaworth, George Donston, and Charles Mellish, junior, Esq.; and Sir Robert Burdett;

who were all the company. The usual hour of dining was soon after four, and the rule of the Club was to have the bill and a bottle brought in at seven. Till this hour all was jollity and good-humour; but Mr. Hewet, happening to start some conversation about the best method of preserving game, setting the laws for that purpose out of the question, Mr. Chaworth and Lord Byron were of different opinions; Mr. Chaworth insisting on severity against poachers and unqualified persons; and Lord Byron declaring that the way to have most game was to take no care of it at all. Mr. Chaworth, in confirmation of what he had said, insisted that Sir Charles Sedley and himself had more game on five acres than Lord Byron had on all his manors. Lord Byron, in reply, proposed a bet of 100 guineas, but this was not laid. Mr. Chaworth then said, that were it not for Sir Charles Sedley's care, and his own, Lord Byron would not have a hare on his estate; and his Lordship asking with a smile, what Sir Charles Sedley's manors were, was answered by Mr. Chaworth,—Nuttall and Bulwell. Lord Byron did not dispute Nuttall, but added, Bulwell was his; on which Mr. Chaworth, with some heat, replied: "If you want information as to Sir Charles Sedley's manors, he lives at Mr. Cooper's, in Dean Street, and, I doubt not, will be ready to give you satisfaction; and, as to myself, your Lordship knows where to find me, in Berkeley Row."

The subject was now dropped; and little was said, when Mr. Chaworth called to settle the reckoning, in doing which the master of the tavern observed him to be flurried. In a few minutes, Mr. Chaworth having paid the bill, went out, and was followed by Mr. Donston, whom Mr. C. asked if he thought he had been short in what he had said; to which Mr. D. replied, "No; he had gone rather too far upon so trifling an occasion, but did not believe that Lord Byron or the company would think any more of it." Mr. Donston then returned to the club-room. Lord Byron now came out, and found Mr. Chaworth still on the stairs: it is doubtful whether his Lordship called upon Mr. Chaworth, or Mr. Chaworth called upon Lord Byron; but both went down to the first landing-place—having dined upon the second floor—and both called a waiter to show an empty room, which the waiter did, having first opened the door, and placed a small tallow-candle, which he had in his hand, on the table; he then retired, when the gentlemen entered, and shut the door after them.

In a few minutes the affair was decided: the bell was rung, but by whom is uncertain: the waiter went up, and perceiving what had happened, ran down very frightened, told his master of the catastrophe, when he ran up to the room, and found the two antagonists standing close together: Mr. Chaworth had his sword in his left hand, and Lord Byron his sword in his right; Lord Byron's left hand was round Mr. Chaworth, and Mr. Chaworth's right hand was round Lord Byron's neck, and over his shoulder. Mr. C. desired Mr. Fynmore, the landlord, to take his sword, and Lord B. delivered up his sword at the same moment: a surgeon was sent for, and came immediately. In the meantime, six of the company entered the room; when Mr. Chaworth said that "he could not live many hours; that he forgave Lord Byron, and hoped the world would; that the affair had passed in the dark, only a small tallow-candle burning in the room; that Lord Byron asked him, if he addressed the observation on the game to Sir

Charles Sedley, or to him?—to which he replied, 'If
you have anything to say, we had better shut the door;'
that while he was doing this, Lord Byron bid him draw,
and in turning he saw his Lordship's sword half-drawn,
on which he whipped out his own sword and made the
first pass; that the sword being through my Lord's
waistcoat, he thought that he had killed him; and,
asking whether he was not mortally wounded, Lord
Byron, while he was speaking, shortened his sword, and
stabbed him in the belly."

When Mr. Mawkins, the surgeon, arrived, he found
Mr. Chaworth sitting by the fire, with the lower part of
his waistcoat open, his shirt bloody, and his hand upon
his belly.   He inquired if he was in immediate danger,
and being answered in the affirmative, he desired his
uncle, Mr. Levinz, might be sent for. In the meantime,
he stated to Mr. Hawkins, that Lord Byron and he (Mr.
Chaworth) entered the room together; that his Lordship said something of the dispute, on which he, Mr.
C., fastened the door, and turning round, perceived his
Lordship with his sword either drawn or nearly so;
on which he instantly drew his own and made a thrust
at him, which he thought had wounded or killed him;
that then perceiving his Lordship shorten his sword to
return the thrust, he thought to have parried it with
his left hand, at which he looked twice, imagining that
he had cut it in the attempt; that he felt the sword
enter his body, and go deep through his back; that
he struggled, and being the stronger man, disarmed his
Lordship, and expressed his apprehension that he had
mortally wounded him; that Lord Byron replied by saying something to the like effect; adding that he hoped
now he would allow him to be as brave a man as any in
the kingdom.

After a little while, Mr. Chaworth seemed to grow stronger, and was removed to his own house : additional medical advice arrived, but no relief could be given him : he continued sensible till his death. Mr. Levinz, his uncle, now arrived with an attorney, to whom Mr. Chaworth gave very sensible and distinct instructions for making his will. The will was then executed, and the attorney, Mr. Partington, committed to writing the last words Mr. Chaworth was heard to say. This writing was handed to Mr. Levinz, and gave rise to a report that a paper was written by the deceased, and sealed up, not to be opened till the time that Lord Byron should be tried; but no paper was written by Mr. Chaworth, and that written by Mr. Partington was as follows : " Sunday morning, the 27th of January, about three of the clock, Mr. Chaworth said, that my Lord's sword was half-drawn, and that he, knowing the man, immediately, or as quick as he could, whipped out his sword, and had the first thrust; that then my Lord wounded him, and he disarmed my Lord, who then said, ' By G—, I have as much courage as any man in England.' "

Lord Byron was committed to the Tower, and was tried before the House of Peers, in Westminster Hall, on the 16th and 17th of April, 1765. Lord Byron's defence was reduced by him into writing, and read by the clerk. The Peers present, including the High Steward, declared Lord Byron, on their honour, to be not guilty of murder, but of manslaughter; with the exception of four Peers, who found him not guilty generally. On this verdict being given, Lord Byron was called upon to say why judgment of manslaughter should not be pronounced upon him. His Lordship immediately claimed the benefit of the 1st Edward VI. cap. 12, a statute, by which, whenever a Peer was convicted of any felony for which a commoner might have Benefit of Clergy, such Peer, on praying the benefit of that Act, was always to be discharged without burning in the hand, or any penal consequence whatever. The claim of Lord Byron being accordingly allowed, he was forthwith discharged on payment of his fees. This singular privilege was supposed to be abrogated by the 7 & 8 Geo. IV. cap. 28, s. 6, which abolished Benefit of Clergy; but some doubt arising on the subject, it was positively put an end to by the 4 & 5 Vict. cap. 22. (See *Celebrated Trials connected with the Aristocracy*, by Mr. Serjeant Burke.)

Mr. Chaworth was the descendant of one of the oldest houses in England, a branch of which obtained an Irish peerage. His grand-niece, the eventual heiress of the family, was Mary Chaworth, the object of the early unrequited love of Lord Byron, the poet. Singularly enough, there was the same degree of relationship between that nobleman and the Lord Byron who killed Mr. Chaworth, as existed between the latter unfortunate gentleman and Mr. Chaworth.*

Several stories are told of the high charges of the Star and Garter Tavern, even in the reign of Queen Anne. The Duke of Ormond, who gave here a dinner to a few friends, was charged twenty-one pounds, six shillings, and eight pence, for four, that is, first and second course, without wine or dessert.

From the *Connoisseur* of 1754, we learn that the fools of quality of that day "drove to the Star and Garter to regale on macaroni, or piddle with an ortolan at White's or Pontac's."

* Abridged from the Romance of London, vol. i. pp. 225–232.

At the Star and Garter, in 1774, was formed the first Cricket Club. Sir Horace Mann, who had promoted cricket in Kent, and the Duke of Dorset and Lord Tankerville, leaders of the Surrey and Hants Eleven, conjointly with other noblemen and gentlemen, formed a committee under the presidency of Sir William Draper. They met at the Star and Garter, and laid down the first rules of cricket, which very rules form the basis of the laws of cricket of this day.

THATCHED-HOUSE TAVERN, ST. JAMES'S-STREET.

" Come and once more together let us greet
    The long-lost pleasures of St. James's-street."—*Tickell.*

Little more than a century and a half ago the parish of St. James was described as "all the houses and grounds comprehended in a place heretofore called ' St. James's Fields' and the confines thereof." Previously to this, the above tavern was most probably a *thatched house.* St. James's-street dates from 1670 : the poets Waller and Pope lived here; Sir Christopher Wren died here, in 1723; as did Gibbon, the historian, in 1794, at Elmsley's, the bookseller's, at No. 76, at the corner of Little St. James's-street. Fox lived next to Brookes's in 1781 ; and Lord Byron lodged at No. 8, in 1811. At the south-west end was the St. James's Coffee-house, taken down in 1806; the foreign and domestic news house of the *Tatler,* and the "fountain-head" of the

Spectator. Thus early, the street had a sort of literary fashion favourable to the growth of taverns and clubs.

The Thatched House, which was taken down in 1814 and 1863, had been for nearly two centuries celebrated for its club meetings, its large public room, and its public dinners, especially those of our universities and great schools. It was one of Swift's favourite haunts: in some birthday verses he sings :—

> " The Deanery-house may well be matched,
> Under correction, with the Thatch'd."

The histories of some of the principal Clubs which which met here, will be found in Vol. I.; as the Brothers, Literary, Dilettanti, and others; (besides a list, page 318.)

The Royal Naval Club held its meetings at the Thatched House, as did some art societies and kindred associations. The large club-room faced St. James's-street, and when lit in the evening with wax-candles in large old glass chandeliers, the Dilettanti pictures could be seen from the pavement of the street. Beneath the tavern front was a range of low-built shops, including that of Rowland, or Rouland, the fashionable coiffeur, who charged five shillings for cutting hair, and made a large fortune by his " incomparable *Huile* Macassar." Through the tavern was a passage to Thatched House-court, in the rear ; and here, in Catherine-Wheel-alley, in the last century, lived the good old widow Delany, after the Doctor's death, as noted in her Autobiography, edited by Lady Llanover. Some of Mrs. Delany's fashionable friends then resided in Dean-street, Soho.

Thatched House-court and the alley have been swept away. Elmsley's was removed for the site of the Conservative Club. In an adjoining house lived the famous Betty, " the queen of apple-women," whom Mason has thus embalmed in his *Heroic Epistle* :—

"And patriot Betty fix her fruitshop here."

It was a famous place for gossip. Walpole says of a story much about, "I should scruple repeating it, if Betty and the waiters at Arthur's did not talk of it publicly." Again, "Would you know what officer's on guard in Betty's fruitshop?"

The Tavern, which has disappeared, was nearly the last relic of old St. James's-street, although its memories survive in various modern Club-houses, and the Thatched House will be kept in mind by the graceful sculpture of the Civil Service Clubhouse, erected upon a portion of the site.

"THE RUNNING FOOTMAN," MAY FAIR.

This sign, in Charles-street, Berkeley Square, carries us back to the days of bad roads, and journeying at snail's pace, when the travelling equipage of the nobility required that one or more men should run in front of the carriage, chiefly as a mark of the rank of the traveller; they were likewise sent on messages, and occasionally for great distances.

The running footman required to be a healthy and active man; he wore a light black cap, a jockey-coat, and carried a pole with at the top a hollow ball, in which he kept a hard-boiled egg and a little white wine, to

serve as refreshment on his journey; and this is supposed to be the origin of the footman's silver-mounted
cane. The Duke of Queensberry, who died in 1810, kept
a running footman longer than his compeers in London;
and Mr. Thoms, in *Notes and Queries*, relates an amusing
anecdote of a man who came to be hired for the duty by
the Duke. His Grace was in the habit of trying their
paces, by seeing how they could run up and down Piccadilly, he watching them and timing them from his
balcony. The man put on a livery before the trial; on
one occasion, a candidate, having run, stood before the
balcony. "You will do very well for me," said the
Duke. "And your livery will do very well for me,"
replied the man, and gave the Duke a last proof of his
ability by running away with it.

The sign in Charles-street represents a young man,
dressed in a kind of livery, and a cap with a feather in
it; he carries the usual pole, and is running; and beneath is "I am the only running Footman," which may
relate to the superior speed of the runner, and this may
be a portrait of a celebrity.

Kindred to the above is the old sign of "The Two
Chairmen," in Warwick-street, Charing Cross,* recalling
the sedans or chairs of Pall Mall; and there is a similar
sign on Hay Hill.

---

* The old Golden Cross Inn, Charing Cross, stood a short
distance west of the present Golden Cross Hotel, No. 452,
Strand. Of the former we read: "April 23, 1643. It was at
this period, by order of the Committee or Commission appointed
by the House, the sign of a tavern, the Golden Cross, at Charing Cross, was taken down, as superstitious and idolatrous."—
In Suffolk-street, Haymarket, was the Tavern before which took
place "the Calves' Head Club" riot.—See Vol. I., p. 27.

PICCADILLY INNS AND TAVERNS.

Piccadilly was long noticed for the variety and extent of its Inns and Taverns, although few remain. At the east end were formerly the Black Bear and White Bear (originally the Fleece), nearly opposite each other. The Black Bear was taken down 1820. The White Bear remains : it occurs in St. Martin's parish-books, 1685 : here Chatelain and Sullivan, the engravers, died; and Benjamin West, the painter, lodged, the first night after his arrival from America. Strype mentions the White Horse Cellar in 1720 ; and the booking-office of the New White Horse Cellar is to this day in " the cellar." The Three Kings stables gateway, No. 75, had two Corinthian pilasters, stated by Disraeli to have belonged to Clarendon House : " the stable-yard at the back presents the features of an old galleried inn-yard, and it is noted as the place from which General Palmer started the first Bath mail-coach." (J. W. Archer : *Vestiges*, part vi.) The Hercules' Pillars (a sign which meant that no habitation was to be found beyond it) stood a few yards west of Hamilton-place, and has been mentioned. The Hercules' Pillars, and another roadside tavern, the Triumphant Car, were standing about 1797, and were mostly frequented by soldiers. Two other Piccadilly inns, the White Horse and Half Moon, both of considerable extent, have given names to streets.

The older and more celebrated house of entertainment was Piccadilly Hall, which appears to have been built by one Robert Baker, in " the fields behind the Mews," leased to him by St. Martin's parish, and sold by his widow to Colonel Panton, who built Panton-

square and Panton-street. Lord Clarendon, in his
History of the Rebellion, speaks of " Mr. Hyde going to
a house called Piccadilly for entertainment and gaming:"
this house, with its gravel-walks and bowling-greens,
extended from the corner of Windmill-street and the
site of Panton-square, as shown in Porter and Faithorne's Map, 1658. Mr. Cunningham found (see
Handbook, 2nd edit. p. 396), in the parish accounts of
St. Martin's, " Robt Backer, of Pickadilley Halle;"
and the receipts for Lammas money paid for the premises as late as 1670. Sir John Suckling, the poet,
was one of the frequenters; and Aubrey remembered
Suckling's " sisters coming to the Peccadillo bowling-
green, crying, for the feare he should lose all their por-
tions." The house was taken down about 1685: a
tennis-court in the rear remained to our time, upon the
site of the Argyll Rooms, Great Windmill-street. The
Society of Antiquaries possess a printed proclamation
(*temp.* Charles II. 1671) against the increase of buildings in Windmill-fields and the fields adjoining Soho;
and in the Plan of 1658, Great Windmill-street consists
of straggling houses, and a windmill in a field west.

Colonel Panton, who is named above, was a celebrated gamester of the time of the Restoration, and in
one night, it is said, he won as many thousands as purchased him an estate of above 1500*l.* a year. " After
this good fortune," says Lucas, " he had such an aver-
sion against all manner of games, that he would never
handle cards or dice again; but lived very handsomely
on his winnings to his dying day, which was in the year
1681. He was the last proprietor of Piccadilly Hall,
and was in possession of land on the site of the streets
and buildings which bear his name, as early as the year

1664. Yet we remember to have seen it stated that Panton-street was named from a particular kind of horse-shoe called a *panton;* and from its contiguity to the Haymarket, this origin was long credited.

At the north-east end of the Haymarket stood the Gaming-house built by the barber of the Earl of Pemboke, and hence called Shaver's Hall: it is described by Garrard, in a letter to Lord Strafford in 1635, as " a new Spring Gardens, erected in the fields beyond the Mews :" its tennis-court remains in James-street.

From a Survey of the Premises, made in 1650, we gather that Shaver's Hall was strongly built of brick, and covered with lead : its large " seller " was divided into six rooms; above these four rooms, and the same in the first storey, to which was a balcony, with a prospect southward to the bowling-alleys. In the second storey were six rooms; and over the same a walk, leaded, and enclosed with rails, "very curiously carved and wrought," as was also the staircase, throughout the house. On the west were large kitchens and coal-house, with lofts over, " as also one faire Tennis Court," of brick, tiled, " well accommodated with all things fitting for the same;" with upper rooms; and at the entrance gate to the upper bowling-green, a parlour-lodge; and a double flight of steps descending to the lower bowling alley; there was still another bowling alley, and an orchard-wall, planted with choice fruit-trees; " as also one pleasant banqueting house, and one other faire and pleasant Roome, called the Greene Roome, and one other Conduit-house, and 2 other Turrets adjoininge to the walls." The ground whereon the said buildings stand, together with 2 fayre Bowling Alleys, orchard gardens, gravily walks, and other green walks, and Courts and Courtyards, containinge, by estimacion, 3 acres and 3 qrs., lying betweene a Roadway leading from Charinge Crosse to Knightsbridge west, now in the possession of Captayne Geeres, and is worth per ann. cl^{li}."*

ISLINGTON TAVERNS.

If you look at a Map of London, in the reign of Queen Elizabeth, the openness of the northern suburbs is very remarkable. Cornhill was then a clear space, and the ground thence to Bishopsgate-street was occupied as gardens. The Spitalfields were entirely open, and Shoreditch church was nearly the last building of London in that direction. Moorfields were used for drying linen; while cattle grazed, and archers shot, in Finsbury Fields, at the verge of which were three windmills. On the western side of Smithfield was a row of trees. Goswell-street was a lonely road, and Islington church stood in the distance, with a few houses and gardens near it. St. Giles's was also a small village, with open country north and west.

The ancient Islington continued to be a sort of dairy-farm for the metropolis. Like her father, Henry VIII., Elizabeth paid frequent visits to this neighbourhood, where some wealthy commoners dwelt; and her partiality to the place left many evidences in old houses, and spots traditionally said to have been visited by the Queen, whose delight it was to go among her people.

Islington retained a few of its Elizabethan houses to

* In Jermyn-street, Haymarket, was the One Tun Tavern, a haunt of Sheridan's; and, upon the site of "the Little Theatre," is the Café de l'Europe.

our times; and its rich dairies were of like antiquity: in the entertainment given to Queen Elizabeth at Kenilworth Castle, in 1575, the Squier Minstrel of Middlesex glorifies Islington with the motto, "*Lac caseus infans ;*" and it is still noted for its cow-keepers. It was once as famous for its cheese-cakes as Chelsea for its buns; and among its other notabilities were custards and stewed "pruans," its mineral spa and its ducking-ponds; Ball's Pond dates from the time of Charles I. At the lower end of Islington, in 1611, were eight inns, principally supported by summer visitors :

> "Hogsdone, *Islington*, and Tothnam Court,
> For cakes and creame had then no small resort."
> Wither's *Britain's Remembrancer*, 1628.

Among the old inns and public-houses were the Crown apparently of the reign of Henry VII., and the Old Queen's Head of about the same date:

> "The Queen's Head and Crown in Islington town,
> Bore, for its brewing, the brightest renown."

Near the Green, the Duke's Head, was kept by Topham, "the strong man of Islington;" in Frog-lane, the Barley-mow, where George Morland painted; at the Old Parr's Head, in Upper-street, Henderson the tragedian first acted; the Three Hats, near the turnpike, was taken down in 1839; and of the Angel, originally a galleried inn, a drawing may be seen at the present inn. Timber gables and rudely-carved brackets are occasionally to be seen in house-fronts; also here and there an old "house of entertainment," which, with the little remaining of "the Green," remind one of Islington village.

The Old Queen's Head was the finest specimen in the neighbourhood of the domestic architecture of the reign of Henry VII. It consisted of three storeys, projecting over each other in front, with bay-windows supported by brackets, and figures carved in wood. The entrance was by a central porch, supported by caryatides of oak, bearing Ionic scrolls. To the left was the Oak Parlour, with carved mantelpiece, of chest-like form; and caryatid jambs, supporting a slab sculptured with the story of Diana and Actæon. The ceiling was a shield, bearing J. M. in a glory, with cherubim, two heads of Roman emperors, with fish, flowers, and other figures, within wreathed borders, with bosses of acorns.

White Conduit House was first built in the fields, in the reign of Charles I., and was named from a stone conduit, 1641, which supplied the Charterhouse with water by a leaden pipe. The tavern was originally a small ale and cake house : Sir William Davenant describes a City wife going to the fields to " sop her cake in milke ;" and Goldsmith speaks of tea-drinking parties here with hot-rolls and butter. White Conduit rolls were nearly as famous as Chelsea buns. The Wheel Pond close by was a noted place for duck-hunting.

In May, 1760, a poetical description of White Conduit House appeared in the *Gentleman's Magazine*. A description of the old place, in 1774, presents a general picture of the tea-garden of that period : " It is formed into walks, prettily disposed. At the end of the principal one is a painting which seems to render it (the walk) in appearance longer than it really is. In the centre of the garden is a fish-pond. There are boxes for company, curiously cut into hedges, adorned with Flemish and other paintings. There are two handsome tea-rooms, and several inferior ones." To these were added a new dancing and tea-saloon, called the Apollo Room. In 1826, the gardens were opened as a minor Vauxhall; and here the charming vocalist, Mrs. Bland, last sang in public. In 1832, the original tavern was taken down, and rebuilt upon a much larger plan : in its principal room 2000 persons could dine. In 1849, these premises were also taken down, the tavern rebuilt upon a smaller scale, and the garden-ground let on building leases.

Cricket was played here by the White Conduit Club, as early as 1799; and one of its attendants, Thomas Lord, subsequently established the Marylebone Club.

White Conduit House was for some years kept by Mr. Christopher Bartholomew, at one time worth 50,000*l.* He had some fortunate hits in the State Lottery, and celebrated his good fortune by a public breakfast in his gardens. He was known to spend upwards of 2000 guineas a day for insurance : fortune forsook him, and ·he passed the latter years of his life in great poverty, partly subsisting on charity. But his gambling propensity led him, in 1807, to purchase with a friend a sixteenth of a lottery-ticket, which was drawn a prize of 20,000*l.*, with his moiety of which he purchased a small annuity, which he soon sold, and died in distress, in 1809.

Bagnigge Wells, on the banks of the Fleet brook, between Clerkenwell and old St. Pancras church, was another tavern of this class. We remember its concert-room and organ, its grottoes, fountain and fishpond, its trim trees, its grotesque costumed figures, and its bust of Nell Gwynne to support the tradition that she had a house here.

A comedy of the seventeenth century has its scene

laid at the Saracen's Head, an old hostelrie, which in
Queen Mary's reign had been hallowed by secret Pro-
testant devotion, and stood between River Lane and the
City Road.

Highbury Barn, upon the site of the barn of the
monks of Canonbury, was another noted tavern. Nearly
opposite Canonbury Tower are the remains of a last-
century tea-garden; and in Barnsbury is a similar relic.
And on the entrance of a coppice of trees is Hornsey
Wood House, a tavern with a delightful prospect.

Islington abounds in chalybeate springs, resembling
the Tunbridge Wells water; one of which was redis-
covered in 1683, in the garden of Sadler's music-house,
subsequently Sadler's Wells Theatre; and at the Sir
Hugh Myddelton's Head tavern was formerly a conver-
sation-picture with twenty-eight portraits of the Sadler's
Wells Club. In Spa Fields, was held " Gooseberry
Fair," where the stalls of gooseberry-fool vied with the
"threepenny tea-booths," and the beer at " my Lord.
Cobham's Head," which denotes the site of the mansion
of Sir John Oldcastle, the Wickliffite, burnt in 1417.

* Canonbury Tavern was in the middle of the last century
a small ale-house. It was taken by a Mr. Lane, who had been
a private soldier : he improved the house, but its celebrity was
gained by the widow Sutton, who kept the place from 1785 to
1808, and built new rooms, and laid out the bowling-green and
tea-gardens. An Assembly was first established here in the year
1810. Nearly the entire premises, which then occupied about
four acres, were situated within the old park wall of the
Priory of St. Bartholomew ; it formed, indeed, a part of the
eastern side of the house ; the ancient fish-pond was also connected with the grounds. The Tavern has been rebuilt.

COPENHAGEN HOUSE.

This old suburban tavern, which stood in Copenhagen Fields, Islington, was cleared away in forming the site of the New Cattle Market.

The house had a curious history. In the time of Nelson, the historian of Islington (1811), it was a house of considerable resort, the situation affording a fine prospect over the western part of the metropolis. Adjoining the house was a small garden, furnished with seats and tables for the accommodation of company; and a fives ground. The principal part of Copenhagen House, although much altered, was probably as old as the time of James I., and is traditionally said to have derived its name from having been the residence of a Danish prince or ambassador during the Great Plague of 1665. Hone, in 1838, says: "It is certain that Copenhagen House has been licensed for the sale of beer, wine, and spirits, upwards of a century; and for refreshments, and as a tea-house, with garden and ground for skittles and Dutch pins, it has been greatly resorted to by Londoners." The date of this hostelry must be older than stated by Hone. Cunningham says: "A public-house or tavern in the parish of Islington, is called Coopenhagen in the map before Bishop Gibson's edition of Camden, 1695."

About the year 1770 this house was kept by a person named Harrington. At his decease the business was continued by his widow, wherein she was assisted for several years by a young woman from Shropshire. This

female assistant afterwards married a person named
Tomes, from whom Hone got much information respecting Copenhagen-house.   In 1780—the time of
the London Riots—a body of the rioters passed on their
way to attack the seat of Lord Mansfield at Caen-wood ;
happily, they passed by without doing any damage, but
Mrs. Harrington and her maid were so much alarmed
that they dispatched a man to Justice Hyde, who sent a
party of soldiers to garrison the place, where they remained
until the riots were ended.   From this spot the view of the
nightly conflagrations in the metropolis must have been
terrific.   Mrs. Tomes says she saw nine fires at one
time.   On the New Year's-day previous to this, Mrs.
Harrington was not so fortunate.   After the family had
retired to rest, a party of burglars forced the kitchen window, and mistaking the salt-box, in the chimney corner,
for a man's head, fired a ball through it.   They then ran
upstairs with a dark lantern, tied the servants, burst
the lower panel of Mrs. Harrington's room door—while
she secreted 50l. between her bed and the mattresses
—and three of them rushed to her bed-side, armed
with a cutlass, crowbar, and a pistol, while a fourth kept
watch outside.   They demanded her money, and as she
denied that she had any, they wrenched her drawers
open with the crowbar, refusing to use the keys she
offered to them.   In these they found about 10l. belonging to her daughter, a little child, whom they threatened
to murder unless she ceased crying ; while they packed
up all the plate, linen, and clothes, which they carried
off.   They then went into the cellar, set all the ale barrels running, broke the necks of the wine bottles, spilt
the other liquors, and slashed a round of beef with their
cutlasses.   From this wanton destruction they returned

to the kitchen, where they ate, drank, and sung; and eventually frightened Mrs. Harrington into delivering up the 50*l.* she had secreted, and it was with difficulty she escaped with her life. Rewards were offered by Government and the parish of Islington for the apprehension of the robbers; and in May following one of them, named Clarkson, was discovered, and hopes of mercy tendered to him if he would discover his accomplices. This man was a watchmaker of Clerkenwell; the other three were tradesmen. They were tried and executed, and Clarkson pardoned. He was, however, afterwards executed for another robbery. In a sense, this robbery was fortunate to Mrs. Harrington. A subscription was raised, which more than covered the loss, and the curiosity of the Londoners induced them to throng to the scene of the robbery. So great was the increase of business that it became necessary to enlarge the premises. Soon afterwards the house was celebrated for fives-playing. This game was our old *hand tennis,* and is a very ancient game. This last addition was almost accidental. " I made the first fives-ball," says Mrs. Tomes, " that was ever thrown up against Copenhagen House. One Hickman, a butcher at Highgate, a countryman of mine, called, and, seeing me counting, we talked about our country sports, and, amongst the rest, *fives.* I told him we'd have a game some day. I laid down the stone myself, and against he came again made a ball. I struck the ball the first blow, he gave it the second—and so we played—and as there was company, they liked the sport, and it got talked of." This was the beginning of fives-play which became so famous at Copenhagen House.

TOPHAM, THE STRONG MAN, AND HIS TAVERNS.

In Upper-street, Islington, was formerly a house with the sign of the Duke's Head, at the south-east corner of Gadd's Row, (now St. Alban's Place), which was remarkable, towards the middle of the last century, on account of its landlord, Thomas Topham, "the strong man of Islington." He was brought up to the trade of a carpenter, but abandoned it soon after his apprenticeship had expired; and about the age of twenty-four became the host of the Red Lion, near the old Hospital of St. Luke, in which house he failed. When he had attained his full growth, his stature was about five feet ten inches, and he soon began to give proof of his superior strength and muscular power. The first public exhibition of his extraordinary strength was that of pulling against a horse, lying upon his back, and placing his feet against the dwarf wall that divided Upper and Lower Moorfields.

By the strength of his fingers, he rolled up a very strong and large pewter dish, which was placed among the curiosities of the British Museum, marked near the edge, " April, 3, 1737, Thomas Topham, of London, carpenter, rolled up this dish (made of the hardest pewter) by the strength of his hands, in the presence of Dr. John Desaguliers," etc. He broke seven or eight pieces of a tobacco-pipe, by the force of his middle finger, having laid them on his first and third fingers. Having thrust the bowl of a strong tobacco-pipe under his garter, his legs being bent, he broke it to pieces by the tendons of his hams, without altering the position of his legs. Another bowl of this kind he broke between his first and second finger, by pressing them together sideways. He took an iron kitchen poker, about a yard long, and three inches round, and bent it nearly to a right angle, by striking upon his bare left arm between the elbow and the wrist. Holding the ends of a poker of like size in his hands, and the middle of it against the back of his neck, he brought both extremities of it together before him; and, what was yet more difficult, pulled it almost straight again. He broke a rope of two inches in circumference; though, from his awkward manner, he was obliged to exert four times more strength than was necessary. He lifted a rolling stone of eight hundred pounds' weight with his hands only, standing in a frame above it, and taking hold of a chain fastened thereto.

But his grand feat was performed in Coldbath Fields, May 28, 1741, in commemoration of the taking of Porto Bello, by Admiral Vernon. At this time Topham was landlord of the Apple-tree, nearly facing the entrance to the House of Correction; here he exhibited the exploit of lifting three hogsheads of water, weighing one thousand eight hundred and thirty-one pounds: he also pulled against one horse, and would have succeeded against two, or even four, had he taken a proper position; but in pulling against two, he was jerked from his seat, and had one of his knees much hurt. Admiral Vernon was present at the above exhibition, in the presence of thousands of spectators; and there is a large print of the strange scene.

Topham subsequently removed to Hog-lane, Shore-

ditch. His wife proved unfaithful to him, which so distressed him that he stabbed her, and so mutilated himself that he died, in the flower of his age.

Many years since, there were several signs in the
metropolis, illustrative of Topham's strength : the last
was one in East Smithfield, where he was represented as
" the Strong Man pulling against two Horses."

THE CASTLE TAVERN, HOLBORN.

This noted tavern, described by Strype, a century and
a half ago, as a house of considerable trade, has been, in
our time, the head-quarters of the Prize Ring, kept by
two of its heroes, Tom Belcher and Tom Spring. Here
was instituted the Daffy Club; and the long room was
adorned with portraits of pugilistic heroes, including
Jem Belcher, Burke, Jackson, Tom Belcher, old Joe
Ward, Dutch Sam, Gregson, Humphreys, Mendoza,
Cribb, Molyneux, Gulley, Randall, Turner, Martin,
Harmer, Spring, Neat, Hickman, Painter, Scroggins,
Tom Owen, etc. ; and among other sporting prints, the
famous dog, Trusty, the present of Lord Camelford to
Jem Belcher, and the victor in fifty battles.   In *Cribb's
Memorial to Congress* is this picture of the great room:—

> " Lent Friday night a bang-up set
> Of milling blades at Belcher's met,
> All high-bred heroes of the Ring,
>   Whose very gammon would delight one ;
> Who, nurs'd beneath the Fancy's wing,
>   Show all her feathers but the white one.

> Brave Tom, the Champion, with an air
> Almost Corinthian, took the chair,
> And kept the coves in quiet tune,
>   By showing such a fist of mutton
> As on a point of order soon
>   Would take the shine from Speaker Sutton.
> And all the lads look'd gay and bright,
>   And gin and genius flashed about;
> And whosoe'er grew unpolite,
>   The well-bred Champion serv'd him out."

In 1828, Belcher retired from the tavern and was succeeded by Tom Spring (Thomas Winter), the immediate successor of Cribb, as Champion of England. Spring prospered at the Castle many years. He died August 17, 1851, in his fifty-sixth year; he was highly respected, and had received several testimonials of public and private esteem; among which were these pieces of plate:—1. The Manchester Cup, presented in 1821. 2. The Hereford Cup, 1823. 3. A noble tankard and a purse, value upwards of five hundred pounds. 4. A silver goblet, from Spring's early patron, Mr. Sant.

Spring's figure was an extremely fine one, and his face and forehead most remarkable. His brow had something of the Greek Jupiter in it, expressing command, energy, determination, and cool courage. Its severity was relieved by the lower part of his countenance, the features of which denoted mildness and playfulness. His actual height was five feet eleven inches and a half; but he could stretch his neck so as to make his admeasurement more than six feet.

MARYLEBONE AND PADDINGTON TAVERNS.

Smith, in his very amusing *Book for a Rainy Day,* tells us that in 1772, beyond Portland Chapel, (now St. Paul's,) the highway was irregular, with here and there a bank of separation; and having crossed the New Road, there was a turnstile, at the entrance of a meadow leading to a little old public-house—the Queen's Head and Artichoke—an odd association: the sign was much weather-beaten, though perhaps once a tolerably good portrait of Queen Elizabeth: the house was reported to have been kept by one of Her Majesty's gardeners.

A little beyond was another turnstile opening also into the fields, over which was a walk to the Jew's Harp Tavern and Tea Gardens. It consisted of a large upper room, ascended by an outside staircase for the accommodation of the company on ball-nights. There were a semicircular enclosure of boxes for tea and ale drinkers; and tables and seats for the smokers, guarded by deal-board soldiers between every box, painted in proper colours. There were trap-ball and tennis grounds, and skittle-grounds. South of the tea-gardens were summer-houses and gardens, where the tenant might be seen on Sunday evening, in a bright scarlet waistcoat, ruffled shirt, and silver shoe-buckles, comfortably taking his tea with his family, honouring a Seven Dials friend with a nod on his peregrination to the famed Wells of Kilburn. Such was the suburban rural enjoyment of a century since on the borders of Marylebone Park.

There is a capital story told of Mr. Speaker Onslow, who, when he could escape from the heated atmosphere of the House of Commons, in his long service of thirty-three years, used to retire to the Jew's Harp. He dressed himself in plain attire, and preferred taking his seat in the chimney-corner of the kitchen, where he took part in the passing joke, and ordinary concerns of the landlord, his family and customers! He continued this practice for a year or two, and thus ingratiated himself with his host and his family, who, not knowing his name, called him "the gentleman," but from his familiar manners, treated him as one of themselves. It happened, however, one day, that the landlord of the Jew's Harp was walking along Parliament-street, when he met the Speaker, in his state-coach, going up with an address to the throne ; and looking narrowly at the chief personage, he was astonished and confounded at recognising the features of the gentleman, his constant customer. He hurried home and communicated the extraordinary intelligence to his wife and family, all of whom were disconcerted at the liberties which, at different times, they had taken with so important a person. In the evening, Mr. Onslow came as usual to the Jew's Harp, with his holiday face and manners, and prepared to take his seat, but found everything in a state of peculiar preparation, and the manners of the landlord and his wife changed from indifference and familiarity to form and obsequiousness : the children were not allowed to climb upon him, and pull his wig as heretofore, and the servants were kept at a distance. He, however, took no notice of the change, but, finding that his name and rank had by some means been discovered, he paid his reckoning, civilly took his departure, and neve visited the house afterwards.

The celebrated Speaker is buried in the family vault
of the Onslows, at Merrow; and in Trinity Church,
Guildford, is a memorial of him—"the figure of the
deceased in a *Roman habit*," and he is resting upon
volumes of the Votes and Journals of the House of
Commons. The monument is overloaded with inscrip-
tions and armorial displays : we suspect that " the
gentleman" of the Jews' Harp chimney-corner would
rather that such indiscriminate ostentation had been
spared, especially " the Roman habit." If we remember
rightly, Speaker Onslow presented to the people of
Merrow, for their church, a cedar-wood pulpit, which
the Churchwardens ordered to be *painted white!*

To return to the taverns. Wilson, our great landscape-painter, was fond of playing at skittles, and frequented the Green Man public-house, in the New-road,
at the end of Norton-street, originally known under the
appellation of the " Farthing Pye-house;" where bits
of mutton were put into a crust shaped like a pie, and
actually sold for a farthing. This house was kept by a
facetious man named Price, of whom there is a mezzo-
tinto portrait : he was an excellent salt-box player, and
frequently accompanied the famous Abel, when playing
on the violoncello. Wilkes was a frequenter of this
house to procure votes for Middlesex, as it was visited
by many opulent freeholders.

The Mother Redcap, at Kentish Town, was a house
of no small terror to travellers in former times. It
has been stated that Mother Redcap was the " Mother
Damnable" of Kentish Town; and that it was at her
house that the notorious Moll Cutpurse, the highway-
woman of the time of Oliver Cromwell, dismounted,
and frequently lodged.

Kentish Town has had some of its old taverns re-built. Here was the Castle Tavern, which had a Per-pendicular stone chimney-piece; the house was taken down in 1849: close to its southern wall was a syca-more planted by Lord Nelson, when a boy, at the en-trance to his uncle's cottage; the tree has been spared. Opposite were the old Assembly-rooms, taken down in 1852 : here was a table with an inscription by an invalid, who recovered his health by walking to this spot every morning to take his breakfast in front of the house.

Bowling-greens were also among the celebrities of Marylebone : where, says the grave John Locke (*Diary*, 1679), a curious stranger " may see several persons of quality bowling, two or three times a week, all the summer." The bowling-green of the Rose of Nor-mandy Tavern and Gaming-house in High-street is supposed to be that referred to in Lady Mary Wortley Montagu's memorable line ; and it is one of the scenes of Captain Macheath's debaucheries, in Gay's *Beggar's Opera.*

The Rose was built some 230 years ago, and was the oldest house in Marylebone parish : it was origi-nally a detached building, used as a house of entertain-ment in connection with the bowling-green at the back ; and in 1659 the place was described as a square brick wall, set with fruit-trees, gravel walks, and the bowling-green ; " all, except the first, double set with quickset hedges, full-grown, and kept in excellent order, and in-dented like town walls." In a map of the Duke of Portland's estate, of 1708, there are shown two bowl-ing-greens, one near the top of High-street, and abut-ting on the grounds of the Old Manor House ; the

other at the back of this house : in connection with the
latter was the Rose Tavern, once much frequented by
persons of the first rank, but latterly in much disre-
pute, and supposed to be referred to by Pennant, who,
when speaking of the Duke of Buckingham's minute
description of the house afterwards the Queen's Palace,
says : " He has omitted his constant visits to the noted
Gaming-house at Marybone ; the place of assemblage
of all the infamous sharpers of the time ;" to whom
his Grace always gave a dinner at the conclusion of
the season ; and his parting toast was, " May as many
of us as remain unhanged next spring meet here
again."

These Bowling-greens were afterwards incorporated
with the well-known Marylebone Gardens, upon the site
of which are now built Beaumont-street, part of Devon-
shire-street, and Devonshire-place. The principal entrance was in High-street. Pepys was here in 1688 :
" Then we abroad to Marrowbone, and there walked in
the Gardens : the first time I was ever there, and a
pretty place it is." In the *London Gazette,* 1691, we
read of " Long's Bowling-green, at the Rose, at Marylebone, half a mile distant from London." The Gardens were at first opened gratis to all classes ; after the
addition of the bowling-greens, the company became
more select, by one shilling entrance-money being
charged, an equivalent being allowed in viands.

An engraving of 1761 shows the Gardens in their
fullest splendour : the centre walk had rows of trees,
with irons for the lamps in the stems ; on either side,
latticed alcoves ; and on the right, the bow-fronted
orchestra with balustrades, supported by columns ; with
a projecting roof, to keep the musicians and singers free

from rain; on the left is a room for balls and suppers.
In 1763, the Gardens were taken by Lowe, the singer;
he kept them until 1769, when he conveyed the
property by assignment, to his creditors; the deed we
remember to have seen in Mr. Sampson Hodgkinson's
Collection at Acton Green: from it we learn that the
premises of Rysbrack, the sculptor, were formerly part
of the Gardens. Nan Cattley and Signor Storace
were among the singers. James Hook, father of Theodore Hook, composed many songs for the Gardens;
and Dr. Arne, catches and glees; and under his direction was played Handel's music, followed by fireworks;
and in 1772, a model-picture of Mount Etna, in erup-
tion. Burlettas from Shakspeare were recited here in
1774. In 1775, Baddeley, the comedian, gave here his
Modern Magic Lantern, including Punch's Election;
next, George Saville Carey his Lecture on Mimicry; and
in 1776, fantoccini, sleight of hand, and representa-
tions of the Boulevards at Paris and Pyramids of Egypt.

Chatterton wrote for the Gardens *The Revenge*, a
burletta, the manuscript of which, together with Chatterton's receipt, given to Henslow, the proprietor of the
Gardens, for the amount paid for the drama, was found
by Mr. Upcott, at a cheesemonger's shop, in the City;
it was published, but its authenticity was at the time
doubted by many eminent critics. (*Crypt*, November,
1827.)

Paddington was long noted for its old Taverns. The
White Lion, Edgware-road, dates 1524, the year when
hops were first imported. At the Red Lion, near the
Harrow-road, tradition says, Shakspeare acted; and
another Red Lion, formerly near the Harrow-road bridge
over the Bourn, is described in an inquisition of Ed-

ward VI. In this road is also an ancient Pack-horse; and the Wheatsheaf, Edgware-road, was a favourite resort of Ben Jonson.*

Kilburn Wells, a noted tea-drinking tavern and garden, sprang up from the fame of the spring of mineral water there.

Bayswater had, within memory, its tea-garden taverns, the most extensive of which were the " physic gardens " of Sir John Hill, who here cultivated his medicinal plants, and prepared from them his tinctures, essences, etc. The ground is now the site of noble mansions. The Bayswater springs, reservoirs, and conduits, in olden times, brought here thousands of pleasure-seekers; as did Shepherd's Bush, with its rural name. Acton, with its wells of mineral water, about the middle of the last century, were in high repute; the assembly-room was then a place of great fashionable resort, but on its decline was converted into tenements. The two noted taverns, the Hats, at Ealing, were much resorted to in the last century, and early in the present.

KENSINGTON AND BROMPTON TAVERNS.

Kensington, on the Great Western road, formerly had its large inns. The coffee-house west of the Palace Road was much resorted to as a tea-drinking place, handy to the gardens.

Kensington, to this day, retains its memorial of the residence of Addison at Holland House, from the period

* Robins's *Paddington, Past and Present.*

of his marriage. The thoroughfare from the Kensington Road to Notting Hill is named Addison Road. At Holland House are shown the table upon which the Essayist wrote; his reputed portrait; and the chamber in which he died.

It has been commonly stated and believed that Addison's marriage with the Countess of Warwick was a most unhappy match; and that, to drown his sorrow, and escape from his termagant wife, he would often slip away from Holland House to the White Horse Inn, which stood at the corner of Lord Holland's Lane, and on the site of the present Holland Arms Inn. Here Addison would enjoy his favourite dish of a fillet of veal, his bottle, and perhaps a friend. He is also stated to have had another way of showing his spite to the Countess, by withdrawing the company from Button's Coffee-house, set up by her Ladyship's old servant. Moreover, Addison is accused of having taught Dryden to drink, so as to hasten his end : how doubly "glorious" old John must have been in his cups. Pope also states that Addison kept such late hours that he was compelled to quit his company. But both these anecdotes are from Spence, and are doubted; and they have done much injury to Addison's character. Miss Aikin, in her *Life of Addison*, endeavours to invalidate these imputations, by reference to the sobriety of Addison's early life. He had a remarkably sound constitution, and could, probably, sit out his companions, and stop short of actual intoxication; indeed, it was said that he was only warmed into the utmost brilliancy of table conversation, by the time that Steele had rendered himself nearly unfit for it. Miss Aikin refers to the tone and temper, the correctness of taste and judgment of Ad-

dison's writings, in proof of his sobriety; and doubts
whether a man, himself stained with the vice of intoxication, would have dared to stigmatize it as in his 569th
Spectator. The idea that domestic unhappiness led him
to contract this dreadful habit, is then repudiated; and
the opposite conclusion supported by the bequest of his
whole property to his lady. "Is it conceivable," asks
Miss Aikin, "that any man would thus 'give and hazard
all he had,' even to his precious only child, in compliment to a woman who should have rendered his last
years miserable by her pride and petulance, and have
driven him out from his home, to pass his comfortless
evenings in the gross indulgence of a tavern." Our
amiable biographer, therefore, equally discredits the
stories of Addison's unhappy marriage, and of his intem-
perate habits.

The White Horse was taken down many years since.
The tradition of its being the tavern frequented by Addison, was common in Kensington when Faulkner
printed his *History,* in 1820.

There was a celebrated visitor at Holland House who,
many years later, partook of "the gross indulgence."
Sheridan was often at Holland House in his latter days;
and Lady Holland told Moore that he used to take a
bottle of wine and a book up to bed with him always;
the *former* alone intended for use. In the morning, he
breakfasted in bed, and had a little brandy or rum in
his tea or coffee; made his appearance between one or
two, and pretending important business, used to set out
for town, but regularly stopped at the Adam and Eve
public-house for a dram, and there ran up a long bill,
which Lord Holland had to pay. This was the old roadside inn, long since taken down.

When the building for the Great Exhibition of 1851 was in course of construction, Alexis Soyer, the celebrated cook from the Reform Club, hired for a term, Gore House, and converted Lady Blessington's well-appointed mansion and grounds into a sort of large *restaurant*, which our poetical cook named "the Symposium." The house was ill planned for the purpose, and underwent much grotesque decoration and *bizarre* embellishment, to meet Soyer's somewhat unorthodox taste; for his chief aim was to show the public "something they had never seen before." The designation of the place—Symposium—led to a dangerous joke: "Ah! I understand," said a wag, "impose-on-'em." Soyer was horrified, and implored the joker not to name his witticism upon 'Change in the City, but he disregarded the *restaurateur's* request, and the pun was often repeated between Cornhill and Kensington.

In the reconstruction and renovation of the place, Soyer was assisted by his friend Mr. George Augustus Sala, who, some years after, when he edited *Temple Bar*, described in his very clever manner, what he saw and thought, whilst for "many moons he slept, and ate, and drank, and walked, and talked, in Gore House, surrounded by the very strangest of company":—

"From February to mid-March a curious medley of carpenters, scene-painters, plumbers, glaziers, gardeners, town-travellers for ironmongers, wine-merchants, and drapers, held high carnival in the place. By-and-by came dukes and duchesses, warriors and statesmen, ambassadors, actors, artists, authors, quack-doctors, ballet-dancers, journalists, Indian princes, Irish members, nearly all that was odd and all that was distinguished, native or foreign, in London town. They wandered up and down the staircases, and in and out of the saloons, quizzing, and talking, and laughing, and flirting sometimes in sly corners. They signed their names in a big book, blazing with gold and morocco, which lay among shavings on a carpenter's bench in the library. Where is that wondrous collection of autographs, that *Libro d'Oro*, now? Mr. Keeley's signature followed suit to that of Lord Carlisle. Fanny Cerito inscribed her pretty name, with that of 'St. Leon' added, next to the signature of the magnificent Duchess of Sutherland. I was at work with the whitewashers on the stairs, and saw Semiramis sweep past. Baron Brunnow met Prof. Holloway on the neutral ground of a page of autographs. Jules Janin's name came close to the laborious *paraphe* of an eminent pugilist. Members of the American Congress found themselves in juxtaposition with Frederick Douglas and the dark gentleman who came as ambassador from Hayti. I remember one Sunday, during that strange time, seeing Mr. Disraeli, Madame Doche, the Author of *Vanity Fair*, a privy councillor, a Sardinian attaché, the Marquis of Normanby, the late Mr. Flexmore the clown, the Editor of *Punch*, and the Wizard of the North, all pressing to enter the whilom boudoir of the Blessington.

"Meanwhile, I and the whitewashers were hard at work. We summoned upholsterers, carvers and gilders to our aid. Troops of men in white caps and jackets began to flit about the lower regions. The gardeners were smothering themselves with roses in the adjacent parterres. Marvellous erections began to rear their heads in the grounds of Gore House. The wilderness had become, not exactly a paradise, but a kind of Garden of Epicurus, in which some of the features of that classical bower of bliss were blended with those of the kingdom of Cockaigne, where pigs are said to run about ready roasted with silver knives and forks stuck in them, and crying, 'Come, eat us; our crackling is delicious, and the sage-and-onions with which we are stuffed distils an odour as sweet as that of freshly gathered violets.' Vans laden with wines, with groceries, with plates and dishes, with glasses and candelabra, and with bales of calico, and still more calico, were perpetually arriving at Gore House. The carriages of the nobility and gentry were blocked up among railway goods-vans and Parcels Delivery carts. The authorities of the place were obliged to send for a detective policeman to mount permanent guard at the Gore, for the swell-mob had found us out, and flying squadrons of felonry hung on the skirts of our distinguished visitors, and harassed their fobs fearfully. Then we sent forth advertisements to the daily papers, and legions of mothers, grandmothers, and aunts brought myriads of newly-washed boys; some chubby and curly-haired, some lanky and straight-locked, from whom we selected the comelier youths, and put them into picturesque garbs, confected for us by Mr. Nicoll. Then we held a competitive examination of pretty girls; and from those who obtained the largest number of marks (of respect and admiration) we chose a bevy of Hebes, whose rosy lips, black eyes and blue eyes, fair hair and dark hair, very nearly drove me crazy in the spring days of 1851.

" And by the end of April we had completely metamorphosed Gore House. I am sure that poor Lady Blessington would not have known her coquettish villa again had she visited it; and I am afraid she would not have been much gratified to see that which the upholsterers, the whitewashers, the hangers of calico, and your humble servant, had wrought. As for the venerable Mr. Wilberforce, who, I believe, occupied Gore House some years before Lady Blessington's tenancy, he would have held up his hands in pious horror to see the changes we had made. A madcap masquerade of bizarre taste and queer fancies had turned Gore House completely inside out. In honest truth, we had played the very dickens with it. The gardens were certainly magnificent; and there was a sloping terrace of flowers in the form of a gigantic shell, and literally crammed with the choicest roses, which has seldom, I believe, been rivalled in ornamental gardening. But the house itself! The library had been kindly dealt by, save that from the ceiling were suspended a crowd of quicksilvered glass globes, which bobbed about like the pendent ostrich-eggs in an Eastern mosque. There was a room called the ' Floriana,' with walls and ceiling fluted with blue and white calico, and stuck all over with spangles. There was the ' Doriana,' also in calico, pink and white, and approached by a portal called the ' door of the dungeon of mystery,' which was studded with huge nails, and garnished with fetters in the well-known Newgate fashion. Looking towards the garden were the Alhambra Terrace and the Venetian Bridge. The back drawing-room was the Night of Stars, or the *Rêverie de l'Etoile polaire ;* the night being represented by a cerulean ceiling painted over with fleecy clouds, and the firmament by hangings of blue gauze spangled with stars cut out of silver-foil paper! Then there was the vestibule of Jupiter Tonans, the walls covered with a salmagundi of the architecture of all nations, from the Acropolis to the Pyramids of Egypt, from Temple Bar to the Tower of Babel. The dining-room became the Hall of Jewels, or the *Salon des Larmes de Danaë*, and the ' Shower of Gems,' with a grand arabesque perforated ceiling, gaudy in gilding and distemper colours. Upstairs there was a room fitted up as a Chinese pagoda, another as an Italian cottage overlooking a vineyard and the Lake of Como ; another as a cavern of ice in the Arctic regions, with sham columns imitating icebergs, and a stuffed white fox—bought cheap at a sale—in the chimney. The grand staircase belonged to me, and I painted its walls with a grotesque nightmare of portraits of people I had never seen, and hundreds more upon whom I had never set eyes save in the print-shops, till I saw the originals grinning, or scowling, or planted in blank amazement before the pictorial libels on the walls.

" In the gardens Sir Charles Fox built for us a huge barrack of wood, glass, and iron, which we called the ' Baronial Hall,' and which we filled with pictures and lithographs, and flags and calico, in our own peculiar fashion. We hired a large grazing-meadow at the back of the gardens, from a worthy Kensington cowkeeper, and having fitted up another barrack at one end of it, called it the ' Pré D'Orsay.' We memorialized the Middlesex magistrates, and, after a great deal of trouble, got a licence enabling us to sell wines and spirits, and to have music and dancing if we so chose. We sprinkled tents and alcoves all over our gardens, and built a gipsies' cavern, and a stalactite pagoda with double windows, in which gold and silver fish floated, And finally, having engaged an army of pages, cooks, scullions, waiters, barmaids, and clerks of the kitchen, we opened this monstrous place on the first of May, 1851, and bade all the world come and dine at SOYER'S SYMPOSIUM."

However, the ungrateful public disregarded the invitation, and poor Alexis Soyer is believed to have lost 4000*l.* by this enterprise. He died a few years after, at the early age of fifty. His friend Mr. Sala has said of him with true pathos :—" He was a vain man ; but he was good and kind and charitable. There are paupers and beggars *even among French cooks,* and Alexis always had his pensioners and his alms-duns, to whom his hand was ever open. He was but a cook, but he was my dear and good friend."

We remember to have heard Soyer say of the writer of these truthful words, in reply to an inquiry as to the artist of the figures upon the staircase-walls, " He is a very clever fellow, of whom you will hear much,"—a prediction which has been fully verified.

Brompton, with its two centuries of Nursery fame, lasted to our time; southward, among " the Groves," were the Florida, Hoop and Toy, and other tea-garden taverns; there remains the Swan, with its bowling-green.

KNIGHTSBRIDGE TAVERNS.

Knightsbridge was formerly a noted " Spring-Garden," with several taverns, of gay and questionable character. Some of the older houses have historical interest. The Rose and Crown, formerly the Oliver Cromwell, has been licensed above three hundred years. It is said to be the house which sheltered Wyat, while his unfortunate Kentish followers rested on the adjacent green. A tradition of the locality also is that Cromwell's body-guard was once quartered here, the probability of which is carefully examined in Davis's *Memorials of Knightsbridge.* The house has been much modernized of late years; "but," says Mr. Davis, "enough still remains in its peculiar chimneys, oval-shaped windows, the low rooms, large yard, and extensive stabling, with the galleries above, and office-like places beneath, to testify to its antiquity and former importance." The Rising Sun, hard by, is a seventeenth century red-brick house, which formerly had much carved work in the rooms, and a good staircase remains.

The Fox and Bull is the third house that has existed under the same sign. The first was Elizabethan with carved and panelled rooms, ornamented ceiling; and it was not until 1799, that the immense fireplaces and dog-irons were removed for stove-grates. This house was pulled down about 1836, and the second immediately built upon its site; this stood till the Albert-gate improvements made the removal of the tavern business to its present situation.*

The original Fox and Bull is traditionally said to have been used by Queen Elizabeth on her visits to Lord

* Stolen Marriages were the source of the old Knightsbridge tavern success; and ten books of marriages and baptisms solemnized here, 1658 to 1752, are preserved. Trinity Chapel, the old edifice, was one of the places where these irregular marriages were solemnized. Thus, in Shadwell's *Sullen Lovers*, Lovell is made to say, "Let's dally no longer; there is a person at Knightsbridge that yokes all stray people together; we'll to him, he'll dispatch us presently, and send us away as lovingly as any two fools that ever yet were condemned to marriage." Some of the entries in this marriage register are suspicious enough—" secrecy for life," or " great secrecy," or " secret for fourteen years " being appended to the names. Mr. Davis, in his *Memorials of Knightsbridge*, was the first to exhume from this document the name of the adventuress " Mrs. Mary Aylif," whom Sir Samuel Morland married as his fourth wife, in 1697. Readers of Pepys will remember how pathetically Morland

Burghley, at Brompton. Its curious sign is said to be the only one of the kind existing. Here for a long time was maintained that Queen Anne style of society, where persons of parts and reputation were to be met with in public rooms. Captain Corbet was for a long time its head; Mr. Shaw, of the War Office, supplied the *London Gazette;* and Mr. Harris, of Covent Garden, his play-bills. Sir Joshua Reynolds is said to have been occasionally a visitor; as also Sir W. Wynn, the patron of Ryland. George Morland, too, was frequently here. The sign was once painted by Sir Joshua, and hung till 1807, when it was blown down and destroyed in a storm. The house is referred to in the *Tatler,* No. 259.

At about where William-street joins Lowndes-square was " an excellent Spring Garden." Among the entries of the Virtuosi, or St. Luke's Club, established by Vandyke, is the following : " Paid and spent at Spring Gardens, by Knightsbridge, forfeiture, 3*l.* 15*s.*" Pepys being at Kensington, " on a frolic," June 16, 1664, "lay in his drawers, and stockings, and waistcoat, till five of the clock, and so up, walked to Knightsbridge, and there eat a mess of cream, and so to St. James's," etc. And, April 24, 1665, the King being in the Park, and sly Pepys being doubtful of being seen in any pleasure, stepped out of the Park to Knightsbridge, and there ate and drank in the coach.

Pepys also speaks of " the World's End," at Knightsbridge, which Mr. Davis thinks could only have been the sign adopted for the Garden; and Pepys, being too soon

wrote, eighteen days after the wedding, that when he had expected to marry an heiress, " I was, about a fortnight since, led as a fool to the stocks, and married a coachman's daughter not worth a shilling."

to go into Hyde Park, went on to Knightsbridge, and there ate and drank at the World's End ; and elsewhere the road going " to the World's End, a drinking-house by the Park, and there merry, and so home late." Congreve, in his *Love for Love,* alludes, in a woman's quarrel, to the place, between Mrs. Frail and Mrs. Foresight, in which the former says: "I don't doubt but you have thought yourself happy in a hackney-coach before now. If I had gone to Knightsbridge, or to Chelsea, or to Spring Garden, or Barn Elms, with a man alone, something might have been said." The house belonging to this Garden stood till about 1826.

Knightsbridge Grove, approached through a stately avenue of trees from the road, was a sporting-house. Here the noted Mrs. Cornelys endeavoured to retrieve her fortunes, after her failure at Carlisle House. In 1785, she gave up her precarious trade. " Ten years after," says Davis's *Memorials of Knightsbridge,* " to the great surprise of the public, she re-appeared at Knightsbridge as Mrs. Smith, a retailer of asses' milk. A suite of breakfast-rooms was opened ; but her former influence could not be recovered. The speculation utterly failed ; and at length she was confined to the Fleet Prison. There she ended her shallow career, dying August 19, 1797."

A once notorious house, the Swan, still exists on the Knightsbridge-road, a little beyond the Green. It is celebrated by Tom Brown. In Otway's *Soldier's Fortune,* 1681, Sir Davy Dunce says :—

" I have surely lost, and ne'er shall find her more. She promised me strictly to stay at home till I came back again ; for ought I know, she may be up three pair of stairs in the Temple now, or, it may be, taking the air as far as Knightsbridge, with

some smooth-faced rogue or another; 'tis a damned house that
Swan,—that Swan at Knightsbridge is a confounded house."

To the Feathers, which stood to the south of Grosvenor-row, an odd anecdote is attached. A Lodge of Odd
Fellows, or some similar society, was in the habit of
holding its meetings in a room at the Feathers; and
on one occasion, when a new member was being initiated
in the mysteries thereof, in rushed two persons, whose
abrupt and unauthorized entrance threw the whole
assemblage into an uproar. Summary punishment was
proposed by an expeditious kick into the street; but,
just as it was about to be bestowed, the secretary recognized one of the intruders as George, Prince of Wales,
afterwards George IV. Circumstances instantly changed:
it indeed was he, out on a nocturnal excursion; and
accordingly it was proposed and carried that the Prince
and his companion should be admitted members. The
Prince was chairman the remainder of the evening; and
the chair in which he sat, ornamented, in consequence,
with the plume, is still preserved in the parlour of the
modern inn in Grosvenor-street West, and over it hangs
a coarsely-executed portrait of the Prince in the robes
of the order. The inn, the hospital, and various small
tenements were removed in 1851, when the present
stately erections were immediately commenced. On
the ground being cleared away, various coins, old horse-
shoes, a few implements of warfare, and some human
remains were discovered.*

Jenny's Whim, another celebrated place of entertainment, has only just entirely disappeared; it was on the
site of St. George's-row. Mr. Davis thinks it to have
been named from the fantastic way in which Jenny, the

* Davis's *Memorials of Knightsbridge.*

first landlady, laid out the garden. Angelo says, it was established by a firework-maker, in the reign of George I. There was a large breakfast-room, and the grounds comprised a bowling-green, alcoves, arbours, and flower-beds; a fish-pond, a cock-pit, and a pond for duck-hunting. In the *Connoisseur*, May 15, 1775, we read: "The lower sort of people had their Ranelaghs and their Vauxhalls as well as the quality. Perrot's inimitable grotto may be seen, for only calling for a pint of beer; and the royal diversion of duck-hunting may be had into the bargain, together with a decanter of Dorchester, for your sixpence, at Jenny's Whim." The large garden here had some amusing deceptions; as by treading on a spring—taking you by surprise—up started different figures, some ugly enough to frighten you—a harlequin, a Mother Shipton, or some terrific animal. In a large piece of water facing the tea-alcoves, large fish or mermaids were showing themselves above the surface." Horace Walpole, in his Letters, occasionally alludes to Jenny's Whim; in one to Montagu he spitefully says—" Here (at Vauxhall) we picked up Lord Granby, arrived very drunk from Jenny's Whim."

Towards the close of the last century, Jenny's Whim began to decline; its morning visitors were not so numerous, and opposition was also powerful. It gradually became forgotten, and at last sank to the condition of a beer-house, and about 1804 the business altogether ceased.*

Jenny's Whim has more than once served the novelist for an illustration; as in *Maids of Honour, a Tale of the Times of George the First:*—" There were gardens,"

* The last relic of "Jenny's Whim" was removed in November, 1865.

says the writer, mentioning the place, "attached to it, and a bowling-green; and parties were frequently made, composed of ladies and gentlemen, to enjoy a day's amusement there in eating strawberries and cream, syllabubs, cake, and taking other refreshments, of which a great variety could be procured, with cider, perry, ale, wine, and other liquors in abundance. The gentlemen played at bowls—some employed themselves at skittles; whilst the ladies amused themselves at a swing, or walked about the garden, admiring the sunflowers, hollyhocks, the Duke of Marlborough cut out of a filbert-tree, and the roses and daisies, currants and gooseberries, that spread their alluring charms in every path.

"This was a favourite rendezvous for lovers in courting time—a day's pleasure at Jenny's Whim being considered by the fair one the most enticing enjoyment that could be offered her; and often the hearts of the most obdurate have given way beneath the influence of its attractions. Jenny's Whim, therefore, had always, during the season, plenty of pleasant parties of young people of both sexes. Sometimes all its chambers were filled, and its gardens thronged by gay and sentimental visitors." *

RANELAGH GARDENS.

This famous place of entertainment was opened in 1742, on the site of the gardens of Ranelagh House, eastward of Chelsea Hospital. It was originally projected by

* In 1755, a quarto satirical tract was published, entitled "Jenny's Whim; or, a Sure Guide to the Nobility, Gentry, and other Eminent Persons in this Metropolis."

Lacy, the patentee of Drury Lane Theatre, as a sort of Winter Vauxhall. There was a Rotunda, with a Doric portico, and arcade and gallery; a Venetian pavilion in a lake, to which the company were rowed in boats; and the grounds were planted with trees and *allées vertes*. The several buildings were designed by Capon, the eminent scene-painter. There were boxes for refreshments, and in each was a painting : in the centre was a heating apparatus, concealed by arches, porticoes and niches, paintings, etc.; and supporting the ceiling, which was decorated with celestial figures, festoons of flowers, and arabesques, and lighted by circles of chandeliers. The Rotunda was opened with a public breakfast, April 5, 1742. Walpole describes the high fashion of Ranelagh : "The prince, princess, duke, much nobility, and much mob besides, were there." " My Lord Chesterfield is so fond of it, that he says he has ordered all his letters to be directed thither." The admission was one shilling ; but the ridottos, with supper and music, were one guinea. Concerts were also given here : Dr. Arne composed the music, Tenducci and Mara sang ; and here were first publicly performed the compositions of the Catch Club. Fireworks and a mimic Etna were next introduced ; and lastly masquerades, described in Fielding's *Amelia*, and satirized in the *Connoisseur*, No. 66, May 1, 1755; wherein the Sunday-evening's tea-drinkings at Ranelagh being laid aside, it is proposed to exhibit " the story of the Fall of Man in a Masquerade."

But the promenade of the Rotunda, to the music of the orchestra and organ, soon declined. " There's your famous Ranelagh, that you make such a fuss about ; why, what a dull place is that !" says Miss Burney's *Evelina*. In 1802, the Installation Ball of the Knights of the Bath was given here; and the Pic-nic Society gave here a breakfast to 2000 persons, when Garnerin ascended in his balloon.   After the Peace Fête, in 1803, for which allegorical scenes were painted by Capon, Ranelagh was deserted, and in 1804, the buildings were removed.

There was subsequently opened in the neighbourhood a New Ranelagh.

CREMORNE TAVERN AND GARDENS.

This property was formerly known as Chelsea Farm, and in 1803, devolved to the Viscount Cremorne, after whom it was named, and who employed Wyatt to build the elegant and commodious mansion.   In the early part of the present century, Cremorne was often visited by George III., and Queen Charlotte, and the Prince of Wales.   In 1825, the house and grounds devolved to Mr. Granville Penn, by whom they were much improved. Next, the beauty of the spot, and its fitness for a pleasure-garden, led to its being opened it to the public as "the Stadium."   After this, the estate fell into other hands, and was appropriated to a very different object. At length, under the proprietorship of Mr. T. B. Simpson, the grounds were laid out with taste, and the tavern enlarged; and the place has prospered for many years as a sort of Vauxhall, with multitudinous amusements, in variety far outnumbering the old proto-gardens.

THE MULBERRY GARDEN,

Upon the site of which is built the northern portion of Buckingham Palace, was planted by order of James I., in 1609, and in the next two reigns became a public garden. Evelyn describes it in 1654 as " ye only place of refreshment about ye towne for persons of ye best quality to be exceedingly cheated at;" and Pepys refers to it as "a silly place," but with "a wilderness somewhat pretty." It is a favourite locality in the gay comedies of Charles II.'s reign.   .

Dryden frequented the Mulberry Garden; and according to a contemporary, the poet ate tarts there with Mrs. Anne Reeve, his mistress. The company sat in arbours, and were regaled with cheesecakes, syllabubs, and sweetened wine; wine-and-water at dinner, and a dish of tea afterwards. Sometimes the ladies wore masks. "The country ladys, for the first month, take up their places in the Mulberry Garden as early as a citizen's wife at a new play."—Sir Charles Sedley's *Mulberry Garden*, 1668.

" A princely palace on that space does rise,
Where Sedley's noble muse found mulberries."—*Dr. King.*

Upon the above part of the garden site was built *Goring House*, let to the Earl of Arlington in 1666, and thence named *Arlington House :* in this year the Earl brought from Holland, for 60*s.*, the first pound of tea received in England ; so that, in all probability, *the first cup of tea made in England was drunk upon the site of Buckingham Palace.*

PIMLICO TAVERNS.

Pimlico is a name of gardens of public entertainment, often mentioned by our early dramatists, and in this respect resembles "Spring Garden." In a rare tract, *Newes from Hogsdon*, 1598, is: "Have at thee, then, my merrie boys, and hey for old Ben Pimlico's nut-browne!" and the place, in or near Hoxton, was afterwards named from him. Ben Jonson has:

> "A second Hogsden,
> In days of Pimlico and eye-bright."—*The Alchemist.*

"Pimlico-path" is a gay resort of his *Bartholomew Fair*; and Meercraft, in *The Devil is an Ass*, says:

> "I'll have thee, Captain Gilthead, and march up
> And take in Pimlico, and kill the bush
> At every tavern."

In 1609, was printed a tract entitled *Pimlyco, or Prince Red Cap, 'tis a Mad World at Hogsden.* Sir Lionel Rash, in Green's *Tu Quoque*, sends his daughter "as far as Pimlico for a draught of Derby ale, that it may bring colour into her cheeks." Massinger mentions,

> "Eating pudding-pies on a Sunday,
> At Pimlico or Islington."—*City Madam.*

Aubrey, in his *Surrey*, speaks of "a Pimlico Garden on Bankside."

Pimlico, the district between Knightsbridge and the Thames, and St. James's Park and Chelsea, was noted for its public gardens: as the Mulberry Garden, now part of the site of Buckingham Palace; the Dwarf Tavern and Gardens, afterwards Spring Gardens, between Ebury-

s 2

street and Belgrave-terrace; the Star and Garter, at the end of Five-Fields-row, famous for its equestrianism, fireworks, and dancing; and the Orange, upon the site of St. Barnabas' church. Here, too, were Ranelagh and New Ranelagh. But the largest garden in Pimlico was Jenny's Whim, already described. In later years it was frequented by crowds from bull-baiting in the adjoining fields. Among the existing old signs are, the Bag o' Nails, Arabella-row, from Ben Jonson's "Bacchanals;" the Compasses, of Cromwell's time (near Grosvenor-row); and the Gun Tavern and Tea-gardens, Queen's-row, with its harbours and costumed figures taken down for the Buckingham Gate improvements. Pimlico is still noted for its ale-breweries.

LAMBETH,—VAUXHALL TAVERNS AND GARDENS, ETC.

On the south bank of the Thames, at the time of the Restoration, were first laid out the New Spring Gardens, at Lambeth (Vauxhall), so called to distinguish them from Spring Garden, Charing Cross. Nearly two centuries of gay existence had Vauxhall Gardens, notwithstanding the proverbial fickleness of our climate, and its ill-adaptation for out-door amusements. The incidents of its history are better known than those of Marylebone or Ranelagh Gardens; so that we shall not here repeat the Vauxhall programmes. The gardens were finally closed in 1859, and the ground is now built upon: a church, of most beautiful design, and a school of art, being the principal edifices.

" Though Vauxhall Gardens retained their plan to the
last, the lamps had long fallen off in their golden fires;
the punch got weaker, the admission-money less; and the
company fell in a like ratio of respectability, and grew
dingy, not to say raffish,—a sorry falling-off from the
Vauxhall crowd of a century since, when it numbered
princes and ambassadors; 'on its tide and torrent of
fashion floated all the beauty of the time; and through
its lighted avenues of trees glided cabinet ministers and
their daughters, royal dukes and their wives, and all the
red-heeled macaronies.' Even fifty years ago, the evening costume of the company was elegant: head-dresses of
flowers and feathers were seen in the promenade, and
the entire place sparkled as did no other place of public
amusement. But low prices brought low company. The
conventional wax-lights got fewer; the punch gave way
to fiery brandy or doctored stout. The semblance of
Vauxhall was still preserved in the orchestra printed
upon the plates and mugs; and the old fire-work bell
tinkled as gaily as ever. But matters grew more seedy;
the place seemed literally worn out; the very trees were
scrubby and singed; and it was high time to say, as
well as see, in letters of lamps, ' Farewell for ever!' " *

Several other taverns and gardens have existed at
different times in this neighbourhood. Cumberland
Gardens' site is now Vauxhall Bridge-road, and Cuper's
Garden was laid out with walks and arbours by Boydell
Cuper, gardener to Thomas, Earl of Arundel, who gave
him some of the mutilated Arundelian marbles (statues),
which Cuper set up in his ground : it was suppressed in

* See the Descriptions of Vauxhall Gardens in *Curiosities of
London*, pp. 745–748. *Walks and Talks about London*, pp. 16–
30. *Romance of London*, vol. iii. pp. 34–44.

1753 : the site is now crossed by Waterloo Bridge Road. Belvidere House and Gardens adjoined Cuper's Garden, in Queen Anne's reign.

The Hercules Inn and Gardens occupied the site of the Asylum for Female Orphans, opened in 1758; and opposite were the Apollo Gardens and the Temple of Flora, Mount-row, opened 1788. A century earlier there existed, in King William's reign, Lambeth Wells, in Three Coney Walk, now Lambeth Walk; it was reputed for its mineral waters, sold at a penny a quart, " the same price paid by St. Thomas's Hospital." About 1750 a Musical Society was held here, and lectures and experiments were given on natural philosophy by Erasmus King, who had been coachman to Dr. Desaguliers. In Stangate-lane, Carlisle-street, is the Bower Saloon, with its theatre and music-room, a pleasure-haunt of our own time. Next is Canterbury Hall, the first established of the great Music Halls of the metropolis.

The Dog and Duck was a place of entertainment in St. George's Fields, where duck-hunting was one of its brutal amusements. The house was taken down upon the rebuilding of Bethlehem Hospital; and the sign-stone, representing a dog squatting upon his haunches, with a duck in his mouth, with the date 1617, is imbedded in the brick wall of the Hospital garden, upon the site of the entrance to the old tavern ; and at the Hospital is a drawing of the Dog and Duck : it was a resort of Hannah More's " Cheapside Apprentice."

Bermondsey Spa, a chalybeate spring, discovered about 1770, was opened, in 1780, as a minor Vauxhall, with fireworks, pictures of still life, and a picture-model of the Siege of Gibraltar, painted by Keyse, the entire apparatus occupying about four acres. He died in 1800, and the garden was shut up about 1805. There are Tokens of the place extant, and the Spa-road is named from it.

A few of the old Southwark taverns have been described. From its being the seat of our early Theatres, the houses of entertainment were here very numerous, in addition to the old historic Inns, which are fast disappearing. In the Beaufoy collection are several Southwark Tavern Tokens; as—The Bore's Head, 1649 (between Nos. 25 and 26 High-street). Next also is a Dogg and Dvcke token, 1651 (St. George's Fields); the Greene Man, 1651 (which remains in Blackman-street); yᵉ Bull Head Taverne, 1667, mentioned by Edward Alleyn, founder of Dulwich College, as one of his resorts; Duke of Suffolk's Head, 1669; and the Swan with Two Necks.

FREEMASONS' LODGES.

Mr. Elmes, in his admirable work, *Sir Christopher Wren and his Times*, 1852, thus glances at the position of Freemasonry in the Metropolis two centuries since, or from the time of the Great Fire :

"In 1666 Wren was nominated deputy Grand Master under Earl Rivers, and distinguished himself above all his predecessors in legislating for the body at large, and in promoting the interests of the lodges under his immediate care. He was Master of the St. Paul's Lodge, which, during the building of the Cathedral, assembled at the Goose and Gridiron in St. Paul's Churchyard, and is now the Lodge of Antiquity, acting by imme-

morial prescription, and regularly presided at its meetings for upwards of eighteen years. During his presidency he presented that Lodge with three mahogany
candlesticks, beautifully carved, and the trowel and
mallet which he used in laying the first stone of the
Cathedral, June 21, 1675, which the brethren of that
ancient and distinguished Lodge still possess and duly
appreciate.

"During the building of the City, Lodges were held
by the fraternity in different places, and several new ones
constituted, which were attended by the leading archi-
tects and the best builders of the day, and amateur
brethren of the mystic craft. In 1674 Earl Rivers resigned his grand-mastership, and George Villiers, Duke
of Buckingham, was elected to the dignified office. He
left the care of the Grand Lodge and the brotherhood
to the deputy Grand Master Wren and his Wardens.
During the short reign of James II., who tolerated no
secret societies but the Jesuits, the Lodges were but
thinly attended; but in 1685, Sir Christopher Wren
was elected Grand Master of the Order, and nominated
Gabriel Cibber, the sculptor, and Edward Strong, the
master mason at St. Paul's and other of the City
churches, as Grand Wardens. The Society has continued with various degrees of success to the present day,
particularly under the grand-masterships of the Prince
of Wales, afterwards King George IV.,* and his brother,
the late Duke of Sussex, and since the death of the
latter, under that of the Earl of Zetland ; and Lodges
under the constitution of the Grand Lodge of England
are held in every part of the habitable globe, as its

* The Prince was initiated in a Lodge at the Key and Garter,
No. 26, Pall Mall.

numerically and annually-increasing lists abundantly show."

Sir Francis Palgrave, in an elaborate paper in the *Edinburgh Review*, April, 1839, however, takes another view of the subject, telling us that "the connexion between the operative masons,* and those whom, without disrespect, we must term a convivial society of good fellows, met at the 'Goose and Gridiron, in St. Paul his Churchyard,' appears to have been finally dissolved about the beginning of the eighteenth century. The theoretical and mystic, for we dare not say ancient, Freemasons, separated from the Worshipful Company of Masons and Citizens of London about the period above mentioned. It appears from an inventory of the contents of the chest of the London Company, that not very long since, it contained 'a book wrote on parchment, and bound or stitched in parchment, containing 113 annals of the antiquity, rise, and progress of the art and mystery of Masonry.' But this document is not now to be found."

There is in existence, and known to persons who take an interest in the History of Freemasonry, a copper-plate List of Freemasons' Lodges in London in the reign of Queen Anne, with a representation of the Signs, and some Masonic ceremony, in which are eleven figures of well-dressed men, in the costume of the above period. There were then 129 Lodges, of which 86 were in London, 36 in English cities, and seven abroad.

Freemasonry evidently sprang up in London at the building of St. Paul's; and many of the oldest Lodges

---

* Hampton Court Palace was built by Freemasons, as appears from the very curious accounts of the expenses of the fabric, extant among the public records of London.

are in the neighbourhood. But the head-quarters of Freemasonry, are the Grand Hall, in the rear of Free-masons' Tavern, 62, Great Queen-street, Lincoln's Inn Fields: it was commenced May 1, 1775, from the designs of Thomas Sandby, R.A., Professor of Architecture in the Royal Academy : 5000*l.* was raised by a Tontine towards the cost; and the Hall was opened and dedi-cated in solemn form, May 23, 1776; Lord Petre, Grand-Master. " It is the first house built in this country with the appropriate symbols of masonry, and with the suitable apartments for the holding of lodges, the initiating, passing, raising, and exalting of brethren." Here are held the Grand and other lodges, which hitherto assembled in the Halls of the City Companies.

Freemasons' Hall, as originally decorated, is shown in a print of the annual procession of Freemasons' Orphans, by T. Stothard, R.A. It is a finely-pro-portioned room, 92 feet by 43 feet, and 60 feet high; and will hold 1500 persons : it was re-decorated in 1846 : the ceiling and coving are richly decorated; above the principal entrance is a large gallery, with an organ; and at the opposite end is a coved recess, flanked by a pair of fluted Ionic columns, and Egyptian doorways ; the sides are decorated with fluted Ionic pilasters; and through-out the room in the frieze are masonic emblems, gilt upon a transparent blue ground. In the intercolumnia-tions are full-length royal and other masonic portraits, including that of the Duke of Sussex, as Grand-Master, by Sir W. Beechey, R.A. In the end recess is a marble statue of the Duke of Sussex, executed for the Grand Lodge, by E. H. Baily, R.A. The statue is seven feet six inches high, and the pedestal six feet ; the Duke wears the robes of a Knight of the Garter, and the Guelphic insignia : at his side is a small altar, sculptured with masonic emblems.

WHITEBAIT TAVERNS.

At what period the lovers of good living first went to eat Whitebait at " the taverns contiguous to the places where the fish is taken," is not very clear. At all events, the houses did not resemble the Brunswick, the West India Dock, the Ship, or the Trafalgar, of the present day, these having much of the architectural pretension of a modern club-house.

Whitebait have long been numbered among the delicacies of our tables; for we find " six dishes of Whitebait " in the funeral feast of the munificent founder of the Charterhouse, given in the Hall of the Stationers' Company, on May 28, 1612—the year before the Globe Theatre was burnt down, and the New River completed. For aught we know these delicious fish may have been served up to Henry VIII. and Queen Elizabeth in their palace at Greenwich, off which place, and Blackwall opposite, Whitebait have been for ages taken in the Thames at flood-tide. To the river-side taverns we must go to enjoy a " Whitebait dinner," for, one of the conditions of success is that the fish should be directly netted out of the river into the cook's cauldron.

About the end of March, or early in April, Whitebait make their appearance in the Thames, and are then small, apparently but just changed from the albuminous state of the young fry. During June, July, and August, immense quantities are consumed by visitors to the different taverns at Greenwich and Blackwall.

Pennant says: Whitebait "are esteemed very delicious when fried with fine flour, and occasion during the season a vast resort of the *lower order of epicures* to the taverns contiguous to the places where they are taken." If this account be correct, there must have been a strange change in the grade of the epicures frequenting Greenwich and Blackwall since Pennant's days; for at present, the fashion of eating Whitebait is sanctioned by the highest authorities, from the Court of St. James's Palace in the West, to the Lord Mayor and *his* court in the East; besides the philosophers of the Royal Society, and her Majesty's Cabinet Ministers. Who, for example, does not recollect such a paragraph as the following, which appeared in the *Morning Post* of the day on which Mr. Yarrell wrote his account of Whitebait, September 10th, 1835 ?—

"Yesterday, the Cabinet Ministers went down the river in the Ordnance barges to Lovegrove's West India Dock Tavern, Blackwall, to partake of their annual fish dinner. Covers were laid for thirty-five gentlemen."

For our own part, we consider the Ministers did not evince their usual good policy in choosing so late a period as September; the Whitebait being finer eating in July or August; so that their "annual fish dinner" must rather be regarded as a sort of prandial wind-up of the parliamentary session than as a specimen of refined epicurism.

We remember many changes in matters concerning Whitebait at Greenwich and Blackwall. Formerly, the taverns were mostly built with weather-board fronts, with bow-windows, so as to command a view of the river. The old Ship, and the Crown and Sceptre, taverns at Greenwich were built in this manner; and some of the Blackwall houses were of humble pretensions: these have disappeared, and handsome architectural piles have been erected in their places. Meanwhile, Whitebait have been sent to the metropolis, by railway, or steamer, where they figure in fishmongers' shops, and tavern *cartes* of almost every degree.

Perhaps the famed delicacy of Whitebait rests as much upon its skilful cookery as upon the freshness of the fish. Dr. Pereira has published the mode of cooking in one of Lovegrave's "bait-kitchens" at Blackwall. The fish should be dressed within an hour after being caught, or they are apt to cling together. They are kept in water, from which they are taken by a skimmer as required; they are then thrown upon a layer of flour, contained in a large napkin, in which they are shaken until completely enveloped in flour; they are then put into a colander, and all the superfluous flour is removed by sifting; the fish are next thrown into hot lard contained in a copper cauldron or stew-pan placed over a charcoal fire; in about two minutes they are removed by a tin skimmer, thrown into a colander to drain, and served up instantly, by placing them on a fish-drainer in a dish. The rapidity of the cooking process is of the utmost importance; and if it be not attended to, the fish will lose their crispness, and be worthless. At table, lemon juice is squeezed over them, and they are seasoned with Cayenne pepper; brown bread and butter is substituted for plain bread; and they are eaten with iced champagne, or punch.

The origin of the Ministers' Fish Dinner, already mentioned, has been thus pleasantly narrated:

Every year, the approach of the close of the Parliamentary Session is indicated by what is termed " the
Ministerial Fish Dinner," in which Whitebait forms a
prominent dish ; and Cabinet Ministers are the company. The Dinner takes place at a principal tavern,
usually at Greenwich, but sometimes at Blackwall : the
dining-room is decorated for the occasion, which par-
takes of a state entertainment. Formerly, however, the
Ministers went down the river from Whitehall in an
Ordnance gilt barge : now, a government steamer is employed. The origin of this annual festivity is told as
follows. On the banks of Dagenham Lake or Reach, in
Essex, many years since, there stood a cottage, occupied by a princely merchant named Preston, a baronet
of Scotland and Nova Scotia, and sometime M.P. for
Dover. He called it his " fishing cottage," and often
in the spring he went thither, with a friend or two, as
a relief to the toils of parliamentary and mercantile
duties. His most frequent guest was the Right Hon.
George Rose, Secretary of the Treasury, and an Elder
Brother of the Trinity House. Many a day did these
two worthies enjoy at Dagenham Reach ; and Mr. Rose
once intimated to Sir Robert, that Mr. Pitt, of whose
friendship they were both justly proud, would, no doubt,
delight in the comfort of such a retreat. A day was
named, and the Premier was invited ; and he was so
well pleased with his reception at the " fishing cottage "
—they were all two if not three bottle men—that, on
taking leave, Mr. Pitt readily accepted an invitation for
the following year.

For a few years, the Premier continued a visitor to
Dagenham, and was always accompanied by Mr. George
Rose. But the distance was considerable ; the going

and coming were somewhat inconvenient for the First
Minister of the Crown. Sir Robert Preston, however,
had his remedy, and he proposed that they should in
future dine nearer London. Greenwich was suggested :
we do not hear of Whitebait in the Dagenham dinners,
and its introduction, probably, dates from the removal
to Greenwich. The party of three was now increased to
four; Mr. Pitt being permitted to bring Lord Camden.
Soon after, a fifth guest was invited—Mr. Charles Long,
afterwards Lord Farnborough. All were still the guests
of Sir Robert Preston; but, one by one, other notables
were invited,—all Tories—and, at last, Lord Camden
considerately remarked, that, as they were all dining at
a tavern, it was but fair that Sir Robert Preston should
be relieved from the expense. It was then arranged
that the dinner should be given, as usual, by Sir Robert
Preston, that is to say, at his invitation; and he insisted
on still contributing a buck and champagne : the rest
of the charges were thenceforth defrayed by the several
guests; and, on this plan, the meeting continued to
take place annually till the death of Mr. Pitt.

Sir Robert was requested, next year, to summon the
several guests, the list of whom, by this time, included
most of the Cabinet Ministers. The time for meeting
was usually after Trinity Monday, a short period before
the end of the Session. By degrees, the meeting, which
was originally purely gastronomic, appears to have assumed, in consequence of the long reign of the Tories,
a political, or semi-political character. Sir Robert
Preston died; but Mr. Long, now Lord Farnborough,
undertook to summon the several guests, the list of
whom was furnished by Sir Robert Preston's private
secretary. Hitherto, the invitations had been sent

privately : now they were dispatched in Cabinet boxes,
and the party was, certainly, for some time, limited to
the Members of the Cabinet. A dinner lubricates ministerial as well as other business; so that the " Ministerial Fish Dinner " may " contribute to the grandeur
and prosperity of our beloved country."

The following Carte is from the last edition of the
Art of Dining, in Murray's *Railway Reading :—*

Fish Dinner at Blackwall or Greenwich.

La tortue à l'Anglaise.
La bisque d'écrevisses.
Le consommé aux quenelles de merlan.
De tortue claire.
Les casseroles de green fat feront le tour de la table.
Les tranches de saumon (crimped).
Le poisson de St. Pierre à la crême.
Le zoutchet de perches.
       ,,   de truites.
       ,,   de flottons.
       ,,   de soles (crimped).
       ,,   de saumon.
       ,,   d'anguilles.
Les lamproies à la Worcester.
Les croques en bouches de laitances de maquereau.
Les boudins de merlans à la reine.

Garnis de persil frit. { Les soles menues frites.
Les petits carrelets ,,
Croquettes de homard.
Les filets d'anguilles.

La truite saumonée à la Tartare.
Le whitebait : *id.* à la diable.

Second Service.

Les petits poulets au cresson—le jambonneau aux épinards.
La Mayonnaise de filets de soles—les filets de merlans
à l'Arpin.

Les petits pois à l'Anglaise—les artichauts à la Barigoule.
La gelée de Marasquin aux fraises—les pets de nonnes.
Les tartelettes aux cerises—les célestines à la fleur d'orange.
Le baba à la compôte d'abricots—le fromage Plombière.

Mr. Walker, in his *Original*, gives an account of a dinner he ordered, at Lovegrove's, at Blackwall, where if you never dined, so much the worse for you :—

" The party will consist of seven men besides myself, and every guest is asked for some reason—upon which good fellowship mainly depends ; for people brought together unconnectedly had, in my opinion, better be kept separately. Eight I hold the golden number, never to be exceeded without weakening the efficacy of concentration. The dinner is to consist of turtle, followed by no other fish but Whitebait, which is to be followed by no other meat but grouse, which are to be succeeded simply by apple-fritters and jelly, pastry on such occasions being quite out of place. With the turtle, of course, there will be punch ; with the Whitebait, champagne ; and with the grouse, claret ; the two former I have ordered to be particularly well iced, and they will all be placed in succession upon the table, so that we can help ourselves as we please. I shall permit no other wines, unless, perchance, a bottle or two of port, if particularly wanted, as I hold variety of wines a great mistake. With respect to the adjuncts, I shall take care that there is cayenne, with lemons cut in halves, not in quarters, within reach of every one, for the turtle, and that brown bread and butter in abundance is set upon the table for the Whitebait. It is no trouble to think of these little matters beforehand, but they make a vast difference in convivial contentment. The dinner will be followed by ices, and a good dessert, after which coffee and one glass of liqueur each, and no more ; so that the present may be enjoyed without inducing retrospective regrets. If the master of a feast wish his party to succeed, he must know how to command ; and not let his guests run riot, each according to his own wild fancy."

THE LONDON TAVERN,

Situated about the middle of the western side of Bishopsgate-street Within, presents in its frontage a mezzanine-storey, and lofty Venetian windows, reminding one of the old-fashioned assembly-room façade. The site of the present tavern was previously occupied by the White Lion Tavern, which was destroyed in an extensive fire on the 7th of November, 1765; it broke out at a peruke-maker's opposite; the flames were carried by a high wind across the street, to the house immediately adjoining the tavern, the fire speedily reaching the corner; the other angles of Cornhill, Gracechurch-street, and Leadenhall-street, were all on fire at the same time, and fifty houses and buildings were destroyed and damaged, including the White Lion and Black Lion Taverns.

Upon the site of the former was founded "The London Tavern," on the Tontine principle; it was commenced in 1767, and completed and opened in September, 1768; Richard B. Jupp, architect. The front is more than 80 feet wide by nearly 70 feet in height.

The Great Dining-room, or "Pillar-room," as it is called, is 40 feet by 33 feet, decorated with medallions and garlands, Corinthian columns and pilasters. At the top of the edifice is the ball-room, extending the whole length of the structure, by 33 feet in width and 30 feet in height, which may be laid out as a banqueting-room for 300 feasters; exclusively of accommodating 150 ladies as spectators in the galleries at each end.

The walls are throughout hung with paintings; and the large room has an organ.

The Turtle is kept in large tanks, which occupy a whole vault, where two tons of turtle may sometimes be seen swimming in one vat. We have to thank Mr. Cunningham for this information, which is noteworthy, independently of its epicurean association,—that "turtles will live in cellars for three months in excellent condition if kept in the same water in which they were brought to this country. To change the water is to lessen the weight and flavour of the turtle." Turtle does not appear in bills of fare of entertainments given by Lord Mayors and Sheriffs between the years 1761 and 1766; and it is not till 1768 that turtle appears by name, and then in the bill of the banquet at the Mansion House to the King of Denmark. The cellars, which consist of the whole basement storey, are filled with barrels of porter, pipes of port, butts of sherry, etc. Then there are a labyrinth of walls of bottle ends, and a region of bins, six bottles deep; the catacombs of Johannisberg, Tokay, and Burgundy. "Still we glide on through rivers of sawdust, through embankments of genial wine. There are twelve hundred of champagne down here; there are between six and seven hundred dozen of claret; corked up in these bins is a capital of from eleven to twelve thousand pounds; these bottles absorb, in simple interest at five per cent., an income amounting to some five or six hundred pounds per annum." *   "It was not, however, solely for uncovering these floods of mighty wines, nor for luxurious feasting that the London Tavern was at first erected, nor for which it is still exclusively famous, since it was always

* *Household Words*, 1852.

T 2

designed to provide a spacious and convenient place for public meetings. One of the earliest printed notices concerning the establishment is of this character, it being the account of a meeting for promoting a public subscription for John Wilkes, on the 12th of February, 1769, at which 3000*l.* were raised, and local committees appointed for the provinces. In the Spring season such meetings and committees of all sorts are equally numerous and conflicting with each other, for they not unfrequently comprise an interesting charitable election or two; and in addition the day's entertainments are often concluded with more than one large dinner, and an evening party for the lady spectators.

" Here, too, may be seen the hasty arrivals of persons for the meetings of the Mexican Bondholders on the second-floor; of a Railway assurance ' up-stairs, and first to the left;' of an asylum election at the end of the passage; and of the party on the ' first-floor to the right,' who had to consider of ' the union of the Gibbleton line to the Great-Trunk-Due-Eastern-Junction.'

" For these business meetings the rooms are arranged with benches, and sumptuously Turkey-carpeted ; the end being provided with a long table for the directors, with an imposing array of papers and pens.

" ' The morn, the noon, the day is pass'd' in the reports, the speeches, the recriminations and defences of these parties, until it is nearly five o'clock. In the very same room the Hooping Cough Asylum Dinner is to take place at six ; and the Mexican Bondholders are stamping and hooting above, on the same floor which in an hour is to support the feast of some Worshipful Company which makes it their hall. The feat appears to be altogether impossible ; nevertheless, it must and will be most accurately performed.

The Secretary has scarcely bound the last piece of red tape round his papers, when four men rush to the four corners of the Turkey carpet, and half of it is rolled up, dust and all. Four other men with the half of a clean carpet bowl it along in the wake of the one displaced. While you are watching the same performance with the remaining half of the floor, a battalion of waiters has fitted up, upon the new half carpet, a row of dining-tables and covered them with table-cloths. While in turn you watch them, the entire apartment is tabled and table-clothed. Thirty men are at this work upon a system, strictly departmental. Rinse and three of his followers lay the knives; Burrows and three more cause the glasses to sparkle on the board. You express your wonder at this magical celerity. Rinse moderately replies that the same game is going on in other four rooms; and this happens six days out of the seven in the dining-room.

When the Banquet was given to Mr. Macready in February, 1851, the London Tavern could not accommodate all the company, because there were seven hundred and odd; and the Hall of Commerce was taken for the dinner. The merchants and brokers were transacting business there at four o'clock; and in two hours, seats, tables, platforms, dinner, wine, gas, and company, were all in. By a quarter before six everything was ready, and a chair placed before each plate. Exactly at six, everything was placed upon the table, and most of the guests were seated.

For effecting these wonderful evolutions, it will be no matter of surprise that we are told that an army of servants, sixty or seventy strong, is retained on the establishment; taking on auxiliary legions during the dining season.

The business of this gigantic establishment is of such extent as to be only carried on by this systematic means. Among the more prominent displays of its resources which take place here are the annual Banquets of the officers of some twenty-eight different regiments, in the month of May. There are likewise given here a very large number of the annual entertainments of the different Charities of London. Twenty-four of the City Companies hold their Banquets here, and transact official business. Several Balls take place here annually. Masonic Lodges are held here; and almost innumerable Meetings, Sales, and Elections for Charities alternate with the more directly festive business of the London Tavern. Each of the departments of so vast an establishment has its special interest. We have glanced at its dining-halls, and its turtle and wine cellars.* To detail its kitchens and the management of its stores and supplies, and consumption, would extend beyond our limit, so that we shall end by remarking that upon no portion of our metropolis is more largely enjoyed the luxury of doing good, and the observance of the rights and duties of goodfellowship, than at the London Tavern.

* The usual allowance at what is called a Turtle-Dinner, is 6 lb. live weight per head. At the Spanish-Dinner, at the City of London Tavern, in 1808, four hundred guests attended, and 2500lb. of turtle were consumed.

For the Banquet at Guildhall, on Lord Mayor's Day, 250 tureens of turtle are provided.

Turtle may be enjoyed in steaks, cutlets, or fins, and as soup, clear and _purée_, at the Albion, London, and Freemasons', and other large taverns. "The Ship and Turtle Tavern," Nos. 129 and 130, Leadenhall-street, is especially famous for its turtle; and from this establishment several of the West-end Club-houses are supplied.

THE CLARENDON HOTEL.

This sumptuous hotel, the reader need scarcely be informed, takes its name from its being built upon a portion of the gardens of Clarendon House gardens, between Albemarle and Bond streets, in each of which the hotel has a frontage. The house was, for a short term, let to the Earl of Chatham, for his town residence.

The Clarendon contains series of apartments, fitted for the reception of princes and their suites, and for nobility. Here are likewise given official banquets on the most costly scale.

Among the records of the house is the *menu* of the dinner given to Lord Chesterfield, on his quitting the office of Master of the Buckhounds, at the Clarendon. The party consisted of thirty; the price was six guineas a head; and the dinner was ordered by Count D'Orsay, who stood almost without a rival amongst connoisseurs in this department of art :—

" *Premier Service.*

"*Potages.*—Printanier : à la reine : *turtle.*
" *Poissons.*—Turbot (*lobster and Dutch sauces*) : saumon à la Tartare : rougets à la cardinal : friture de morue : *whitebait.*
"*Relevés.*—Filet de bœuf à la Napolitaine : dindon à la chipolata : timballe de macaroni : *haunch of venison.*
" *Entrées.*—Croquettes de volaille : petits pâtés aux huîtres : côtelettes d'agneau : purée de champignons : côtelettes d'agneau aux points d'asperge : fricandeau de veau à l'oseille : ris de veau piqué aux tomates : côtelettes de pigeons à la Dusselle : chartreuse de légumes aux faisans: filets de cannetons à la Bigarrade : boudins à la Richelieu : sauté de volaille aux truffes : pâté de mouton monté.
"*Côté.*—Bœuf rôti : jambon : salade.

"*Second Service.*

"*Rôts.*—Chapons, quails, turkey poults, *green goose.*

"*Entremets.*— Asperges : haricot à la Française : mayonnaise de homard : gelée Macédoine : aspics d'œufs de pluvier : Charlotte Russe: gelée au Marasquin : crême marbre : corbeille de pâtisserie : vol-au-vent de rhubarb : tourte d'abricots : corbeille des meringues: dressed crab: salade au gélantine.—Champignons aux fines herbes.

"*Relevés.*—Soufflé à la vanille : Nesselrode pudding : Adelaide sandwiches : fondus. Pièces montées," etc.

The reader will not fail to observe how well the English dishes,—turtle, whitebait, and venison,—relieve the French in this dinner : and what a breadth, depth, solidity, and dignity they add to it. Green goose, also, may rank as English, the goose being held in little honour, with the exception of its liver, by the French ; but we think Comte D'Orsay did quite right in inserting it. The execution is said to have been pretty nearly on a par with the conception, and the whole entertainment was crowned with the most inspiriting success. The price was not unusually large.*

FREEMASONS' TAVERN, GREAT QUEEN-STREET.

This well-appointed tavern, built by William Tyler, in 1786, and since considerably enlarged, in addition to the usual appointments, possesses the great advantage of Freemasons' Hall, wherein take place some of our

* *The Art of Dining.* Murray, 1852.

leading public festivals and anniversary dinners, the latter mostly in May and June. Here was given the farewell dinner to John Philip Kemble, upon his retirement from the stage, in 1817; the public dinner, on his birthday, to James Hogg, the Ettrick Shepherd, in 1832; Mollard, who has published an excellent *Art of Cookery*, was many years *Maître d'Hôtel*, and proprietor of the Freemasons' Tavern.

In the Hall meet the Madrigal Society, the Melodists' and other musical clubs : and the annual dinners of the Theatrical Fund, Artists' Societies, and other public institutions, are given here.

Freemasons' Hall has obtained some notoriety as the arena in which were delivered and acted the Addresses at the Anniversary Dinners of the Literary Fund, upon whose eccentricities we find the following amusing note in the latest edition of the *Rejected Addresses* :—

"The annotator's first personal knowledge of William Thomas Fitzgerald, was at Harry Greville's Pic-Nic Theatre, in Tottenham-street, where he personated Zanga in a wig too small for his head. The second time of seeing him was at the table of old Lord Dudley, who familiarly called him Fitz, but forgot to name him in his will. The Viscount's son, however, liberally supplied the omission by a donation of five thousand pounds. The third and last time of encountering him was at an anniversary dinner of the Literary Fund, at the Freemasons' Tavern. Both parties, as two of the stewards, met their brethren in a small room about half-an-hour before dinner. The lampooner, out of delicacy, kept aloof from the poet. The latter, however, made up to him, when the following dialogue took place :

" Fitzgerald (with good humour). ' Mr.——, I mean to recite after dinner.'

" Mr. ——. ' Do you?'

" Fitzgerald. ' Yes: you'll have more of God bless the Regent and the Duke of York !'

" The whole of this imitation, (one of the Rejected Addresses,) after a lapse of twenty years, appears to the authors too personal and sarcastic; but they may shelter themselves under a very broad mantle :—

> " Let hoarse Fitzgerald bawl
> His creaking couplets in a tavern-hall."—*Byron.*

" Fitzgerald actually sent in an address to the Committee on the 31st of August, 1812. It was published among the other *Genuine Rejected Addresses*, in one volume, in that year. The following is an extract :—

> " The troubled shade of Garrick, hovering near,
> Dropt on the burning pile a pitying tear."

" What a pity that, like Sterne's recording angel, it did not succeed in blotting the fire out for ever ! That falling, why not adopt Gulliver's remedy ?"

Upon the " Rejected," the *Edinburgh Review* notes:— " The first piece, under the name of the loyal Mr. Fitzgerald, though as good we suppose as the original, is not very interesting. Whether it be very like Mr. Fitzgerald or not, however, it must be allowed that the vulgarity, servility, and gross absurdity of the newspaper scribblers is well rendered."

THE ALBION, ALDERSGATE-STREET.

This extensive establishment has long been famed for its good dinners, and its excellent wines. Here take place the majority of the banquets of the Corporation of London, the Sheriffs' Inauguration Dinners, as well as those of Civic Companies and Committees, and such festivals, public and private, as are usually held at taverns of the highest class.

The farewell Dinners given by the East India Company to the Governors-General of India, usually take place at the Albion. " Here likewise (after dinner) the annual trade sales of the principal London publishers take place," revivifying the olden printing and book glories of Aldersgate and Little Britain.

The *cuisine* of the Albion has long been celebrated for its *recherché* character. Among the traditions of the tavern it is told that a dinner was once given here, under the auspices of the *gourmand* Alderman Sir William Curtis, which cost the party between thirty and forty pounds apiece. It might well have cost twice as much, for amongst other acts of extravagance, they dispatched a special messenger to Westphalia to choose a ham. There is likewise told a bet as to the comparative merits of the Albion and York House (Bath) dinners, which was to have been formally decided by a dinner of unparalleled munificence, and nearly equal cost at each ; but it became a drawn bet, the Albion beating in the first course, and the York House in the second. Still, these are reminiscences on which, we frankly own, no great reliance is to be placed.

Lord Southampton once gave a dinner at the Albion, at ten guineas a head; and the ordinary price for the best dinner at this house (including wine) is three guineas.*

ST. JAMES'S HALL.

This new building which is externally concealed by houses, except the fronts, in Piccadilly and Regent-street, consists of a greater Hall and two minor Halls, which are let for Concerts, Lectures, etc., and also form part of the Tavern establishment, two of the Halls being used as public dining-rooms. The principal Hall, larger than St. Martin's, but smaller than Exeter Hall, is 140 feet long, 60 feet wide, and 60 feet high. At one end is a semicircular recess, in which stands the large organ. The noble room has been decorated by Mr. Owen Jones with singularly light, rich, and festive effect : the grand feature being the roof, which is blue and white, red and gold, in Alhambresque patterns. The lighting is quite novel, and consists of gas-stars, depending from the roof, which thus appears spangled.

The superb decoration and effective lighting, render this a truly festive Hall, with abundant space to set off the banquet displays. The first Public Dinner was given here on June 2, 1858, when Mr. Robert Stephenson, the eminent engineer, presided, and a silver salver and claret-jug, with a sum of money—altogether

* *The Art of Dining.*—Murray, 1852.

in value 2678*l.*—were presented to Mr. F. Petit Smith, in recognition of his bringing into general use the System of Screw Propulsion; the testimonial being purchased by 138 subscribers, chiefly eminent naval officers, ship-builders, ship-owners, and men of science.

In the following month, (20th of July,) a banquet was given here to Mr. Charles Kean, F.S.A., in testimony of his having exalted the English theatre—of his public merits and private virtues. The Duke of Newcastle presided: there was a brilliant presence of guests, and nearly four hundred ladies were in the galleries. Subsequently, in the Hall was presented to Mr. Kean the magnificent service of plate, purchased by public subscription.

The success of these intellectual banquets proved a most auspicious inauguration of St. James's Hall for—

" The feast of reason and the flow of soul."

THEATRICAL TAVERNS.

Among these establishments, the Eagle, in the City-road, deserves mention. It occupies the site of the Shepherd and Shepherdess, a tavern and tea-garden of some seventy-five years since. To the Eagle is annexed a large theatre.

Sadler's Wells was, at one period, a tavern theatre, where the audience took their wine while they sat and witnessed the performances.

APPENDIX.

BEEFSTEAK SOCIETY.

(Vol. I. page 149.)

We find in Smith's *Book for a Rainy Day* the following record respecting the Beefsteak Society, or, as
he calls it, in an unorthodox way, Club :—

" Mr. John Nixon, of Basinghall-street, gave me the
following information. Mr. Nixon, as Secretary, had possession of the original book. Lambert's Club was first
held in Covent Garden theatre [other accounts state, in
the Lincoln's-Inn-Fields theatre,] in the upper room
called the ' Thunder and Lightning ;' then in one
even with the two-shilling gallery ; next in an apartment even with the boxes ; and afterwards in a lower
room, where they remained until the fire. After that
time, Mr. Harris insisted upon it, as the playhouse was
a new building, that the Club should not be held there.
They then went to the Bedford Coffee-house, next-door.
Upon the ceiling of the dining-room they placed Lambert's original gridiron, which had been saved from the
fire. They had a kitchen, a cook, a wine-cellar, etc.,
entirely independent of the Bedford Hotel.

"There was also a Society held at Robins's room, called 'The Ad Libitum,' of which Mr. Nixon had the books; but it was a totally different Society, quite unconnected with the Beefsteak Club."

WHITE'S CLUB.

(Vol. I. page 121.)

The following humorous Address was supposed to have been written by Colonel Lyttelton, brother to Sir George Lyttelton, in 1752, on His Majesty's return from Hanover, when numberless Addresses were presented. White's was then a Chocolate-house, near St. James's Palace, and was the famous gaming-house, where most of the nobility had meetings and a Society :—

" The Gamesters' Address to the King.

" Most Righteous Sovereign,

" May it please your Majesty, we, the Lords, Knights, etc., of the Society of White's, beg leave to throw ourselves at your Majesty's feet (our honours and consciences lying under the *table,* and our fortunes being ever at stake), and congratulate your Majesty's happy return to these kingdoms which assemble us together, to the great advantage of some, the ruin of others, and the unspeakable satisfaction of all, both us, our wives, and children. We beg leave to acknowledge your Majesty's great goodness and lenity, in allowing us to break those laws, which we ourselves have made, and you have sanctified and confirmed : while your Majesty alone religiously observes and regards them. And we beg leave to assure your Majesty of our most unfeigned loyalty and attachment to your sacred person; and that next to the Kings of Diamonds, Clubs, Spades, and Hearts, we love, honour, and adore you."

To which His Majesty was pleased to return this most gracious answer:—

"My Lords and Gentlemen,

"I return you my thanks for your loyal address; but while I have such rivals in your affection, as you tell me of, I can neither think it worth preserving or regarding. I look upon you yourselves as a *pack* of *cards*, and shall *deal* with you accordingly."—*Cole's MSS.* vol. xxxi. p. 171,—in the British Museum.

In *Richardsoniana* we read: " Very often the taste of running perpetually after diversions is not a mark of any pleasure taken in them, but of none taken in ourselves. This sallying abroad is only from uneasiness at home, which is in every one's self. Like a gentleman who overlooking them at White's at piquet, till three or four in the morning: on a dispute they referred to him; when he protested he knew nothing of the game; ' Zounds,' say they, ' and sit here till this time?'—' Gentlemen, I'm married !'—' Oh ! Sir, we beg pardon.' "

THE ROYAL ACADEMY CLUB.

This Club consisted exclusively of Members of the Royal Academy. Nollekens, the sculptor, for many years, made one at the table; and so strongly was he bent upon saving all he could privately conceal, that he did not mind paying two guineas a year for his admission-ticket, in order to indulge himself with a few nutmegs, which he contrived to pocket privately; for as red-wine negus was the principal beverage, nutmegs were used. Now, it generally happened, if another bowl was wanted, that the nutmegs were missing. Nollekens, who had frequently been seen to pocket them, was one day requested by Rossi the sculptor, to see if they had not fallen under the table; upon which Nollekens actually went crawling beneath, upon his hands and knees, pretending to look for them, though at that very time they were in his waistcoat-pocket. He was so old a stager at this monopoly of nutmegs, that he would sometimes engage the maker of the negus in conversation, looking him full in the face, whilst he, slyly and unobserved, as he thought, conveyed away the spice; like the fellow who is stealing the bank-note from the blind man, in Hogarth's admirable print of the Royal Cockpit.—*Smith's Nollekens and his Times*, vol. i. p. 225.

DESTRUCTION OF TAVERNS BY FIRE.

On the morning of the 25th of March, 1748, a most calamitous and destructive fire commenced at a peruke-maker's, named Eldridge, in Exchange Alley, Cornhill; and within twelve hours totally destroyed between 90 and 100 houses, besides damaging many others. The flames spread in three directions at once, and extending into Cornhill, consumed about twenty houses there, including the London Assurance Office; the Fleece and the Three Tuns Taverns; and Tom's and the Rainbow Coffee-houses. In Exchange Alley, the Swan Tavern, with Garraway's, Jonathan's and the Jerusalem Coffee-houses, were burnt down; and in the contiguous avenues and Birchin-lane, the George and Vulture Tavern, with several other coffee-houses, underwent a like fate. Mr. Eldridge, with his wife, children, and servants, all perished in the flames. The value of the effects and merchandise destroyed was computed at 200,000*l.*, exclusive of that of the numerous buildings.

In the above fire was consumed the house in which was born the poet Gray; and the injury which his property sustained on the occasion, induced him to sink a great part of the remainder in purchasing an annuity: his father had been an Exchange broker. The house was within a few doors of Birchin-lane.

THE TZAR OF MUSCOVY'S HEAD, TOWER-STREET.

Close to Tower-hill, and not far from the site of the Rose tavern, is a small tavern, or public-house, which received its sign in commemoration of the convivial eccentricities of an Emperor, one of the most extraordinary characters that ever appeared on the great theatre of the world—" who gave a polish to his nation and was himself a savage."

Such was Peter the Great, who, with his suite, consisting of Menzikoff, and some others, came to London on the twenty-first of January, 1698, principally with the view of acquiring information on matters connected with naval architecture. We have little evidence that during his residence here Peter ever worked as a shipwright in Deptford Dockyard, as is generally believed. He was, however, very fond of sailing and managing boats and a yacht on the Thames; and his great delight was to get a small decked-boat, belonging to the Dockyard, and taking only Menzikoff, and three or four others of his suite, to work the vessel with them, he being the helmsman. Now, the great failing of Peter was his love of strong liquors. He and his companions having finished their day's work, used to resort to a public-house in Great Tower-street, close to Tower-hill, to smoke their pipes, and drink beer and brandy. The landlord, in gratitude for the imperial custom, had the Tzar of Muscovy's head painted, and put up for his sign, which continued till the year 1808, when a person of the name

u 2

292 CLUB LIFE OF LONDON.

of Waxel took a fancy to the old sign, and offered the
then occupier of the house to paint him a new one for it.
A copy was accordingly made from the original, as the
sign of "The Tzar of the Muscovy," looking like a
Tartar. The house has, however, been rebuilt, and the
sign removed, but the name remains.

ROSE TAVERN, TOWER-STREET.

In Tower-street, before the Great Fire, was the Rose
tavern, which, upon the 4th of January, 1649, was the
scene of a memorable explosion of gunpowder, and
miraculous preservation. It appears that over-against
the wall of Allhallows Barking churchyard, was the
house of a ship-chandler, who, about seven o'clock at
night, being busy in his shop, barreling up gunpowder,
it took fire, and in the twinkling of an eye, blew up not
only that, but all the houses thereabout, to the number
(towards the street and in back alleys) of fifty or sixty.
The number of persons destroyed by this blow could
never be known, for the next house but one was the
Rose tavern, a house never (at that time of night) but
full of company; and that day the parish-dinner was
at the house. And in three or four days, after digging, they continually found heads, arms, legs, and half
bodies, miserably torn and scorched; besides many
whole bodies, not so much as their clothes singed.

In the course of this accident, says the narrator (Mr.
Leybourne, in Strype), " I will instance two; the one a
dead, the other a living monument. In the digging

(strange to relate) they found the mistress of the house of the Rose tavern, sitting in her bar, and one of the drawers standing by the bar's side, with a pot in his hand, only stifled with dust and smoke; their bodies being preserved whole by means of great timbers falling across one another. This is one. Another is this :— The next morning there was found upon the upper leads of Barking church, a young child lying in a cradle, as newly laid in bed, neither the child nor the cradle having the least sign of any fire or other hurt. It was never known whose child it was, so that one of the parish kept it as a memorial; for in the year 1666 I saw the child, grown to be then a proper maiden, and came to the man that kept her at that time, where he was drinking at a tavern with some other company then present. And he told us she was the child so found in the cradle upon the church leads as aforesaid."

According to a tablet which hangs beneath the organ gallery of the church, the quantity of gunpowder exploded in this catastrophe was twenty-seven barrels. Tower-street was wholly destroyed in the Great Fire of 1666.

THE NAG'S HEAD TAVERN, CHEAPSIDE.

As you pass through Cheapside, you may observe upon the front of the old house, No. 39, the sign-stone of a "Nag's Head:" this is presumed to have been the sign of the Nag's Head Tavern, which is described as at the Cheapside corner of Friday-street. This house

obtained some notoriety from its having been the pretended scene of the consecration of Matthew Parker,
Archbishop of Canterbury, in the reign of Queen Elizabeth, at that critical period when the English Protestant
or Reformed Church was in its infancy. Pennant thus
relates the scandalous story. " It was pretended by the
adversaries of our religion, that a certain number of
ecclesiastics, in their hurry to take possession of the
vacant see, assembled here, where they were to undergo
the ceremony from Anthony Kitchen, alias Dunstan,
bishop of Landaff, a sort of occasional conformist who
had taken the oaths of supremacy to Elizabeth. Bonner,
Bishop of London, (then confined in the Tower,) hearing
of it, sent his chaplain to Kitchen, threatening him
with excommunication, in case he proceeded. The pre-
late therefore refused to perform the ceremony : on
which, say the Roman Catholics, Parker and the other
candidates, rather than defer possession of their dioceses,
determined to consecrate one another ; which, says the
story, they did without any sort of scruple, and Scorey
began with Parker, who instantly rose Archbishop of
Canterbury. The refutation of this tale may be read in
Strype's *Life of Archbishop Parker*, at p. 57. A view
of the Nag's Head Tavern and its sign, is preserved in
La Serre's prints, Entrée de la Reyne Mère du Roy,
1638, and is copied in Wilkinson's *Londina Illustrata*.

The Roman Catholics laid the scene in the tavern : the
real consecration took place in the adjoining church of
St. Mary-le-Bow. As the form then adopted has been
the subject of much controversy, the following note,
from a letter of Dr. Pusey, dated Dec. 4, 1865, may be
quoted here :

" The form adopted at the *confirmation* of Archbishop

Parker was carefully framed on the old form used in the *confirmations* by Archbishop Chichele" (which was the point for which I examined the registers in the Lambeth library). The words used in the *consecrations* of the bishops confirmed by Chichele do not occur in the registers. The words used by the consecrators of Parker, " *Accipe Spiritum Sanctum,*" were used in the later Pontificals, as in that of Exeter, Lacy's (*Maskell, Monumenta Ritualia,* iii. 258). Roman Catholic writers admit that *that* only is essential to consecration which the English service-book retained—prayer during the service, which should have reference to the office of bishops, and the imposition of hands. And in fact Cardinal Pole engaged to retain in their orders those who had been so ordained under Edward VI., and his act was confirmed by Paul IV. (*Sanders de Schism. Angl.,* L. iii. 350).

THE HUMMUMS, COVENT GARDEN.

" Hammam " is the Arabic word for a bagnio, or bath, such as was originally "The Hummums," in Covent Garden, before it became an hotel.

There is a marvellous ghost story connected with this house, where died Parson Ford, who makes so conspicuous a figure in Hogarth's *Midnight Modern Conversation.* The narrative is thus given in Boswell's *Johnson* by Croker :—

" *Boswell.* Was there not a story of Parson Ford's ghost having appeared ?

" *Johnson.* Sir, it was believed. A waiter at the Hummums, in which house Ford died, had been absent for some time, and returned, not knowing that Ford was dead. Going down to the cellar, according to the story, he met him ; going down again, he met him a second

time. When he came up, he asked some people of the
house what Ford could be doing there. They told him
Ford was dead. The waiter took a fever, in which he
lay for some time. When he recovered, he said he had a
message to deliver to some woman from Ford; but he
was not to tell what or to whom. He walked out; he
was followed; but somewhere about St. Paul's they lost
him. He came back and said he had delivered it, and
the women exclaimed, ' Then we are all undone.' Dr.
Pallet, who was not a credulous man, inquired into the
truth of this story, and he said the evidence was irresistible. My wife went to the Hummums; (it is a place where
people get themselves cupped.) I believe she went with
intention to hear about this story of Ford. At first they
were unwilling to tell her; but after they had talked to
her, she came away satisfied that it was true. To be sure,
the man had a fever; and this vision may have been the
beginning of it. But if the message to the women, and
their behaviour upon it, were true, as related, there was
something supernatural. That rests upon his word, and
there it remains."

ORIGIN OF TAVERN SIGNS.

The cognisances of many illustrious persons connected
with the Middle Ages are still preserved in the signs
attached to our taverns and inns. Thus the White Hart
with the golden chain was the badge of King Richard II.;
the Antelope was that of King Henry IV.; the Feathers
was the cognisance of Henry VI.; and the White Swan

was the device of Edward of Lancaster, his ill-fated heir slain at the battle of Tewkesbury.

Before the Great Fire of London, in 1666, almost all the liveries of the great feudal lords were preserved at these houses of public resort. Many of their heraldic signs were then unfortunately lost: but the Bear and Ragged Staff, the ensign of the famed Warwick, still exists as a sign: while the Star of the Lords of Oxford, the brilliancy of which decided the fate of the battle of Barnet; the Lion of Norfolk, which shone so conspicuously on Bosworth field; the Sun of the ill-omened house of York, together with the Red and White Rose, either simply or conjointly, carry the historian and the antiquary back to a distant period, although now disguised in the gaudy colouring of a freshly-painted signboard.

The White Horse was the standard of the Saxons before and after their coming into England. It was a proper emblem of victory and triumph, as we read in Ovid and elsewhere. The White Horse is to this day the ensign of the county of Kent, as we see upon hop-pockets and bags; and throughout the county it is a favourite inn-sign.

The Saracen's Head inn-sign originated in the age of the Crusades. By some it is thought to have been adopted in memory of the father of St. Thomas à Becket, who was a Saracen. Selden thus explains it: "Do not undervalue an enemy by whom you have been worsted. When our countrymen came home from fighting with the Saracens, and were beaten by them, they pictured them with huge, big, terrible faces (as you still see the sign of the Saracen's Head is), when in truth they were like other men. But this they did to save their own credit. Still more direct is the explanation in Richard the Crusader causing a Saracen's head to be served up to the ambassadors of Saladin. May it not also have some reference to the Saracen's Head of the Quintain, a military exercise antecedent to jousts and tournaments?

The custom of placing a Bush at Tavern doors has already been noticed; we add a few notes :—In the preface to the *Law of Drinking*, keeping a public-house is called the trade of the ivy-bush : the bush was a sign so very general, that probably from thence arose the proverb "good wine needs no bush," or indication as to where it was sold. In *Good Newes and Bad Newes*, 1622, a host says :—

> "I rather will take down my bush and sign
> Than live by means of riotous expense."

The ancient method of putting a bough of a tree upon anything, to signify that it was for disposal, is still exemplified by an old besom (or birch broom) being placed at the mast-head of a vessel that is intended for sale. In Dekker's *Wonderful Yeare*, 1603, is the passage " Spied a bush at the end of a pole, the ancient badge of a countrey ale-house." And in Harris's *Drunkard's Cup*, p. 299, " Nay, if the house be not with an ivie bush, let him have his tooles about him, nutmegs, rosemary, tobacco, with other the appurtenances, and he knows how of puddle ale to make a cup of English wine." From a passage in *Whimzies, or a new Cast of Characters*, 1631, it would seem that signs in alehouses succeeded birch poles.

It is usual in some counties, particularly Staffordshire, to hang a bush at the door of an ale-house, or mug-house. Sir Thomas Browne considers that the human faces depicted on sign-boards, for the sun and moon, are relics of paganism, and that they originally meant Apollo and Diana. This has been noticed in Hudibras—

> " Tell me but what's the nat'ral cause
> Why on a sign no painter draws
> The full moon ever, but the half."

A Bell sign-stone may be seen on the house-front, No. 26, Great Knight-Rider-street : it bears the date 1668, and is boldly carved; whether it is of tavern or other trade it is hard to say : the house appears to be of the above date.

The Bell, in Great Carter-lane, in this neighbourhood, has been taken down : it was an interesting place, for, hence, October 25, 1598, Richard Quiney addressed to his "loveing good ffrend and countryman, Mr. Wm. Schackespere," (then living in Southwark, near the Bear-garden), a letter for a loan of thirty pounds ; which letter we have seen in the possession of Mr. R. Bell Wheler, at Stratford-upon-Avon : it is believed to be the only existing letter addressed to Shakspere.

The Bull, Bishopsgate, is noteworthy ; for the yard of this inn supplied a stage to our early actors, before James Burbadge and his fellows obtained a patent from Queen Elizabeth for erecting a permanent building for theatrical entertainments. Tarleton often played here. Anthony Bacon, the brother of Francis, lived in a house in Bishopsgate-street, not far from the Bull Inn, to the great concern of his mother, who not only dreaded that the plays and interludes acted at the Bull might corrupt his servants, but on her own son's account objected to the parish as being without a godly clergyman.

Gerard's Hall, Basing-lane, had the fine Norman crypt of the ancient hall of the Sisars for its wine-cellar; besides the tutelar effigies of "Gerard the gyant," a fair specimen of a London sign, *temp.* Charles II. Here also was shown the staff used by Gerard in the wars, and a ladder to ascend to the top of the staff; and in the neighbouring church of St. Mildred, Bread-street, hangs a huge tilting-helmet, said to have been worn by the said giant. The staff, Stow thinks, may rather have been used as a May-pole, and to stand in the hall decked with evergreens at Christmas; the ladder serving for decking the pole and hall-roof.

Fosbroke says, that the Bell Savage is a strange corruption of the Queen of Sheba; the Bell Savage, of which the device was a savage man standing by a bell, is supposed to be derived from the French, Belle Sauvage, on account of a beautiful savage having been once shown there; by others it is considered, with more probability, to have been so named in compliment to some ancient landlady of the celebrated inn upon Ludgate-hill, whose surname was Savage, as in the Close-rolls of the thirty-first year of the reign of Henry VI. is an entry of a grant of that inn to "John Frensch, gentilman," and called " Savage's Ynne," *alias* the " Bell on the Hoof."

The token of the house is—" HENRY YOVNG AT YE. An Indian woman holding an arrow and a bow.—℞. ON LVDGATE HILL. In the field, H. M. Y.

" There is a tradition [Mr. Akerman writes] that the origin of this sign, and not only of the inn, but also of the name of the court in which it is situate, was derived from that of Isabella Savage, whose property they once were, and who conveyed them by deed to the Cutlers' Company. This, we may observe, is a mistake. The name of the person who left the Bell Savage to the Cutlers' Company was Craythorne, not Savage."

In Flecknoe's *Ænigmatical Characters*, 1665, in alluding to "your fanatick reformers," he says, "as for the signs, they have pretty well begun the reformation already, changing the sign of the Salutation of the Angel and our Lady into the Shouldier and Citizen, and the Catherine Wheel into the Cat and Wheel, so that there only wants their making the Dragon to kill St. George, and the Devil to tweak St. Dunstan by the nose, to make the reformation compleat. Such ridiculous work they make of their reformation, and so zealous are they against all mirth and jollity, as they would pluck down the sign of the Cat and Fiddle, too, if it durst but play so loud as they might hear it."

The sign In God is our Hope is still to be seen at a public-house on the western road between Cranford and Slough. Coryatt mentions the Ave Maria, with verses, as the sign of an alehouse abroad, and a street where all the signs on one side were of birds. The Swan with Two Nicks, or Necks, as it is commonly called, was so termed from the two nicks or marks, to make known that it was a swan of the Vintners' Company; the swans of that company having two semicircular pieces cut from the upper mandible of the swan, one on each side, which are called nicks. The origin of the Bolt-in-Tun is thus explained. The bolt was the arrow shot from a cross-bow, and the tun or barrel was used as the target, and in this device the bolt is painted sticking in the bunghole. It appears not unreasonable to conclude, that hitting the bung was as great an object in crossbow-shooting as it is to a member of a Toxophilite Club to strike the target in the bull's eye. The sign of the

Three Loggerheads is two grotesque wooden heads, with
the inscription "Here we three Loggerheads be," the
reader being the third. The Honest Lawyer is depicted
at a beershop at Stepney; the device is a lawyer with
his head under his arm, to prevent his telling lies.

The Lamb and Lark has reference to a well-known
proverb that we should go to bed with the lamb and
rise with the lark. The Eagle and Child, *vulgo* Bird
and Baby, is by some persons imagined to allude to
Jupiter taking Ganymede; others suppose that it merely
commemorates the fact of a child having been carried
off by an eagle; but this sign is from the arms of the
Derby family (eagle and child) who had a house at Lambeth, where is the Bird and Baby.

The Green Man and Still should be a green man (or
man who deals in *green herbs*) with a bundle of pepper-
mint or pennyroyal under his arm, which he brings to
be distilled.

Upon the modern building of the Bull and Mouth
has been conferred the more elegant name of the Queen's
Hotel. Now the former is a corruption of Boulogne
Mouth, and the sign was put up to commemorate the
destruction of the French flotilla at the mouth of
Boulogne harbour in the reign of Henry VIII. This
absurd corruption has been perpetuated by a carving in
stone of a bull and a human face with an enormous
mouth. The Bull and Gate, palpably, has the like
origin; as at the *Gate* of Boulogne the treaty of capitu-
lation to the English was signed.

The Spread Eagle, which constitutes the arms of
Austria and Russia, originated with Charlemagne, and
was in England introduced out of compliment to some
German potentate.

The oddest sign we know is now called The Mischief, in Oxford-street, and our remembrance of this dates over half a century, when the street was called Oxford-road, then unpaved, is truly Hogarthian. It was at that time called the Man loaded with Mischief, *i. e.* a wife, two squalling brats, a monkey, a cat, a jackdaw, etc. The perpetrator of this libel on the other sex, we suppose, was some poor henpecked individual.*

On the subject of sign combinations, a writer in *Notes and Queries* says :—" This subject has been taken up by a literary contemporary, and some ingenious but far-fetched attempts at explanation have been made, deduced from languages the publican is not likely to have heard of. The following seem at least to be undoubtedly English : The Sun and Whalebone, Cock and Bell, Ram and Teazle, Cow and Snuffers, Crow and Horse-shoe, Hoop and Pie,—*cum multis aliis.* I have some remembrance of a very simple solution of the cause of the incongruity, which was this : The lease being out of (say) the sign of The Ram, or the tenant had left for some cause, and gone to the sign of The Teazle; wishing to be known, and followed by as many of his old connexion as possible, and also to secure the new, he took his old sign with him, and set it up beside the other, and the house soon became known as The Ram and Teazle. After some time the signs required re-painting or renewing, and as one board was more convenient than two, the 'emblems,' as poor Dick Tinto calls them, were depicted together, and hence rose the puzzle."

There have been some strange guesses. Some have thought the Goat and Compasses to be a corruption of

* Communicated to the *Builder* by Mr. Rhodes.

"God encompasseth us," but it has been much more directly traced as follows, by Sir Edmund Head, who has communicated the same to Mr. P. Cunningham: "At Cologne, in the church of Santa Maria in Capitolio, is a flat stone on the floor, professing to be the Grabstein der Brüder und Schwester eines ehrbaren Wein- und Fass-Ampts, Anno 1693; that is, I suppose, a vault belonging to the Wine Coopers' Company. The arms exhibit a shield with a pair of compasses, an axe, and a dray, or truck, with goats for supporters. In a country, like England, dealing so much at one time in Rhenish wine, a more likely origin for such a sign could hardly be imagined."

The Pig in the Pound might formerly be seen towards the east end of Oxford-street, not far from "The Mischief."

The Magpie and Horseshoe may be seen in Fetter-lane: the ominous import attached to the bird and the shoe may account for this association in the sign: we can imagine ready bibbers going to houses with this sign "for luck."

The George, Snow-hill, is a good specimen of a carved sign-stone of—

> "St. George that swing'd the dragon,
> And sits on horseback at mine hoste's door."

INDEX

TO THE FIRST VOLUME.

——◆——

INDEX

TO THE SECOND VOLUME.

—✦—

𝕮𝖔𝖋𝖋𝖊𝖊-𝖍𝖔𝖚𝖘𝖊𝖘.

Taverns.

f.

THE END.

JOHN EDWARD TAYLOR, PRINTER,
LITTLE QUEEN STREET, LINCOLN'S INN FIELDS.

www.ingramcontent.com/pod-product-compliance
Lightning Source LLC
Chambersburg PA
CBHW021124270326
41929CB00009B/1031